D0151853

FOR KIM TUCCI:
    AN INSPIRING TEACHER,
WHOSE OWN BOOK SHOULD
BE WORTH READING.
    ALL THE BEST,
        MIKE MURRAY
            APRIL 8, 1992

TEACHING
MASS
COMMUNICATION

TEACHING MASS COMMUNICATION

A Guide to Better Instruction

EDITED BY
Michael D. Murray
AND
Anthony J. Ferri

 PRAEGER

New York
Westport, Connecticut
London

Library of Congress Cataloging-in-Publication Data

Teaching mass communication : a guide to better instruction / edited
  by Michael D. Murray and Anthony J. Ferri.
       p. cm.
    Includes bibliographical references and index.
       ISBN 0-275-94156-6
       1. Mass Media—Study and teaching (Higher) I. Murray, Michael D.
  II. Ferri, Anthony J.
  P91.3.T44   1992
  302.23'071'1—dc20   91-28831

British Library Cataloguing in Publication Data is available.

Copyright © 1992 by Michael D. Murray and Anthony J. Ferri

All rights reserved. No portion of this book may be
reproduced, by any process or technique, without the
express written consent of the publisher.

Library of Congress Catalog Card Number: 91-28831
ISBN: 0-275-94156-6

First published in 1992

Praeger Publishers, One Madison Avenue, New York, NY 10010
An imprint of Greenwood Publishing Group, Inc.

Printed in the United States of America

∞™

The paper used in this book complies with the
Permanent Paper Standard issued by the National
Information Standards Organization (Z39.48-1984).

10 9 8 7 6 5 4 3 2 1

CONTENTS

PREFACE

This manuscript has had a number of lives since its birth. Suffice to say that we are very pleased to see its entry into the published world.

The intent of this book is to offer an instructional guidebook for faculty who teach mass communication courses. While most instructors probably use a course text along with one or two others for lecture material, there are few if any books that tell you how to teach courses in mass communication. While no single work can cover every aspect and every course, we believe this book will give most instructors and administrators an excellent foundation from which to plan and teach mass communication courses found in contemporary programs.

Putting a book together is somewhat like producing a play or movie; there are many people who have had some part in the overall process. First, thanks to the people at Praeger, and especially Anne Davidson, who supported this work. We want to thank the contributors for their efforts. We also want to thank the Greenspun School of Communication at the University of Nevada, Las Vegas for a generous grant supporting our editorial efforts. Our word processor worked many a weekend and late night for this book, so thanks to Leslie Gorr of UNLV.

Michael Murray would like to acknowledge the support and inspiration of his wife, Carol, and his daughters Ellen and Katherine.

Anthony Ferri would like to thank Michael Murray for his support and confidence. He would also like to acknowledge the support and inspiration of his wife, Margaret, his son Steven, and his daughter Theresa.

TEACHING MASS COMMUNICATION

INTRODUCTION

This text represents an effort to offer the beginning teacher a number of ideas about coursework in a still-developing field. Mass communication programs and departments have sprung up in large measure because of the need to fuse traditional curricula in journalism, speech, broadcasting, advertising, and public relations. Some colleges and departments have taken strong philosophical stands on formalized training, assuming some very sound, well-reasoned arguments concerning course content, orientation of curriculum, and even the name by which they will be known. Indeed, we still hear of squabbles in the field over whether the term "mass media" or "mass communication" should be used. Should an academic unit in mass communication be associated with a department of "communication" or "communications," "speech," or "journalism"? Some schools have settled comfortably in departments of "communication studies." Other tradition-bound institutions have kept subunits separated.

It is the intent of this book to contribute to the second wave of development and understanding in the field by offering those perspectives on teaching the courses most often found currently as part of the rubric of mass communication. In seeking out original essays from teachers and scholars currently in the field, the editors intentionally ignored the positioning of the individual within an institutional framework. Some of the authors are affiliated with major journalism schools and others call small departments of communication or mass communication their home. Also, in reviewing the background of the various contributors, you will find that they represent a wide variety of academic philosophies and points of view. Most have, in addition to their extensive teaching careers, substantive professional experience in the field and, in many cases, administrative backgrounds that include working with beginning teachers and graduate students.

Recent studies have shown that beginning teachers are often responsible for as much as a quarter of all undergraduate coursework at some of America's biggest schools. Survey data of teaching assistants has found that only half of all academic departments provide university "teachers in training" with any formal teacher education, even though two-thirds have assumed sole responsibility for classes by their second year on the job. Beyond the department level, it was found that only a quarter of the schools surveyed provided campus-wide training programs, and even those opportunities were not mandatory at most institutions. Ironically, in terms of sheer numbers, teaching assistants on some campuses are on a par with regular faculty when it comes to contact with undergraduate students.[1] Obviously, this situation needs to be addressed.

Clearly, more attention needs to be paid to the preparation beginning teachers receive. Perhaps, as some educators have recently suggested, this should begin with an examination of who these aspirants to academe are, including their motivations for entering higher education. Fortunately, many schools are beginning to view teacher training as an investment, with an apprenticeship for the professorship as a model, getting away from the view of teaching assistants as merely a source of supplementary labor, and offering a graduated program in which close monitoring, peer observation, and specialized workshops become part of the teacher training routine.

In the more specialized fields of mass communication, some introspection on these issues has already begun.[2] This book, therefore, assumes that the student of the field has a familiarity with the basics, in addition to a desire to improve performance in specialty areas consistent with current demands as well as in the so-called bread-and-butter courses. In broadcasting, for example, where production classes are among the most popular with undergraduate students, this creates challenges since graduate students tend to concentrate, as one might expect, on research-and-effects-type research specialization. Fortunately, again we find the quality of instruction improving due to much introspection and organized efforts to support development opportunities at almost every level.

Having pointed out what we hope are obvious prerequisites, we will leave it to others of those administration "types" among us to deal with the challenge of getting those high-demand skills courses taught while satisfying institutional needs for scholarly productivity.

A round-table discussion of leading educators in the field offers hope that vitality of instruction is being considered in conjunction with alternative models in mass communication education, calling for balance in education. In that discussion, for example, Sharon Murphy, Communication Dean of Marquette University, argued for a balanced curriculum with fundamentals such as principles of communication to be taught in conjunction with tough writing standards. Also good news is the fact that in the same publication in which the round-table appeared, the *Gannett Center Journal*, another article focusing on top schools listed "quality of teaching" as its first criterion and backed it up with specific references to good teachers.[3]

Beyond individual professors and institutions, a variety of service and training programs have begun to enhance the teaching of mass communication. The Poynter Institute for Media Studies in St. Petersburg, Florida, provides continuing education and advanced study in the field, serving as a bridge between practitioners and teachers. The Freedom Forum Media Studies Center (formerly The Gannett Center for Media Studies), under the directorship of Everette Dennis, offers both research and teaching enhancement programs, including a specialized program to assist administrators in the field. Professor Dennis has also personally addressed the educational mission head-on in a study which, among other things, searched for proposals to improve curricula. Individual divisions of the Association for Education in Journalism and Mass Communication (AEJMC), Speech Communication Association (SCA), Broadcast Education Association (BEA), and the International Communication Association (ICA), among others, have provided teacher training programs and, in some cases, shared composite course outlines for scrutiny by beginning instructors.

The SCA has contributed to the field of mass communication through its support of a specialized division of mass communication and both *Critical Studies in Mass Communication* and a pedagogically oriented journal, *Communication Education*. Similarly, the AEJMC supports scholarly study through its Mass Communication and Society division, its *Mass Comm Review* journal, and the association's instructional journal, *Journalism Educator*. The BEA is, of course, exclusively devoted to broadcast issues, with two specialized journals including *Feedback*, which frequently carries articles of interest to those teaching broadcasting courses.

Coincidentally, the leadership of three of these national media-related academic organizations—the Association for Communication Administration (ACA), the Association for Education of Journalism and Mass Communication (AEJMC), and the BEA—met jointly for the first time and agreed to work toward closer cooperation, beginning with the publication of a single directory of all academic programs in the communication disciplines. The data base was compiled and published by Indiana University–Purdue University at Indianapolis. Edited by Garland Ellmore, it provides a useful overview of institutions to the beginning teacher. This kind of development adds to the sense of optimism and a willingness to share ideas in a still-new field.

The editors are hopeful that this book will aid in the encouragement of an integrative approach—one that can be utilized in two primary contexts: for the beginning teacher of mass communication and the seasoned instructor who would like to get an added perspective on particular coursework. It is, therefore, a resource book for the classroom teacher. The text evaluates methods in a variety of courses in the field, including those in print, broadcast/film, advertising, and public relations. It may also be used as a textbook for methods of teaching mass communication or for the mass communication-for-teachers classes. It provides an overview of the field and presents options for treating issues in each area for those attempting to keep abreast in an ever-changing media environment.

Additionally, the text offers insight into the course planning process—the issues to be addressed, the organization of coursework, review of literature, nature of key assignments, the use and availability of teaching aids, textbooks, grading, and course evaluation. In many cases, authors share their work habits and focus on the popular periodicals and journals they use on a regular basis to keep current on developments related to a particular course. Some are obvious choices and others reflect a particular bias, philosophy, or even organizational affiliation of the author. This is meant to give the careful reader a complete and personal view of coursework as it is taught, rather than to offer "the perfect course" presented in an idealized or unrealistic setting. As most of the authors explain, each class is presented as it is taught but with some options, which each individual instructor may want to consider.

NOTES

1. See Peter Monaghan, "University Officials Deplore the Lack of Adequate Training Given to Teaching Assistants, Ponder How to Improve It," *Chronicle of Higher Education* (November 29, 1989): A17.

2. Gerold Baldasty, "Teaching Sources: Help Is at Hand," *Clio Among the Media* (Spring 1991): 5–6.

3. See James Boylan and Norman H. Sims, "Stand and Deliver: Six Teachers Who Made a Difference," *Gannett Center Journal* (Spring 1988): 49–60; and "Eleven Exemplary Journalism Schools," *Gannett Center Journal* (Spring 1988): 68–76.

Part I

THE INTRODUCTORY COURSE

The first two chapters include overviews for teaching the so-called window-to-the-field courses, both in mass communication and broadcasting. Content, textbook, and assignment considerations are integrated with information including, in chapter 1, a rather detailed profile of the current teacher of this course. In chapter 2, Don Godfrey offers perspective as one who has seen this course diminished somewhat by some of those likely to draw the assignment—the beginning graduate student, the media professional on part-time assignment, or the instructor of twenty or more years in the classroom. His viewpoint? The challenge to be involved in the first student experience in the field should be approached as an exciting one, even in the context of the large lecture hall environment that today it frequently demands.

Godfrey draws on twenty years of experience teaching the course on a number of college campuses, professional broadcasting experience at some of the nation's top stations, acquaintanceships he has made in those contexts, as well as a close association with the Broadcast Education Association (BEA) from which his course objectives and content recommendations are derived. Textbook options, such as the tried and proven major choice, Sydney Head and Christopher Sterling's *Broadcasting in America*, are reviewed and form the basis of comparison for other available alternatives. Because of the nature of the course, Godfrey suggests that the goals of the course and nature of the student be carefully coordinated with text selection.

A review of sources in the field will prove especially valuable to the novice teacher and students—whether aspiring professional broadcasters or merely consumer-conscious undergraduates seeking a more informed background in broadcasting. This overview includes both professional trade and academic journals in the field, as well as journalism reviews and suggestions on how one might apply newspaper criticism to localized issues. With a firm commitment to principles culled from close professional ties, Godfrey presents what would be viewed as a traditional course with such topics as historical background, regulatory and business concerns, programming, and research issues. As one might expect, he follows this up with a discussion of which sections require the most attention and again draws on his experience as editor of BEA's *Directory of Broadcast Archives* to suggest classroom supplements to instruction, based on availability and his insights from many years of teaching the course. These suggestions include 16 mm films, recordings, and recommendations on off-air use of material with an eye toward avoiding potential copyright problems. This chapter concludes with a review of classroom assignments focusing on student preparation of critical essays, the traditional term paper assignment, and an oral history paper—a provocative and more detailed alternative. Godfrey's advice is most sound and well seasoned.

Co-editor of this book, Anthony J. Ferri begins chapter 3 on the basic public relations course by contrasting the everyday world of teaching classes and the glitz and glamour of Las Vegas, Nevada, the city in which he lives and works. His goal is to provide students with an insight into both the profession of public relations, a most misunderstood field, and its process. Like many of the authors in this section, Ferri takes time to review the position of this course in relation to others that may be available in the curriculum.

Ferri discusses assignments relative to the all-purpose class and those with a broader base in a sequence, beginning with a definition of terms to distinguish it from others such as advertising. He then offers a very detailed topical outline of areas for consideration in this course and a listing of major assignments recommended for the class including special projects, as well as a short list of texts for consideration by the public relations instructor. He also offers the reader some valuable advice on testing policies, selection of guest speakers, and supplementary reading material.

In chapter 4, Gary Burns discusses the place of film in the communication curriculum and its popularity as an area of study. He then offers views on course structure and content, including considerations of a filmmaking component as a means of merging theory and practice—a popular option when costs can be incurred as part of laboratory fees. On the other hand, this chapter presumes that a film production component is not well suited to the course under study, with the next logical question being whether a historical or aesthetic approach would be most appropriate since both employ similar kinds of considerations—with the instructor showing many of the same touchstone films.

Burns explores categories of film ranging from primitive to experimental and suggests that units of the class be built around film screenings. When, on a semester basis, additional weeks are available, the author recommends the use of American film genres from the studio years, theatrical adaptations, and personal favorites with selection criteria for each. For film selection he offers important sources such as the critics poll from *Sight and Sound* magazine, and reviews five basic texts—both historical and aesthetic in scope—and two major reference works worth noting.

To his credit, Burns also discusses the sticky question of film rental costs, which, in the real world of higher education, unfortunately sometimes helps to dictate course content with respect to screenings. He recommends institutional programming in VHS video format with the caveat that this often creates both aesthetic and access problems. Beyond that thorny and never-ending issue, Burns raises the logistical questions faced in scheduling films for classroom use which vary in length and the issue alluded to earlier regarding the use of lab fees for equipment use, film development, or rental costs. Class size is assumed to be quite large for this course, so objective tests are the norm with research papers prohibitive unless the instructor has some graduate assistance for grading purposes. In spite of some of the limitations he notes, Burns paints a generally encouraging picture for instructors in the basic film course—a course which frequently sets the tone for an entire film curriculum at some of the bigger or more specialized institutions.

Regardless of institutional size and scope, almost all schools endorse the use of internships in one form or other. Chapter 5, Internship Programs, begins with an analysis of the course description, placement opportunities, and models for successful administration. Included in this section are questions regarding eligibility of students and a specific run-down on required coursework for various types of internships. S. Scott Whitlow addresses the issue of compensation for interns, workload, and evaluation within the context of a proven success story at Kentucky. She also offers the reader helpful suggestions on how meaningful objectives can be measured as part of the intern contract and factors worth considering when the details of a weekly journal and summary report are included as part of intern requirements. She recommends preparation of a press release at the midterm of the student's internship experience and an Internship Overview Kit which is used as an intern hunting strategy and a screening tool. Whitlow gives careful consideration to the wide variety of factors that help to determine the importance of a student's internship opportunity.

Chapter 1

THE BASIC COURSE IN MASS COMMUNICATION

Michael D. Murray

Perhaps the greatest challenge facing the instructor of the Introduction to Mass Communication course is deciding what material to cover and to what depth. Given a typical fifteen- or sixteen-week semester format, or an even shorter quarter system with a ten-week period, in which to offer an overview of the field, the instructor may feel as if he or she faces an incredible obstacle of time versus content. To help compensate for this situation, the instructor may wish to begin each term with a detailed questionnaire to be administered during the initial class meeting. This can be employed to discover the extent of media familiarity and use, find key areas of interest, and bolster content of important but limited exposure among members of the class.

Over the past fifteen years, interest has increased considerably in advertising and public relations, and many schools have struggled with personnel and facilities to meet the demands of an advanced curriculum in those areas. The fact that so many students have targeted these areas of interest offers the instructor an insight on strategies for classroom use or a focal point for class discussion for other areas such as film, with the discussion centering on broadcast promotion of major motion pictures.

Once the questionnaire is administered, the instructor needs to formulate a plan to engage the students most effectively. This particular course is often viewed as something of an insurance policy for many departments in that it assures the faculty that, regardless of the students' specialty areas and major areas of interest, they will be provided with some basic historical background of the American mass media and will gain at least some grounding in the important issues related to content in all of the various areas. The questionnaire can help to identify areas of interest—asking the students to list or number each area according to their level of interest as well as asking them to identify whatever future goals they may have in mind.

BACKGROUND

Planning begins with a statement of purpose and course objectives. These usually address the philosophical boundaries of the course, specific goals, and what the parameters for achievement in the course will be. Planning should take place with an eye toward available resources—deciding on the course structure, the nature and type of assignments, and the number and design of tests. The objectives of my introductory course include two components: one general and philosophical in nature, the other specific and related to the acquisition of skills. The first is designed to alert the student to the survey nature of the course and the fact that we are going to examine the forces shaping the American mass media.

The student needs to understand at the outset that this course provides a little bit of everything, "a window to the field," with less depth than we would like. Secondly, we want the student to understand that the course has a critical component—that objectives include the acquisition of evaluative tools for assessing media performance and that, in addition, we will treat the theories advanced to explain the American mass media and its performance. In this way, we satisfy the need to incorporate exposure to the field and the role evaluation of media performance play, both in our culture and our everyday life. In doing so, we also set the tone for the class, which, even at the beginning stage, attracts both budding practitioners and those with a purely consumer orientation. Obviously, meeting the needs of a diversified group with different expectations requires ingenuity on the part of the instructor in devising lesson plans and developing strategies for involvement on the part of students.

One popular activity to engender involvement is, of course, the group project. Course information forms are used to assign groups usually of five to seven members. A wide variety of media-related issues are available for exploration and study by students in this class. I try to get each group of students to focus on a general area based on their expressed interest, meet with the groups individually at the outset for in-class discussion of possible topics, and try to avoid presenting a laundry list of topics (as is their desire) for fear that they will merely mimic what prior groups have done in this course.

The description of the assignment spells out that each student group identify three to five possible topics for review by the instructor. In this way, we avoid a misunderstanding with respect to topics that may be beyond the scope of an introductory course. The study may incorporate a survey, a historical review, or an assessment of a current policy or new technology. I have recently incorporated peer review of in-class group presentations as a means of assessing effectiveness and impact, although I reserve all grading of the assignment itself, which constitutes 10 percent of each student's grade.

The class presentations are limited to a half-hour for each group and also result in a written summary of group findings, five to seven pages in length. When this assignment is made, I alert the class that I will also be using a sociogram to help evaluate individual group members' contributions. This lets them know that I will be getting feedback for individual group members to the extent and nature of each person's activity, with the grade for the assignment reflecting both overall and individual performance. I sometimes describe the use of a sociogram as a "gestapo-type" tactic but have found it to work wonders in avoiding disputes regarding levels of contributions by participants and instances in which a minority of group members participated and did all the work in preparing presentation of findings to both the class and myself. Use of the sociogram also has the effect of encouraging atten-dance—an important consideration in a contemporary setting, espe-cially when the instructor is turning over bits and pieces of class time for group planning activity, as is the practice in my course.

Giving individual students an alternative to the group assignment can be worthwhile in some select cases, although generally it is not to be encouraged. One alternative I have used is a fifteen- to twenty-page term paper, offered in instances in which all but one or two of the group members agree on the use of extensive out-of-class meet-ings. I have found it difficult to demand high levels of outside activity in the form of meeting time in the context of a commuter campus. On the other hand, an instructor's "hidden agenda" for making the group assignment in an introductory course may include the desire to encourage interaction among those students with similar interests. Obviously, alternatives complicate this goal, which explains why they are to be discouraged.

In a class of 50 to as many as 100 students, I usually have fewer than a half-dozen students requesting the term paper option. Of course, for many instructors, particularly at the present time, the emphasis would undoubtedly be reversed, with some kind of individual writing or term assignment being of greater importance.

In the event that you elect to assign group projects or term papers, an information questionnaire of the type mentioned earlier allows you to group students by interest area or assign paper topics rather than leaving assignments open-ended and thus avoiding potential plagiarism questions. Also listed on the questionnaire are items related to the student's use of the media. Included are questions about the newspaper press. Which newspapers do you read regularly and what part of the paper do you read first? Students are asked to identify their favorite columnist, most highly thought-of local broadcast news anchor and reporter, and the current film they would most likely recommend to a friend. This gives the instructor an index of students' attitudes toward and use of various aspects of the media. Students tell about their favorite advertising campaign, most frequently read magazine, and most popular author. Given an urban location, this assignment can also provide clues as to which guest speakers might be most effective for a classroom visit.

Inviting into the classroom a promotion or advertising specialist such as the creator of the Anheuser Busch Spuds McKenzie or "Know When to Say When" television campaigns makes an impression with the class and provides them with background on what many may have once identified as a favorite contemporary advertising campaign. Having a local columnist or broadcaster visit the campus to discuss his or her career can also assist a class in gaining perspective on a field or a particular media market, as described in detail later in the chapter on news writing.

In surveying the class's newspaper readership, I ask not only what paper they read and what areas receive most of their attention, but how often they read and with what degree of retention. In this regard, in structuring the class I allow for the use of current events quizzes to be sure that they are staying current and up to date with news events. This assignment is discussed in another section but generally provides another degree of assurance that the students understand the importance of keeping up with what is going on in the world. In surveying alumni, it is interesting to note how many of my former students regard this assignment as having been one of the most meaningful of their college career, or at least the one they best remember.

In addition to the problem of facing overwhelming content and shortness of time in which to convey basic information, a second major challenge develops in the context of what the placement of information should be—the order of presentation. Most of the major media textbooks in the field are segmented, with print occupying at least a chapter or two. Although the need for texts providing an integrative approach is well documented, few publishers acknowledge or use this approach. If they did, the instructor would still be faced with the question of how best to convey material from a variety of areas of the field, particularly when a historical model is utilized and the instructor is forced to provide background on simultaneous developments in related fields.

ORGANIZATION

Taking a media-based content approach to the subject, as most introductory mass communication courses do, focuses attention at the start with a theoretical overview of the field progressing through print, broadcast, advertising/public relations, and film. The historic development of each medium is usually accompanied by perspective on production—the process of getting the product out, whatever it may be. The historic firsts are presented alongside special topics such as press associations, which do not fall neatly into print or broadcast. These topics are usually subject to scrutiny during a week's time and placed early in the course. Areas such as magazine and book publishing demand attention beyond the newspaper press and the role of government. Economic and ethical considerations are, unfortunately, usually tagged onto the end of the course, along with whatever prognostications the instructor and/or textbook author are willing to venture.

Because of the assignments I have held at urban schools, I have also tried to devote one unit of instruction in each content topic segment of the course to the local media scene. A specialty in media history and in the status of the market has enhanced this attempt to localize content and provide a base of information. For example, a slide presentation of historic front pages from local newspapers was created, revolving around a lecture organized for the *St. Louis Post-Dispatch* "Newspaper in Education" program, geared toward primary and secondary school teachers. The slide set which was prepared for the author by the newspaper's photography department was based on a book the publisher put out centering on major historical events. The lecture I have adopted for use in the introductory course presents a biographical account of the life of founder Joseph Pulitzer and major local, national, and international coverage by the *Post-Dispatch*.

A similar lecture on the local broadcasting scene was a by-product of a consulting assignment—a short station history prepared by the author, providing an overview of the first station in the market, also the first Pulitzer station in the country, KSD-TV, now KSDK. The occasion was the station's fortieth anniversary. The history, which was excerpted in the *Post-Dispatch* on the anniversary date in 1987, was also adapted for classroom use and supplemented with slides to offer a comparative look at the broadcast market. Many instructors employ the slide programs of Vis-Com, Inc., a Minneapolis-based company specializing in historic front pages, to present information of national significance. In addition, I employ local coverage of major media events such as the "War of the Worlds" broadcast to stimulate additional interest in early broadcasting. Excerpts of both the broadcast itself, available on tape and recording, are integrated with readings from the local press the day after the broadcast, presented along with the reaction to it.

Localization adds a unique perspective and clarifies the impact of the broadcast in a more direct way. While on the faculty of Virginia Tech, I surveyed and shared reactions reported from papers in Roanoke, Richmond, and northern Virginia—the home base for most of that student population. At the University of Louisville, mostly an urban, commuter school, I used the *Courier-Journal* and *Times* as my source for these talks. In each instance, I found a greater degree of receptivity to these events in this context and more easily related to other sources such as Hadley Cantril's study of the Orson Welles's broadcast, *The Invasion from Mars*, which includes testimony by those affected by the broadcast, as well as a published script.[1]

As an additional means of introducing the field of popular radio programming, I frequently show the class a three-part documentary entitled "Those Great Radio Comedians." As an adjunct to covering the history of broadcast news, we screen the film "This Is Edward R. Murrow" or one of Murrow's best CBS Reports documentaries, such as "Harvest of Shame." In the film section of the course, I usually show some classic shorts from the early years of American film and excerpts from classic documentaries such as *Nanook of the North* or the German film *Triumph of the Will*. Both of these films are, of course, of historical importance for different reasons, and they offer the classic contrast in documentary style and motivation. If you are based in a big city, many of these films are available free for school use from the public library or the local school system.

Many 16 mm films are available through major state institutions which have invested heavily in film. These include Indiana University and the University of Missouri–Columbia. At my current institution, we have access to state and local school system library holdings in film, and we also purchased a number of classic films for classroom use. Many of the classics are now available in video format. The pluses and minuses of use in small format are discussed in chapter 4, Introduction to Film, but it will suffice to say that the small format can increase film use but sometimes create scheduling problems, as well as aesthetic considerations. The other obvious consideration, when viewed from the perspective of the entire curriculum, is the importance of coordinating use of films. If the students see the same films over and over again in different classes, they may lose sight of their importance, although the argument could be made that even this is justified when viewed from another perspective. A discussion with colleagues with respect to their approach and their use of visual aids is always important, especially when viewed with departmental budgets in mind.

Much attention has been devoted recently to mass media trends including concentrated ownership and the legal battles among media owner giants and apparent breaches of public faith in press performance.[2] The so-called new technology is also a hot topic, often reserved for the concluding or "futures" section of the course and frequently selected as a subject for group projects. These can be used as a means of treating topics of special interest to students while providing some variation in the mode of delivery of course content. Even more complex is the challenge of integrating issues from two or three areas when a more or less chronological approach has been taken within a certain subject area. Fortunately, some texts have added comparative chapters to treat these issues late in the book.

TEXTS

Structuring the basic course is, in part, dependent on textbook selection, as it is with most other introductory coursework. For many years, a limited number of texts occupied the Introduction to Mass Communication or Mass Media textbook market. These first attempts at surveying the media landscape were tied to curricular development. The typical college course in mass communication evolved in the context of the departments of speech communication or journalism schools as a logical adjunct to developing courses in broadcasting, film, advertising, and print journalism, sometimes taught, particularly at the smaller schools, in an English department. This growth in course offerings accompanied a tremendous upsurge in school enrollment in the 1960s and 1970s and the evolution of mass communication programs and eclectic departments of communication. One introductory text by Professor Edwin Emery, Phillip Ault, and Warren Agee dominated a very limited market at the start of this growth period. This text, still in use, set the standard in media textbook publishing and was widely used.

Text selection is frequently the indirect by-product of graduate training. In my case, as a young assistant professor fresh from graduate school in the early 1970s, it was flattering indeed being asked to design a large lecture introductory course in mass communication that would provide an overview of the areas of advertising, broadcasting, film, journalism, and public relations. About the same time, a textbook publisher, Science Research Associates, requested an evaluation of a new text covering the mass communication landscape. Authored by Don Pember of the University of Washington, *Mass Media in America* offered undergraduates a comparative examination of historical/critical content in mass media written in a lively manner and supplemented with a number of illustrations. Since I sought a chronological approach and a critical outlook representing both humanities and social science perspectives, I found the book useful and have adopted it, off and on, for nearly twenty years of classroom use.

When I reviewed Pember's second edition for a refereed scholarly publication in subsequent years, I pointed to suggestions I had made earlier to the publisher concerning the selection of examples with which I was most familiar and those with which I disagreed. As in most publishing ventures, some counsel was heeded and some ignored. But in spite of the omissions, I continued to rate the text quite highly and indicated that the revised edition was an improvement. I found that this book's distinct critical viewpoint was absent from many of the introductory texts that were beginning to spring up in answer to an ever-growing market.

The Emery, Ault, and Agee text continued to hold a strong position in the area as well as another text by Edwin Emery, a very comprehensive scholarly history of the press, a favorite among journalism professors discussed here in chapter 14, Mass Communication History. Emery, distinguished professor now emeritus from the University of Minnesota, won a variety of awards for this book, which has been updated to include other areas under the co-authorship of his son Michael, also a distinguished scholar and educator, currently department chair at California State University–Northridge. This book, *The Press in America*, currently competes in the marketplace and, because of its orientation, is particularly popular among media historians.

As the interest in media studies has continued to grow, other major textbook publishers have entered the competition, and books by the Emerys and Don Pember compete in a crowded field, authored by scholars from a wide variety of backgrounds and perspectives. Leading texts in the area include:

Sam Becker and Churchill Roberts, *Discovering Mass Communication* (New York: Harper Collins, 1991).

Shirley Biagi, *Media/Impact* (Belmont, CA: Wadsworth, 1990).

Jay Black and Jennings Bryant, *Introduction to Mass Communication*, 3rd ed. (Dubuque, IA: William C. Brown, 1992).

Melvin L. DeFleur and Everette E. Dennis, *Understanding Mass Communication*, 4th ed. (Palo Alto, CA: Houghton Mifflin, 1991).

Joseph R. Dominick, *The Dynamics of Mass Communication*, 3rd ed. (New York: McGraw-Hill, 1990).

John Merrill, John Lee, and Edward Jay Friedlander, *Modern Mass Media* (New York: Harper Collins, 1990).

Edward J. Whetmore, *Mediamerica*, 3rd ed. (Belmont, CA: Wadsworth, 1987).

One other well-received new entry is *Mass Media in the Informative Age* (Englewood Cliffs, NJ: Prentice-Hall, 1990) by Thomas Pasqua, James Buckalew, Robert Rayfield, and James Tankard. Similar to many new texts, it includes a bank of test questions, but also eight videotapes to enhance student learning. Another recent addition includes John Vivian's *The Media of Mass Communication* (Boston: Allyn & Bacon, 1991), a test bank of 800 questions, lecture resources, an annotated text for teacher's use, and a video tie-in with the Cable News Network (CNN), including taped interviews with such media luminaries as Lee Rich of MGM United Artists and CNN founder Ted Turner. All of these significant contributions to the literature are widely used across the country in the introductory media course. Becker and Roberts's text is highly regarded because of its comparative nature and the up-to-date, technological information. The book by Merrill, Lee, and Friedlander is probably the most eclectic and graphically sophisticated. Shirley Biagi's entry prides itself on minority treatment, while Edward Whetmore takes more of a popular culture approach, with significant contributions in the broadcasting area. Vivian's new book is noteworthy because of its format—a popular magazine style, with boxed profiles of major media leaders and issues. The text also has a publication tie-in with *Messages: The*

Washington Post Media Companion. These are only a few of a multitude of publications covering media content. Some of the most recent entries into the market include not only a teacher's manual for planning purposes but a bank of test questions and teaching aids.

Again, since available texts frequently reflect the background, primary interest, and expertise of the author, the beginning instructor is advised to investigate the textbook writers for clues to their orientation toward the media and their experience in the field. In this way, the instructor can help alert himself or herself to potential biases, strengths, weaknesses, and a good "fit" with the teacher's orientation and background.

INSTRUCTOR BACKGROUND

Who teaches the introductory course in mass communication? It varies, of course, from campus to campus. At some schools with fully developed doctoral programs, large lecture introductory courses are staffed by teams of graduate students usually under the supervision of an experienced faculty member, with each student offering a lecture in his or her specialty area—discussing a topic related to an area of expertise or perhaps a potential dissertation topic. Obviously, without careful supervision, training, and coordination, this approach could lead to a very disjointed, structurally unsound course.

On the opposite end of the spectrum are those schools that try to place their best-known, most prominent senior faculty member in the course, thus assuring students at the introductory level that they will be coming into contact with the best the school has to offer, getting these undergraduates off on the right foot with the academic department or school of communications. Such is the case at the celebrated University of Missouri–Columbia Journalism School, where the beginning required course for mass communication students, one with a distinctive historical focus, traditionally has been taught by a nationally recognized media historian, dating back to the distinguished Frank Luther Mott, author of *American Journalism* and a former Missouri dean.

In either case, under most circumstances the choice of instructor, seen from a content orientation, is always going to be limited to some extent by academic specialty and work experience in the field. In other words, faculty members, just like textbook authors and students, come from a particular background with special interests and life experiences. In the case of the senior professor, because of the nature of academia and scholarship leading to promotion and tenure, the person is likely to have a highly structured and specialized program of research that can hinder the generalist's approach of an introductory course. For this reason, the regular instructor of this survey course needs to identify those areas in which he or she requires regular exposure to literature or, in the case of a beginner, make a conscious effort to identify basic sources in various subfields. The challenge to gain basic knowledge is often most acute when an individual comes to the field from a highly specialized program of graduate study. It is not unusual, for example, for a journalism student to have little acquaintance with film study, given a structured journalism sequence at the undergraduate level and a highly specialized program of graduate study. By the same token, a film student may have had little exposure to the print area and may require some specialized reading and study to come up to speed with those trained in newspaper journalism or journalism history where Pulitzer and Hearst are "household names." This challenge is often present in the field of mass communication because of the diversity of avenues through which instructors enter the field and the kind of affiliations they bring with them.

It has been said that most scholars subscribe to only three or four academic journals in their field, and two of the three are received as part of a professional membership. Since there are over two dozen academic and professional organizations touching on various facets of media study, we can surmise that someone attempting to keep abreast in the field faces a unique task, unparalleled in academia. Leading academic organizations with mass media components include specialized groups discussed earlier, such as the Broadcast Education Association (BEA) affiliated with the trade organization, the National Association of Broadcasters (NAB), and more general groups with mass media or mass communication and society subdivisions. These include the Speech Communication Association (SCA); the Association for Education in Journalism and Mass Communication (AEJMC), which has a specialized accrediting procedure; the International Communication Association (ICA); the American Journalism Historians Association (AJHA); and a good deal more.

As mentioned in the Introduction, many of these groups publish major academic journals in the field: *Critical Studies in Mass Communication* (SCA); AEJMC publishes *Journalism Educator, Journalism Quarterly,* and *Journalism Monographs,* as well as *Mass Comm Review,* put forth by the Mass Communication and Society Division of that organization. Beyond these, the ICA publishes *Communication Theory* and the BEA produces both the *Journal of Broadcasting and Electronic Media* and *Feedback,* a publication with a pedagogical orientation for broadcasting instructors. Other specialized publications include the *Journal of Advertising, Journal of Advertising Research, Communication Research, Newspaper Research Journal, Public Opinion Quarterly,* and *Public Relations Review.*

The professional and trade organizations in such fields as print journalism, broadcasting, advertising, public relations, and film also contribute a large body of information on issues in the various subfields. Publications such as *Advertising Age, American Film, Billboard, Broadcasting, Radio and Records, Editor and Publisher, Hollywood Reporter,* and *Variety* all address issues of the day and news from the media beat in various specialty areas. This volume of opinion and news offers the media scholar an overwhelming number of choices with which to keep up. Of course, many of these publications are available only through organizational membership. *The Quill,* for example, is offered only to members of the Society of Professional Journalists/Sigma Delta Chi, although many of the topical issues addressed in the publication are often discussed in the most popular reviews in the field, *The Columbia Journalism Review* and the *Washington Journalism Review.* Most of the academic journals in the field are, of course, available through library subscription or professional membership.

Memberships play a varying degree of importance in the life of the media teacher. In a presidential address for the AEJMC based on a major study, David Weaver, the Roy Howard Professor at Indiana University, challenged mass communication teachers to become more eclectic in their scholarly work and professional relationships. Weaver reported on trends among professors in mass communication and allied fields, suggesting a distinction between those entering the academy from a professional media career and those who received most of their training and media exposure through advanced education in the area.

Weaver estimated a total of nearly four thousand full-time professors in the field or less than one percent of the nearly half-million college professors in the United States—by industry standards, a small group indeed. Perhaps more intriguing was the categorization of mass communication faculty. Using a telephone sample, the group of mass communication faculty was broken into four distinct classes:[3]

1. Eclectics—those who divide their time between both professional and academic channels of communication;
2. Industry Isolates—those who spend their time exclusively with professional sources of information;

3. Academic Isolates—those pursuing only academic memberships and scholarly journals to the exclusion of industry information;
4. Outliers—those who appear to be isolated entirely from both professionals in the field and their academic peers in mass communication.

Weaver suggested that less than half, about 40 percent, of those contacted for the study qualified as eclectics, even though one would hope that those placed in charge of the introductory mass communication course would have eclectic tastes and interests representing a variety of sources and currency in the field, particularly in the specialty area. In the final analysis, this survey further demonstrates the diversity of faculty in the field and reinforces the need to see to it that those faculty charged with instruction in the general survey course represent an eclectic approach in order to provide consistency and a comprehensive introduction to the field.[4]

In terms of preparation, the ideal candidate for an introductory mass media assignment would have at least a minimum of practical work-related experience in one of the prominent areas of mass communication and a familiarity with the other areas ordinarily gained through advanced graduate study in the field. In light of the Weaver findings, a commitment to staying abreast in the field by a regular program of reading and research is an obvious necessity given the apparent care with which some members of the academic community view their scholarly obligations.

In his 1982 survey for the Mass Communication and Society division of AEJMC, Roy Moore, a major contributor to this book and author of chapter 12 on the Mass Communication Law course, found that in the large lecture mass communication course, almost a third of those sampled were full professors and that nearly 90 percent had extensive teaching experience. The mean for the sample was thirteen years of experience, with a range of two to thirty-two years. Over half of those surveyed held doctorates. This finding, although now somewhat dated, goes against the popular perception that the introductory course is taught by graduate students or the most junior faculty members. It would seem that in the field of mass communication, beginning undergraduate students are being exposed to tenured faculty—those who have succeeded in balancing teaching responsibilities with a program of research. This reflects positively on the field and its faculty, a fact sometimes forgotten in the evaluation process, particularly when conducted solely by undergraduates in a required course.

Once requested to survey attitudes toward course evaluation among teachers in the field, I remember reading a response from a veteran teacher who said, in effect, that she valued student opinion above all else and thought formal student evaluations were an excellent and very valid source of information on teaching effectiveness. The instructor added that she had always received very favorable evaluations, but that if she ever started receiving negative evaluations she would probably start to view the process of collecting student opinion of teaching as being a totally worthless endeavor. This perhaps sums up the attitudes some of us hold of how others view our classroom performance—a very personal, highly ego-involved process in which young people, sometimes fresh from the nation's high schools, reflect on how we—seasoned scholars—convey a lifetime of accumulated knowledge, often in specialized areas in which we hold a national reputation among peers. On the other hand, in the introductory course, regular assessment is perhaps the best indicator of how well the stated objectives of a program are met in line with articulated goals and available resources.

That is to say, the Introduction to Mass Communication course is often the place where parameters of student learning in the field are generally set and expectations of demands are engendered to students in the program and the entire academic community or campus. Frequently instructors take time out in this course to discuss important issues of the day, particularly interrelated issues with broad implications, debated within an institutional framework. For all intents and purposes this is where students start to decide the important questions and parameters of the discipline—what's important and what's not. It is also used as a sounding board and "window on the field" for students unsure of a major in communication or journalism. Because of the importance of this course to the rest of the curriculum, the ideal evaluative instrument would include not only questions regarding course content and quality of instruction but would attempt to get at the specifics employed regarding the overall mission of the course. It would include specific questions regarding use of films, audio-visual aids, and guests brought in to speak from the outside. In short, it would reflect on how effectively the stage had been set for further study in the field.

NOTES

1. For additional source information, see Michael D. Murray and Jack Colldeweigh, "More Help for the Harried Professor: A Selected Program of Tapes in Print and Broadcast Journalism," *Resources in Education* (August

1978) from AEJMC Proceedings, 1978 Annual Meeting, College Park, Maryland.

2. For a summary of arguments, see Ben H. Bagdikian, "Special Issue: The Lords of the Global Village," *The Nation* 248 (June 12, 1989), no. 23, 805–20; See also Ben H. Bagdikian, *The Media Monopoly*, 2nd ed. Boston: Beacon Press, 1987.

3. See David Weaver and G. Cleveland Wilhoit, "A Profile of the JMC Educator," *Journalism Educator* (Summer 1988): 33.

4. More recently, Melvin Mencher commented on the need to recognize cultural and racial differences in our courses to improve coverage. See "Confronting Our Critics and Ourselves," *Journalism Educator* (Winter 1990): 67.

Chapter 2

INTRODUCTION TO BROADCASTING

Donald G. Godfrey

"The age of civilization based on reading, on written literature, is over," Martin Esslin has declared.[1] This is a statement that creates shock, bewilderment, anger, and reflection. However, no matter what your view on the impact of today's media on society, there is no denying its influence is broad. Our culture is engulfed in a telecommunications revolution, bombarded with more information than is possible to assimilate. Donis A. Dondis expressed this same concern when she implied that we are a visually illiterate society.[2] The instructor of An Introduction to Broadcasting faces these issues as they relate to both the consumers and the budding practitioners who are enrolled in the course.

Broadcasting and telecommunications have revolutionized the heart of our nation's culture, business, and communications. The coming of this revolution has greatly affected our homes, our family, and the way of life of our entire society. "It is no accident that the rise of printed literature coincided with the Renaissance and Reformation."[3] Likewise, it is no accident that the information society of today has coincided with the rise of telecommunications and broadcast technology; in fact, the catalyst of the movement has been the preeminent position of broadcasting in our society. These facts make the Introduction to Broadcasting course one of the most exciting and challenging of the curriculum.

BACKGROUND

Teaching the introductory course on American broadcasting is an assignment often dismissed too casually by the new graduate student who sees it only as temporary duty, by the media professional who has difficulty sifting twenty years of experience into a meaningful organization pattern, and by the professor who finds little excitement in that "same ole 100–200 level stuff." It is, however, an exciting opportunity to be the first—the first to bring a new world of insight into the minds of those eager consumers of our media, and the first to direct and establish the foundation of information for those who aspire to careers in the field. As one colleague noted, "It is just fun to take the sex appeal out of the media." There is no denying the impact of radio and television communications. It has permeated almost every facet of our lives. Teaching this course is to uncover some of those mysteries.

The responsibility of one who approaches the introductory class is not to be taken lightly. The introductory course serves as an important springboard for upper-division and job-related courses, and the instructor has a responsibility of basic consumer education. The long-range goal is to elevate the standards of the industry and the consumer. In this broader perspective, the course is to introduce hundreds of students to the world of broadcasting and telecommunications. A former colleague, Robert Guy, program director for KING-TV, used to tell the story of a luncheon he attended with several university presidents, deans, and academic officers of the West. Bob earned a Ph.D. in marketing, he had passed through the academic ranks, and in later years he had returned to work in commercial broadcasting. At the luncheon, members at the table were asked to introduce themselves and tell a little bit about their work. Following Bob's introduction, everyone in the room sat silently; finally one of the university presidents spoke, with some indignation: "You're the man responsible for that garbage we're seeing on our television!" Without any hesitation, Bob responded, "You folks in education have had a captive audience for over a hundred years and you've failed to elevate the status of the American public!" This is our consumer challenge! This is the challenge of those who will shortly enter and direct the industry.

ORGANIZATION

Utilizing the terms of a syllabus, a simple statement of purpose would read: The purpose of the course is to examine the American broadcasting system, its historical basis, its philosophical foundation, and its systems, patterns, functions, and problems of communication.

The Broadcast Education Association's composite course outline lists four course content objectives: (1) to acquaint the student with the historical setting of broadcasting—past, present, and trends toward the future; (2) to acquaint the student with the basic structure of American broadcasting; (3) to acquaint the student with the basic operation of broadcasting stations; (4) to help the student to form critical judgment of broadcast programming, to understand the communicative aspects of mass advertising, and to analyze the effect of broadcasting on society.

These directives provide a general overview and focus on the course content. Now, what do you want your students to gain from this course, both in terms of behavioral as well as content objectives? As a colleague stated, "My students will never watch television or listen to radio in the same way again, and they'll enjoy it more!" The BEA's published behavioral objectives for students who complete the course are as follows:

1. Identify significant contributions of selected individuals in the development of broadcasting;
2. Identify significant elements in the structure and organization of the broadcasting industry;
3. Explain the basic formulas used in broadcast sales and audience measurement;
4. Define or identify selected terminology related to the broadcasting industry;
5. Explain the growth and formation of regulatory agencies that relate to broadcasting, particularly the Federal Communications Commission;
6. Explain the organization and departmental functions of a broadcast station;
7. Explain the organization of trends and innovations in broadcasting;
8. Outline various local radio and television programming services in his/her own area.[4]

Note in the above BEA objectives the continued use of the words "identify/define." In that respect they are very much like the content objectives. However, the instructor must so direct the course to emphasize the functional meaning of the terms in order to accomplish behavioral objectives; otherwise the terms become a list of meaningless jargon.

One primary objective appears in both the content and behavioral objectives: to acquaint the students with the elements and operational systems of the business of broadcasting. In other words, it is important once the basic operational systems are understood that students know how these components interrelate. Do not lose sight of the fact that broadcasting is a communications business and, while some see this as a criticism, an equal number view it as a compliment.

TEXTS

The selection of a text depends on the individual experience of the instructor and the makeup of your student body. You'll want to check with faculty colleagues, see what is currently being used, and ask their rationale for a particular selection. Ask about the new and revised editions of available texts. Write the publishing companies and request examination copies. Most are happy to provide free review texts.

Perhaps the book referred to most often by those who have taught the course is Sydney Head's *Broadcasting in America* (Boston: Houghton Mifflin, 1990). It has recently been updated by Professor Christopher Sterling. This text is this author's first choice, especially if the course is used as a screening course or if it is for career orientation. In the days of this author's undergraduate work, not one student liked the text, and that fact has not changed. However, a diligent instructor guided everyone through it, and over the years this publication became a most valuable reference source. Now there are two major criticisms of Head's textbook. First, as one colleague noted, "It's almost a reference text." It is not a text that is difficult to read; it is simply detailed. However, is that a criticism or a compliment? It would not be an understatement to say that almost every major work published on the industry has cited the work of Sydney Head. The second criticism of this text relates to the inclusion of the introductory chapters on early technology. These chapters lead off the textbook, and they are difficult, even for many instructors. The solution? Simply review the material and cover in lecture form those elements you see as important. Then start your students' reading schedule with whatever chapters you wish. A textbook should not dictate a syllabus or a course layout. It is a secondary document supporting and enriching the major content directives set by the instructor as he or she views a specific set of objectives and student clientele. So take the textbook of your choice and arrange the reading schedule to complement and enrich your own organizational approach. There are also many other texts. They include:

John R. Bittner, *Broadcasting and Telecommunication: An Introduction*, 2nd ed. (Englewood Cliffs, NJ: Prentice Hall, 1985).

Joseph Dominick, Barry L. Sherman, and Gary Copeland, *Broadcasting/Cable and Beyond* (New York: McGraw-Hill, 1989).

Eugene S. Foster, *Understanding Broadcasting* (Reading, MA: Addison-Wesley, 1982).

Leslie F. Smith, *Perspectives on Radio and Television: Telecommunications in the United States*, 3rd ed. (New York: Harper & Row, 1990).

Marvin Smith, *Radio, TV & Cable: A Telecommunications Approach* (New York: Holt Rinehart & Winston, 1985).

These texts are easily read and are used by many schools where the consumer literacy objectives are balanced with career preparation. The consumer does not always need the depth of *Broadcasting in America* as does the practitioner. Actually, it would be difficult for the new instructor to err in the selection of a text. There are a number of fine works. Supplementary texts have proven invaluable to this author. These include:

Elizabeth J. Heighton and Don R. Cunningham, *Advertising in the Broadcast and Cable Media*, 2nd ed. (Belmont, CA: Wadsworth, 1984). This text supplements your advertising discussion and the understanding of business and sales relationships. Other supporting publications of particular interest are cited in the bibliography.

Frank J. Kahn, *Documents of American Broadcasting*, 4th ed. (New York: Prentice Hall, 1984). Provides just exactly what its title implies: the acts, codes, and laws relative to governing the broadcast system. You can extract some of these documents for distribution in class. Then each individual word, phrase, and paragraph can be discussed.

Christopher Sterling and John Kittross, *Stay Tuned: A Concise History of American Broadcasting*, 2nd ed. (Belmont, CA: Wadsworth, 1990). A comprehensive American history text. As a new instructor, if you desire more detail on any given historical topic, it is provided in *Stay Tuned*. The text is well documented and it is easy to follow up on specific references.

One of the most commonly used pieces of supplemental reading is *Broadcasting Magazine*, the industry's trade journal. Students not familiar with the terminology of the industry are at times frustrated by the depth of some articles; however, this provides an opportunity to teach, to define terminology in its operational context, and to relate current developments to the course content. Start by having students read the programming section and get them interested in following the ratings. Then as the course proceeds, their interest will expand and you can relate specific articles to the course. *Broadcasting Magazine*'s circulation department also offers a student discount.

Another valuable supplement can be found in the columns of your local papers. Today more and more papers offer columns by a staff "broadcast critic," which can be invaluable for localizing your course materials. Some of these critics will be merely program reviewers, and while that does serve a readership purpose, your interest will be primarily with those critics who are watching the media within your community, localizing national media trends, and functioning as a consumer information reporter/ critic as well as a reviewer of national programs.

Other periodicals important to broadcasting include *Radio-Television Age; Radio Only; TV Guide; The Journal of Broadcasting and Electronic Media;* and *Journal of Communication.*

Again, the new instructor need only relate those materials complementary to interest and content. This author will never forget that first introductory course assignment. It was anticipated with excitement! Preparation seemed adequate, but after three weeks into the course, all the material had been covered, and the final exam was yet eight weeks away. A kind mentor was solicited and the course was prepared one day at a time, one week at a time, one semester/quarter at a time. The outline that follows is a compilation of what this author has developed, and it is in line with BEA directives. It is important that a new instructor mold his or her outline in relation to personal experience. Even if you have not had any professional experience, don't assume that you cannot relate from an educated point of view. Sharing is an important part of the thinking and learning process. As Fred Friendly notes in most of his seminars, "The responsibility of a teacher [is] to make learning so intense you can escape only by thinking." Teaching is far more than the relation of old war stories. Stories can enrich, but the essential component of teaching is to guide your students through an experiential learning process, relate to them, dialogue with them, and challenge their own thoughts.

Here is a working outline developed by the author over the last twenty years of teaching the course. For purposes of this chapter it is in traditional outline form. For the syllabus, the roman numeral designations are changed to Week I/Monday, Wednesday, Friday, and so forth.

I. The History of the American System
   A. Wireless Communication—The Industrial Age and the
       Era of What Historians Refer to as American Imperialism
      1. James Clerk Maxwell—electromagnetic theory
      2. Heinrich Hertz—puts theory to practice
      3. Marconi—the inventor and entrepreneur
      4. Lee De Forest—audio tube
   B. From Wireless to Radio
      1. Experiment era
         a. The inventors
         b. Point-to-point communication
         c. Ship-to-shore
      2. Non-commercial era—World War I
         a. World War I—Navy
         B. Patent problems
      3. Commercial era—patterns begin to emerge
         a. KDKA/CFCF—first and precedents
         b. WEAF–AT&T contributions
         c. RCA development
      4. The networks emerge
         a. AT&T
         b. NBC Red & Blue
         c. CBS

II. Government Regulation and Broadcasting—Imperialism to
     the Roaring Twenties
   A. Wireless Ship Act
   B. Radio Act of 1912
   C. Legislation of the 1920s
      1. Hoover Conference—the question of regulation
      2. U.S. vs. Zenith
      3. Attorney general's opinion
      4. The period of chaos
   D. The 1927 Radio Act
      1. Basic hypothesis
         a. Channels belong to the people
         b. Radio is a unique service

          c.   Service must be equally distributed

          d.   Not all are eligible for a channel

          e.   Radio is protected by the First Amendment

          f.   Government has regulatory power

          g.   Those powers are not absolute

    2.   Definition of broadcasting

    3.   Federal Radio Commission takes over

    4.   Major personalities and issues

          a.   Coolidge   —a quiet, do-nothing president

          b.   Hoover   —the great humanitarian

                            — rugged individualism

                            —Father of American System

              White   —the great negotiator

              Dill   —the progressive

              Roosevelt   —the New Deal

E.   The Communications Act of 1934

    1.   Three additional responsibilities

    2.   Reflects the New Deal and Roosevelt

F.   Importance of the Elasticity of these Acts

    1.   Issues of the time compared to issues of our time

    2.   How would you resolve the issues?

III.   Broadcasting Patterns Emerge in Response to a Need—From the Roaring Twenties, the New Deal, the Depression, Isolationism vs. One World, and World War II

    A.   Development of Syndication

    B.   Broadcast Music Incorporated

    C.   Press Radio War Prepares Foundation for News Organizations

    D.   Networks Develop Affiliates

        1.   Network affiliate relationship history

        2.   Contractual relationship

    E.   Networks Grow

        1.   Chain broadcasting investigations

        2.   Growth of CBS, NBC, Mutual, and ABC

F. FM Broadcasting
    1. Edwin Armstrong
    2. The business resistance
G. Review Chart—Broadcasting System USA Style
H. Post-War and War Effects
I. Radio's Golden Age—play program excerpts
J. The Freeze
K. Radio in Transition
    1. Problem of programming
    2. Local programming

IV. Television
    A. Historical Development
        1. Farnsworth
        2. CBS/NBC systems
        3. Radio patterns/organizations in place
    B. Post-War Programming
    C. Color Television Development
    D. Early Life Programming—play excerpts

V. The Business of Broadcast Communication
    A. Television Station Organization and Functions
        1. Departmental organization and function
        2. Distribution systems
            a. UHF/VHF/translators/satellites
            b. Cable stations
        3. Unions
        4. Technical and market designations
    B. Radio Station Types and Organizations
        1. Formats
        2. Technical designations and meaning
    C. Broadcast Advertising
    D. Types of Advertising
    E. Mechanics in the Sale of Time
        1. National spot
        2. Network advertising
        3. Local advertising

F.   Functions of the Advertising Agency and Station Rep

VI.   Broadcast Programming
  A.   Brief Overview of Programming Law
    1.   Great Lakes opinion
    2.   Blue Book precedent
    3.   Marketplace decisions
  B.   Daily Operations and Program Law
    1.   Section 315
    2.   Will the Fairness Doctrine be revised once again?
    3.   Obscenity
    4.   Public records
    5.   Censorship
    6.   Advertising and fairness
  C.   Television Station Programming
    1.   Seven principles of programming
    2.   Programming cycles
    3.   Today's costs
    4.   The social diamond and audience composition
    5.   Challenges in scheduling
    6.   Strategies in scheduling

VII.   Audience Research
  A.   Rating Service Information
  B.   Ratings and Share Defined
  C.   Major Ratings Firms and Methodology
  D.   Ratings and Market Definitions
  E.   Simplified Ratings Breakout
  F.   Value of Ratings
  G.   Demographic and Psychographic Ratings
  H.   Criticism of Rating
  I.   Growing Body of Audience Research Data
    1.   Research firms
    2.   Station research

VIII.   The Business of Broadcast News
  A.   What Is News?

B. The Station's Newsroom
C. Programming the News for Profit
D. Gathering and Disseminating the News

IX. Educational/Public Broadcasting
A. Sixth Report and Order
B. Public vs. Educational Defined
C. Earning a Non-Profit
D. Television and the Teacher
1. In the classroom
2. Effects on the classroom

X. New Technology
A. Multipoint Distribution
B. Subscription Television
C. Direct Broadcast Satellites
D. High Definition Television
E. Etc. as time permits—with emphasis on
1. Benefits to the audience
2. Effects on the industry
3. Business opportunity/marketplace

XI. Cable Television
A. System Description
B. Regulation
C. Programming and Potential

XII. A Look Toward the Future
A. Programming
B. Regulation
C. Marketplace

In the outline Sections I and II, it is particularly important that students see the events in the context of their historical environment. For example, the development of the wireless came during the late industrial era. It is one of the inventions that came after the head of the patent office declared it would close, because all that could be invented had already been invented. Also, the Navy might have played a completely different role had it not been for the exigencies of World War I. Perhaps the most glaring historical context omission occurs in discussions of the development of broadcast regulation, Section II. It is true that the industry wanted regulation; it is true that the 1927 Radio Act was passed as the result of a great deal of pressure from both the radio industry and the public (because of the period of chaos); however, it is equally true that these laws were developed and affected by the context of people and time.[5] The modernism versus fundamentalism controversy, for example, sparked the famous debates between Clarence Darrow and William Jennings Bryan. These debates were broadcast, as was the Scopes trial, and they led to serious discussions revolving around broadcast censorship.

Legislators responded to such environments and discussed these questions and others as they drafted what is now communication law. In relating these to students, simply ask: What is the difference between the censorship questions then and now? The business ethic ruled the roost of American government during the Roaring Twenties. How did the legislature respond to that? Can you see how their discussions are reflected in the fundamental hypotheses of the Radio Act? What is the difference between the business ethics of the 1920s and today's business ethics? As you respond to these questions, you will find even political slogans cycling through the decades. It is important that you discuss, just briefly, the political and cultural environment. These were real people and actual events whose decisions and circumstances affect our lives today.

One of the most important supplementary resources is your local broadcast community, which provides opportunities for both students and instructors. The course is enhanced by carefully selected guest speakers. Don't be afraid to ask anyone, even those at the top—a local critic whose articles you've been reading, the managers of stations and talent. Most will enjoy the experience. There is just one word of caution. You want individuals who will enrich the curriculum through their experience, not stand on a soap box and expose their ego.

There are supplemental films and audio materials available through your audio-visual department or films you can use through an exchange service with other universities. The following represents this author's favorites:

Braverman Productions' *Televisionland* is a composite film of the history of television. It gives the students a good laugh as well as an under-standing of the early days of television programming.

Braverman Productions' *The Making of Live Television* is a dated look at the behind-the-scenes Emmy Awards from a production point of view. If your television production professor is not using this film in one of the basic production classes, use it for this introductory course during your discussion of programming.

Clio Award Films

These are simply reels of award-winning commercials compiled annually. The commercials are always excellent productions gathered from all over the world. They are generally available with some cooperation from your local Ad Club.

The Arbitron Ratings Company and the Associated Press have also produced films for classroom use, which are available with just a phone call. It is wise to plan well ahead to assure your booking. The Associated Press film is excellent and works well during Section VIII. The Arbitron film, unfortunately, is weak. You may want to preview it before you make a decision. It contains an enjoyable clip from the WKRP television series, which provides a good introduction to Section VII on ratings. While the film is weak, Arbitron is anxious to assist and will provide printed information and old ratings books for class examination.

Old radio programs are available from many sources. Some can even be purchased at your local variety store today. Play those programs you enjoy and relate your enthusiasm to the class. Many instructors use the Orson Welles Mercury Theatre of the Air "War of the Worlds." This is a good piece to illustrate the societal effects of our media, but in the opinion of this author, there are better examples of Orson Welles's work and better examples of radio's golden age. Several directories list institutional collections where you can acquire selections from radio's golden age. For example, *Reruns on File* is a directory consisting primarily of collections available for academic use and research.[6] Most will lend programs at minimal or no cost for classroom use.

The industry is calling for improved writing skills from our graduates, and as a result, many schools are requiring some form of writing assignment in almost every class. In the introductory class this can take on several forms. The first is the traditional term paper. The second is to have your students write critical one- to three-page essays on programs or specific topics of discussion. These two exercises are traditional and easily tooled into the course. A third exercise used periodically by this author—and as a writing option—is an oral history paper. This is a bit unusual, but with the proper preparation, it can be a very successful exercise.

The stated purpose of the "final oral history paper option" is to record the historical insight of people who "have enchanted us with accounts of their lives in another era." The development of this project requires the student to do many of the same things a term paper would accomplish.

The success of the interview depends on preparation. During the interview the most important thing the student can do is to be quiet and listen. Let the mind of the subject tell the story as the interviewer listens and asks open-ended questions. It is a good idea to consult Gary Shumway's pamphlet "An Oral History Primer."[7]

There are similarities between a good oral history and a good term paper. One difference this author has noted is that those students who opt to undertake an oral history and successfully complete the assignment return with a far greater appreciation for the historical foundation of our industry and an excitement for history.

A few words of caution with this assignment. First, do it yourself with a member of your own family or a local professional before you make the assignment. Second, have the students submit at least three names of proposed interview subjects and then you assign them one. This will avoid duplication and bother to your local broadcast pioneers who do not want to be interviewed every semester. Finally, don't be reluctant to let them interview their own family members. All that really matters is the requirement that the subject be over sixty-five years of age.

Evaluation is simply a matter of weighing exams and writing projects. The larger the class the more likely you will be to use the objective tests. Most instructors will weigh a 75/25 balance between tests and papers. If you are a new instructor, you might also request the instructor's manual of your text. These are usually helpful in making up those multiple choice questions. No matter what your testing mechanism and your writing assignments, stress concepts and organization. It is important that your professional students understand this foundation. It is important that those who are merely consumers understand general operations. Don't lose sight of your behavioral and content objectives and the fact that they can elevate their own individual tastes by understanding and making clear decisions on their own media habits.

CONCLUSION

Introduction to Broadcasting can be one of the most exciting courses you will teach. This author has taught it periodically for twenty years, and each time it is different. There are different personalities to every class, and as you have heard before, "The only constant in the broadcast industry is change." It is exciting to see the students change, to help them in understanding systems and information flow operations and in developing their own standards. It is exciting to watch the lights go on and the glamour disappear from their eyes. A greater understanding of our industry results in an educated consumer and an uplifted practitioner.

NOTES

1. Martin Esslin, *The Age of Television* (San Francisco: W. H. Freeman & Co., 1982), 4–6.

2. Donis A. Dondis, *A Primer of Visual Literacy* (Cambridge, MA: MIT Press, 1973), 11.

3. Edward Jay Whetmore, *Mediamerica*, 2nd ed. (Belmont, CA: Wadsworth, 1982), 5.

4. "BEA Composite Course Outline: 2A," Broadcast Education Association, Temple University, n.d.

5. Donald G. Godfrey, "The 1927 Radio Act: People and Politics," *Journalism History* 4:3 (Autumn 1977): 74–78.

6. Donald G. Godfrey, ed., *Reruns on File* (Hillsdale, NJ: Lawrence Erlbaum Associates, Inc., 1991).

7. Gary L. Shumway and William G. Hartley, *An Oral History Primer* (Fullerton, CA: Shumway & Hartley, 1980). Professor Shumway teaches in the department of history at California State University–Fullerton.

Chapter 3

INTRODUCTION TO PUBLIC RELATIONS

Anthony J. Ferri

What images come to mind when I say "Las Vegas"? The desert, gambling, and bright lights? It's a safe bet, if you'll pardon the pun, that you will not consider things like families, neighborhoods, churches, and a university as part of this city. And yet, away from the casinos on "the Strip," Las Vegas is your typical American city. One consequence of these images is that many people come to Las Vegas every year to gamble and have fun, attracted by the mystique of the desert and the party atmosphere of the Strip. The local casinos and community do little to change this impression, and actually promote the illusion of the twenty-four hour play town. Another consequence may be a negative association between gambling and the credibility of the local university. Does the image of a typical American university with faculty busily researching contemporary issues and teaching serious-minded students clash with your image of the gambling city of America? If the answer is yes, then we may have a public relations problem. I tell my students that we are all practicing public relations when we interact with people off campus, either locally or out of town. For this and many other reasons, public relations is both a desirable and relevant area of study and research.

BACKGROUND

Teaching the introductory public relations course gives the instructor the chance to explore contemporary issues in the context of communication theory and principles. I think you will find that this chapter, along with your own areas of expertise or knowledge, will equip you sufficiently to prepare an interesting and challenging course for your students.

Although it is desirable and feasible to inform students about the process and profession of public relations, it is unrealistic to expect to train them to be public relations experts in one course. Even if you include a practical project in the course, it must be made clear to the students that they are only being introduced to the process and profession. Public relations is both a process and a profession, and you should expect your students, after completing your course, to know how public relations works and who are the major participants. If they want to become professionals or practitioners in the field, additional course work and experience will be necessary.

ORGANIZATION

The organization of the course is a function of the curriculum in which it is taught. There are at least two types of introductory classes in public relations. One is the "all purpose" class, which means that it is the only public relations class in your curriculum. In this course you introduce the history and theory of public relations and incorporate applied projects. The other type is the introductory class of a public relations major or sequence.

The implications for these typologies on course structure can be seen in the number of projects included. For the all-purpose class, the instructor might want to incorporate two of the three assignments described later in this chapter. If you have a public relations sequence or a major that includes a number of public relations classes, then the case study project would suffice. Even if you choose not to have any student projects, the course material outlined in this chapter should provide your students with sufficient knowledge of public relations.

It is important to develop some terms that will help indicate important relationships among the major players in public relations. I use the word "organization" to denote any company, institution, or person using public relations. Organizations are the clients of public relations. The "practitioner" is the public relations person or agency practicing public relations. As obvious as these terms may seem, students find it very useful to have such terms defined. As the instructor, you will find things are much easier to explain when you define these major participants in the process.

Regardless of the type of course or textbook used, certain subject areas or units are necessary in the introductory class. A unit can be one class or a week of classes, depending on the importance you want to assign to that subject area. The subjects are in order of presentation.

Defining Public Relations

This subject is so important because it dictates what you and your students will expect from the term "public relations." I like to open this unit with definitions from the students themselves. In my experience, two types of definitions emerge—their academic definition and their personal or connotative definition. The academic definition includes things like "communication is persuasion," or "public relations is designed to bring people together." Their connotative or personal definition usually portrays public relations as a superficial, misleading process, often portrayed in popular vernacular as "just PR."

I use these definitions in order to determine my students' impressions and expectations of public relations as well as to demonstrate the difference between the process as practiced in the field or "real world" versus the prescriptive or academic definition. This may lead to a discussion about what role educational institutions have in advancing the practice of public relations and what input professional practitioners should provide these institutions. Should academic institutions lead the public relations profession through research of the process?

Since public relations varies in the way it is practiced in the field and the manner in which it is examined by academics, it is helpful to develop a definition that offers direction and reference for your instructional needs and is fairly accurate in terms of application. The ideal definition of public relations would accurately portray the realities in the field and the potentials of the practice. Rex Harlow's attempt at such a definition serves as a guide for the course described in this chapter, since the heart of this definition is a desirable and workable focus for the study of public relations.[1] Public relations creates public support and understanding for client organizations. What I add to this definition is the notion of relationships. Public relations is a process of communication relationships among practitioners, organizations, and publics in which the practitioners try to develop the most favorable relationships between their client organizations and publics.

It is important to tell your students that this is a prescriptive definition and an ideal one at that. Educational institutions lead the practitioners through theory and research, and practitioners apply what we learn. Thus, a public relations definition for the class may not match what is out there in the field at this point.

Many students confuse advertising and public relations. The best way to distinguish advertising and public relations is to define advertising as a tool used by marketing professionals to sell products and services, while public relations is a broader process where people use advertising to promote images and ideas.

In addition to lecture material on people like Ivy Lee and Edward Bernays[2] (almost every text will include useful biographies and historical analyses), you can engage your students in the history of public relations by having them help you outline the careers of contemporary persons in public relations and explain how those practitioners have defined or changed the profession and practice. It is not necessary to restrict these discussions to public relations professionals. You can examine how the president of the United States or your university president uses public relations and how this use has expanded or limited the practice. It is important to get your students to see how persons practicing or using public relations change the process and purpose through their efforts and needs.

Human and mass communication theories lay the groundwork for the study and practice of public relations. While the variables within the theories may be recognizable to the reader, it is recommended that a good reading and analysis of theoretical works is desirable and advisable.

I like to start with a discussion of epistemologies. I explain to students that there are different ways of knowing and that all are used in public relations: pragmatics, authority, and empiricism. Pragmatics is really experience, as I define it. Public relations practitioners operate via this epistemology or way of knowing when they use previous successful cases in order to solve problems. It is experience without reason. When practitioners do something because a consultant or even a professor of communication tells them it is correct, they are behaving according to authority. The use of scientific studies, either developed by the practitioner or read in a journal, is the practice of empiricism. It is experience with reason. Most practitioners operate via pragmatics and authority.

A number of variables and theories are applicable to the study of public relations. The following list highlights the major areas of study. It is not necessary to spend separate units on each area, but it is desirable to spend part of a unit on each. Also, you will find that these variables and theories will overlap subject areas in the course. This is beneficial since it will help promote the concept of theoretical grounding for your students.

Credibility. Credibility is a source's competence or trustworthiness in the minds of his or her audience. The essence of public relations is to create credible messages about a client to various audiences. This is somewhat difficult with a profession that is suspect by the stereotype of the name public relations.

Definition of Communication. Many introductory texts of communication will offer contemporary theories of communication that introduce the important concepts of sender, message, channel, receiver, and feedback. The concept of "trace," as defined by DeFleur and Ball-Rokeach, is also useful in a lecture on communication since it focuses on one of the key factors of communication—meaning.[3] A trace is any experience that has been permanently recorded in memory. Symbols have meaning for us, in part, because of particular trace configurations we associate with those symbols. My understanding of the word "pasta," for instance, might embrace a number of images including my grandmother cooking this dish, or a recent outing at some Italian restaurant. Since every individual has different experiences, one's ability to understand symbols the way others do is limited. The difficulty of communicating meaningful messages to others is an important theme in the course. When you discuss the simple press release in class, for instance, it is desirable to reiterate the relationship between trace and meaning so that students learn how important it is for practitioners to visualize the reader of the release and to consider the types of symbols that would be significant to him or her.

Communication Contexts. Differentiating the contexts in which persons and groups communicate is helpful in a public relations class since public relations operates on different levels. While mass communication is a major channel for external public relations, face-to-face and group communication are important for internal relations. The major contexts to consider are face-to-face or one-to-one; group communication; organizational (how organizations interact and communicate internally); and mass communication.

Persuasion Theories. One of the goals of public relations is to create support for the organization. This involves persuading publics to accept the organization through positive attitudes and actions. There are many persuasion texts that will give you the major theories and research. Whatever theories you include, remember the following points. First, some students will want to generalize the theories you present beyond their limits, while others will expect the theories to be as utilitarian as a coin-operated machine. It will be your job to present the theories as general models for analysis of public relations relationships. Some of the relevant persuasion theories are psychological balance; expectancy-value or other motivational theories; and sociocultural approach to persuasion.

Symbolic Communication. Theories focusing on semantics, connotation, and nonverbal communication are important for understanding the use of language in public relations. Practitioners spend much time and effort on developing words which connote positive images for their organizations. In marketing, for example, auto companies "downsize" a car; they do not make it smaller. "Used cars" are "pre-owned." The tobacco industry has realized that the connotations and attitudes associated with cigarettes and cancer are so strong that they have tried to shift the focus of public debate away from the health issue and more toward less loaded issues and images like smokers' rights.

A discussion of logotypes in this unit is warranted. Blending theories of symbolic communication and the use of logotypes or logos by organizations gives the student another sense of theoretical grounding.

Organization and Structure of Public Relations

Employees and Agencies. Students should know how public relations is housed within organizations and how it is practiced outside organizations (advertising and public relations agencies). Public relations as practiced within a company department is different from public relations performed by professional, outside agencies. Practitioners working within a company department are really employees and may have a lower level of credibility from a corporate executive's view than an outside agency. This has an impact on the success of public relations programs.

Titles and Euphemisms. Public relations is not called public relations by many practitioners. Euphemisms like "public information officer" are used in government, for example. The subject of titles is important for two reasons. First, it shows students that public relations is a broader field than they might think. All those non-public relations titles for public relations people mask the full extent of the size of the profession. Secondly, the use of euphemisms is usually a sign that the profession is not entirely comfortable with the title and its connotation.

Problem Solving Sequence

Most public relations texts now describe a process of public relations that includes research, planning, implementation, and evaluation. It is a useful sequence of activities to prescribe. It needs to be made clear, however, that it is a prescribed sequence of activities and not a scientific theory.

The first part of the process, the research stage, includes both informal and formal analyses of the client's standing in the minds of its publics. Essentially, in this part of the process practitioners seek to find what the organization's publics know and how they feel about the organization.

Informal methods of research include press clippings (handled by clipping services companies contracted by the client), field reports by sales staff, focus groups, and personal conversations between practitioners and relevant publics. The formal methods include scientific surveys (usually done by advertising agencies for a client).

Sometimes students question the importance of covering this area in a public relations class since they associate communication and not research with the profession. It is useful here to tell your students that even though most practitioners do not personally conduct formal research projects, a knowledge of the typical methods and terms is necessary for the practitioner who uses a professional research agency.

Other important topics included under formal research are sampling procedures, survey instrumentation and questionnaire design, and descriptive statistics. All of these subjects are covered rather clearly in most basic survey or statistics books.

The second part of the process is the planning stage. The most important aspect includes these questions: what is the purpose of a public relations plan and what should be in it. The purpose of any plan is to produce some blueprint from which the practitioner can act. Obviously, in many situations a plan is not feasible due to time constraints. However, for long-term or continuous public relations efforts, like a public relations campaign, a plan serves as the map. Additionally, a plan should be seen as a persuasive document by which the practitioner tries to sell the public relations campaign or strategy to the employer or client organization.

The contents of the plan should include (1) statement of the problem and analysis of relevant data (the research results in stage one); (2) the objectives of the campaign (specific outcomes like "to motivate a particular target public to attend an open house"); (3) the communications plan (campaign theme, relevant media, specific messages); (4)

the action plan (noncommunicative events like an open house) if warranted; (5) budget (costs of services, hardware, and personnel needed); and (6) a sequence calendar (what needs to be done and when).

The third stage in the process is the implementation of the plan from stage two. In order to expand this topic in class, the instructor should examine what parts of the communication and action plans might be affected by real world events. What happens, for instance, if the planned open house is held on a day of rain and lightning?

The fourth and final stage of the process is the evaluation of the campaign. Essentially, this includes a monitoring of the attitudes and beliefs first studied in stage one. It is a before-and-after process whereby the practitioner tries to assess the impact of the communication and action plans on the feelings and knowledge of the target publics. In the "real world" of public relations such systematic evaluation is not always done, but when it is, practitioners will contract with some research company to do follow-up survey work. The topics of survey research and statistics are relevant here.

A "public" in public relations is any group of people who affect or are affected by an organization. The broad range of this definition is an indication of the arbitrary notion of the concept "public." Publics are defined by public relations practitioners in terms of strategies and goals: what does the organization need or want to do and which groups of people help, mediate, or hinder the cause. Typically publics are divided according to organizational placement (internal, external) and socioeconomics (business, gender, profession).

The best way to demonstrate the concept of publics for students is to dissect their own university, college, or high school. The internal publics are easiest to outline, and in class I have students tell me what publics to put on the chalkboard. These internal publics are instructors, nonteaching staff, administrators, and the students. The tricky part is outlining the external publics. For the typical university the publics would include the community, high school seniors and grads, business leaders, and the state legislature.

One of the most important areas to emphasize in an introductory public relations class is media relations. The mass media are the principal channels for information dissemination for organizations. How to manage or manipulate the media to help get organizational messages across to publics, for free, is what media relations is all about.

Some of the major topics in this unit include media organizations (typical structure of local and national television and newspaper units); power of the media (lectures based on empirically based texts in the field); publicity materials (press releases, news conferences); and interviewing (how to be interviewed and how to control the interview process).

The crafting and hard work necessary for effective publicity are areas that must be made salient and significant for public relations students. Even the most finely crafted press release cannot guarantee media coverage or even attention to an organizational story. The basic premise in publicity is that in order to get media coverage of the client organization's story or point of view, and without cost, the practitioner must give "legitimate" news to those news media. "Legitimate" means information that the editors normally publish or broadcast.

We all have had problems with products or services, and thus we are all experts on consumer relations. For this and many other reasons, consumer relations is an interesting unit in public relations. You may want to start this area with some illustrations solicited from your class. Typical consumer complaint areas that your students will share include airline, auto, and appliance problems. In addition to how practitioners handle complaints, consumer relations will also offer some very dramatic case studies like product tampering (e.g., the Tylenol product tampering case of 1982). Today, not only are companies pitching their products and services through advertising, they are also trying to position these products and services within a world of changing technologies and socioeconomic environments. The airline industry, for example, is subject to the increasing fear of flying as a result of dramatic crashes. Regardless of the actual safety of this mode of transportation, the perception of safety is what affects consumers' fear of flying, and this is one very good reason why public relations people are needed in that industry.

Most students work either full- or part-time and you can expect that they will gladly share their stories about their problems or challenges at work. Employee relations is a subject that can illustrate the public relations process in a way to which students can relate. I start this unit by asking students to respond to the following questions: (1) How do you know when you have done something good or bad on the job? (2) How is important information sent to you, personally? These and other similar questions generate the stories and discussions about employee relations.

Since even the most basic forms of public relations involve some aspect of constitutional issues, some discussion of the legal framework in which practitioners work is necessitated in the introductory class. Whether it involves possible libel considerations in the company newsletter or employee rights of privacy, the need for practitioners to cover all legal bases is very important, and thus of interest to the public relations student.

A note of caution is in order. While I try to avoid esoteric subjects or ones well beyond my expertise, I do incorporate the legal subject area in most of my public relations courses. It is advisable, however, to inform your students of your own expertise and suggest that they always seek professional legal advice on the job if they become practitioners. Again, the course is an introduction to the process of public relations, and only an introduction.

Three exams is an effective number for the introductory class. Quizzes could be added, but they are not really necessary. Exams and/or quizzes should be worth about 65 to 75 percent of the final grade. Even if you include a major student project like a public relations proposal, you should limit the value of the practical aspects of the course, since it is introductory. The student assignments are designed to illustrate the process, and not serve as training for the profession.

Students can be given a public relations client or they can find their own as a proposal project. This client can be a local business, nonprofit organization, or even your own university, college, or school. Your students must provide the client with a public relations proposal for a particular problem. They are to provide a proposal only and not its implementation. The value of this type of project is that it allows students the time to focus on the research and planning aspects of public relations. Also, it gives your client a chance to see if your students are capable of providing effective public relations ideas, thus building a bridge for future classes. This project is most successful as a group project, with about five students per group.

The major components are:

Research and Analysis of the Problem. The students provide the client with formal and informal data on the target publics as well as any other data relevant to the problem. Students will need some instruction and training on the use of focus groups and/or basic survey methods. Supplementary readings on research methods are particularly helpful.

Public Relations Strategy. This component includes the communications and action plans necessary to solve the problems. Specifics would include the relevant media, publics, and specific messages needed and overall campaign theme. In other words, what resources are necessary to get and hold the attention of the target publics or to get them to do something? While the fund-raising event is a relatively simple one to plan (simple in terms of determining publics and media), more complex campaigns can be developed (e.g., changing the image of your university or school from just the local college or school to a nationally recognized educational institution in the minds of targeted local publics).

Budget. The students need to cost out all relevant resources from printing of brochures to the "free" services supplied by companies and media interested in becoming sponsors in the case of a fund-raising event.

Two themes need to be addressed when you explain this section of the plan to your students. First, they need to really think through all possible costs and sort them out. For example, they will need to telephone a number of printers to find the best price, quality, and delivery (finish date) package. The second theme is that public relations is seen as an expense center. It is difficult for management of organizations to see what it is that public relations people accomplish, other than press releases and advertisements.

Calendar. An outline needs to be included, indicating what parts of the communications and action plans need to be staged when, and for how long. The importance of the calendar is that it forces the practitioner to be organized and realistic about the plan's outcomes.

Students can either find a client themselves or be given one by the instructor for an output project. Unlike the proposal project, students are expected to produce output of some kind, like a whole or part of a publicity campaign. It is assumed that the client either provides relevant research or is not too concerned about detailed research. An example of the latter might be an open house where research is not the formal survey type, but would be fact-finding and resource documentation (e.g., what are the competing events in the community for that date; what resources are needed; etc.).

Numerous nonprofit organizations have fund-raising needs or other similar projects that lend themselves to workable, desirable outputs for students. Whatever the project or client, the main tasks that should be included in these projects would be (1) resource development (facts on what and who is needed for the project); (2) publicity materials (from press releases to videotape promotionals if your department has the equipment); and (3) a clearly organized and staged event or campaign (open house; fundraiser; press conference; or image campaign for your university or school). This project works best as a group project with five students per group.

Another alternative is assignment of individual projects. These are original case studies researched and written by students individually and independently (not in groups). Their task is simple. They need to summarize an actual public relations case and interview the major participants. Essentially, students must look to the local companies and institutions in the community to find one that has had some public relations problem or success and set out to document the case through an interview of the practitioner(s) in the case. Students are encouraged to use the problem-solving sequence (research, planning, implementation, evaluation) as a way to organize and evaluate the material for the case study.

The assignment has two important goals. First, it allows the student to view public relations from an actual and unique perspective. Second, it allows students to interact or at least communicate directly with public relations people. (Students' first contact with the outside world of practitioners usually is in their first job interview.)

TEXTS

There are now numerous introductory texts to choose from, and it is very important for the instructor to examine as many as possible. The major considerations in selecting an effective text follow.

First, most texts will include more material than you will need or want. It might be useful to start with such a broad-based text the first time you teach the class, and then let your experience with the course help you decide on some future text.

Second, read the text for overall readability and interest. Put yourself in your students' shoes and read. Are there any general principles or themes after, say, five chapters? If there are not, then what would you expect your students to remember? If there are fifteen overall important units you want to cover in your course and the text covers twenty-five, there is little likelihood that you will be able to maintain your students' attention and interest.

Third, and finally, get the publishers to supply you with all the ancillary products. Many publishers today will give you student and faculty workbooks, exam questions, and computer software (for exams and grading). The computer software is especially important if you have large classes.

With these considerations in mind, here is just a short list from which to choose:

Otis Basin and Craig Aronoff, *Public Relations: The Profession and the Practice*, 2nd ed. (Dubuque, IA: William C. Brown, 1988).

Scott M. Cutlip, Allen H. Center, and Glen M. Broom, *Effective Public Relations*, 6th ed. (Englewood Cliffs, NJ: Prentice-Hall, Inc., 1985).

Ray Eldon Hiebert, ed., *Precision Public Relations* (New York: Longman, 1988).

Robert T. Reilly, *Public Relations in Action*, 2nd ed. (Englewood Cliffs, NJ: Prentice-Hall, 1987).

Fraser P. Seitel, *The Practice of Public Relations*, 4th ed. (Columbus, OH: Merrill Publishing, 1989).

CONCLUSION

It is important to have both a fair and reality-based grading system for the group projects. Since the students will be providing either a proposal or finished product to a client, it is only reasonable to expect them to be evaluated based on this output. Clients judge the services and products on their quality, price, and usefulness. Thus, the proposal or finished product as a whole should play a significant part in the grading. Have the client give you a grade for each group's output so that you can have some frame of reference, but let both the client and students know that you will assign the grade based on a set of criteria you have developed. The group project itself should be worth about 25 or 30 percent of the final grade. Additionally, all students in a group should receive the same grade for the project produced by that group.

It is only fair to allow students to help you interpret who was doing the real work on the project. Thus, a smaller percentage of the student's final grade should be based on participation (about 5 to 10 percent). What I do is have students grade themselves in their group on the basis of reliability (number of meetings made and whether on time), input (overall ideas and other forms of contribution), and collegiality (how much support and reinforcement contributed to others in the group). I give students a form that lists statements reflecting the above categories and add Likert type scales (Strongly Agree—to Strongly Disagree) to the statements. On this same form I ask them to put down an overall percentage or letter grade representing the overall value of that student's contribution. A form is filled out by the student for each person in the group, including him- or herself.

I have students fill out these forms twice during the semester. Sometime before mid-semester exams, I have them fill out the form.

I calculate the "grades" and use them for feedback to share with students individually, so that I can motivate them to do better if it is indicated. Students fill out the second form at the end of the course. You can use the grades from both forms and average them out in order to calculate each student's participation grade in the course.

Case studies should be evaluated on the basis of thoroughness (number of interviews, sources), clarity and organization, and copy (typed, no typos, no spelling errors). Inevitably you will find yourself wondering whether your job is to be a "cheerleader" for the public relations profession or simply an academic observer. At some point in the course you might talk about "effective" public relations techniques or what a practitioner "ought to do" in order to be successful in a certain context. Such prescriptive analysis may be reinforced by students asking you to list the skills necessary to become a practitioner. I find it helpful to clearly define or redefine my purpose to my students. I tell them that I am an instructor full-time and do consulting part-time. My main jobs are researching and teaching.

NOTES

1. Rex F. Harlow, "Building a Public Relations Definition," *Public Relations Review* 2 (Winter 1976): 34–42.

2. For an overview, see chapter 2 in Scott M. Cutlip, Allen H. Center, and Glen M. Broom, *Effective Public Relations*, 6th ed. (Englewood Cliffs, NJ: Prentice-Hall, Inc., 1985): 22–57; see also Dennis L. Wilcox, Phillip H. Ault, and Warren K. Agee, *Public Relations: Strategies and Tactics*, 2nd ed. (New York: Harper & Row, 1989): 35–64.

3. Melvin L. DeFleur and Sandra Ball-Rokeach, *Theories of Mass Communication*, 4th ed. (New York: Longman, 1982): 125–30.

Chapter 4

INTRODUCTION TO FILM

Gary Burns

During the late 1890s and early 1900s, when film was very young, it was not quite clear whether film was an entirely new art or merely a sort of "theatre without words." Before long, filmmakers such as D.W. Griffith, Charles Chaplin, and Sergei Eisenstein demonstrated that film was not only a new art, but one with power to move millions of people as they had never been moved before. Despite its great popularity, or perhaps because of it, film has seldom held a secure place in the school curriculum, either at the college or secondary level. This has changed somewhat in the past twenty years or so, to the point that a 1980 study by the American Film Institute reported that 227 four-year colleges offered bachelor's degrees in film, with another 209 schools offering courses in film (or television) but no degree. The same study reported that there were 12,526 film majors, with about 200,000 students taking film or television courses every semester.[1]

BACKGROUND

In almost every film curriculum, there is probably a course called Introduction to Film, or something similar. It is the one course to have if you have only one, and it is the course most students should take first in a well-developed film curriculum. Thus, the course must often serve two purposes: (1) to provide a thorough overview of film for the student who will never take another film course, and (2) to provide a foundation for students who will take other film courses. Along with these purposes often comes an imperative to emphasize film's importance among the arts and humanities, since the course carries general education credit at many colleges.

There are numerous ways to structure the Introduction to Film course so as to meet the needs of the different types of students who typically enroll. The most basic structural issue is whether the course will have any production component. Some teachers favor including a film production assignment in order to integrate theory and practice.[2] And it cannot be denied that one of the best ways to learn about film is to make a film. Reasons one might decide *not* to use a production exercise include the expense of equipment and film stock, large class size, availability of film production elsewhere in the curriculum, and the fact that (for better or worse) practical experience would not at most universities be considered a form of humanistic inquiry.

Another issue has arisen recently in discussions of the place of film production in the curriculum—namely, whether film production should be taught together with video production, separately from video production, or not at all.[3] This controversy is too complicated to explore here, but it is something that a teacher might have to address if he or she intends to teach film production, either in Introduction to Film or elsewhere.

For purposes of this chapter, I will assume that there is no production component in the Introduction to Film course. This leaves the teacher two major approaches to choose from—historical and aesthetic. The historical approach presents a canon of films in chronological order, whereas the aesthetic approach focuses on the structural components or processes of film (script, lighting, sound, editing, etc.) and on major ways of looking at film critically (genres, authors, movements, feminism, etc.).[4] In practice, the historical and aesthetic approaches may yield very similar results, primarily because it is difficult to deviate very far from the canon of films accepted as important by the academic community.

Citizen Kane is the clearest case in point. Students arrive having seen the latest installment of *Friday the 13th*, but not *Citizen Kane*. They must see *Citizen Kane*, regardless of whether the course is structured historically or aesthetically. Thus one strikes a blow for cultural literacy, although perhaps not of the sort E. D. Hirsch and Allan Bloom had in mind.

Beyond *Citizen Kane*, the "touchstones" are somewhat contestable, as they should be, but there is nonetheless a canon that, if not built on specific films, at least acknowledges certain categories:

1. Primitives—something by the Lumières, Méliès, and Porter; perhaps Edison/Dickson, Hepworth, Cohl, etc.

2. Griffith—*The Birth of a Nation, Intolerance, Broken Blossoms, Way Down East*, or a short or two for those more "intolerant" of silents.

3. Silent comedy—*The Gold Rush* or something else by Chaplin; something by Keaton.

4. Soviet classics—often *Battleship Potemkin* (sometimes only the Odessa Steps sequence).

5. German Expressionism—*The Cabinet of Dr. Caligari, Metropolis*, etc.

6. Renoir—*The Rules of the Game, Grand Illusion*.

7. Italian Neorealism or second wave—something by Rossellini, DeSica, or Fellini.

8. French New Wave—often something by Godard or Truffaut.

9. Hitchcock—*North by Northwest, Psycho*, etc.

10. Recent American film—*Bonnie and Clyde, The Graduate*, etc.

11. Documentary—*Nanook of the North, Triumph of the Will, Night and Fog, The River*, etc.

12. Experimental—*Un Chien andalou, Meshes of the Afternoon*, etc.

The units in the course will typically be built around film screenings, so that the scheme above, plus *Citizen Kane*, would yield thirteen units, each of which would normally represent one week in a college course. Some units can easily be combined—for example, one might easily show a few primitives and a Griffith, Chaplin, or Keaton short all in one screening, although my preference is to use an entire week for each unit as listed above.

In a semester course lasting fifteen weeks, two more units would be needed to round out the list of thirteen given above. Normally I use an American genre film from the studio years (usually *My Darling Clementine*) and a theatrical adaptation (such as Welles's *Macbeth*). Students, of course, prefer films that are fictional, in color, with sound, in English, recent, American, and in a familiar genre. It is entirely appropriate to take this into account and also to include personal favorites. Classes are better when students and teacher alike enjoy the material that is under consideration. Thus teachers who wish to make the class as accessible as possible to impatient or finicky students will probably prefer to use more American studio films than I have listed. This skirts the canonical system, since American studio films tend not to be included in the canon, with occasional unexplainable exceptions, such as *The Searchers*. Selection criteria for studio films might include such general matters as whether the film is critically well regarded, maintaining a balance of films from different historical periods, and avoiding excessive duplication of genres or authors while still allowing for a certain amount of comparative analysis.

The purest expression of the canon appears every ten years in the critics' poll published in *Sight and Sound* magazine.[5] But one can get a sense of what the "classic" films are by reading practically any film textbook. Despite scholars' frequent protestations that ten-best lists and similar projects are exercises in futility and pedantry, it is no surprise that practically every film textbook devotes considerable space to *Citizen Kane* (the best film of all time, according to every *Sight and Sound* poll since 1962), plus suitable coverage to "runners-up" and historical milestone films (*The Rules of the Game, Battleship Potemkin, The Birth of a Nation,* etc.). The development of such a canon, formal or informal, is inevitable and in fact useful, for without it there would be no "mainstream" and therefore no way to position oneself, as teacher or student, in support or opposition with respect to it. Even in order to make sense of avant-garde film (which, paradoxically, has its own canon), it is necessary to be aware of the kind of system the avant-garde is supposedly reacting against. In addition to providing a glimpse of the canon, practically every film textbook demonstrates some way to organize the subject of film either historically or aesthetically.

TEXTS

There are two main categories of textbooks that the teacher of Introduction to Film should look at. On the one hand, there are the History of Film textbooks. These, of course, are designed for the course called History of Film, which at many schools would be a follow-up course or sequence to the Introduction to Film course. However, if the curriculum does not separate Introduction from History, a history text might be a wise choice in the Introduction to Film class, at least as a supplementary text. All the major history texts give some attention to aesthetics, and the teacher's lectures can fill in any important aesthetic details omitted in the books.

The major History of Film texts include:

David A. Cook, *A History of Narrative Film*, 2nd ed. (New York: Norton, 1990).

Jack C. Ellis, *A History of Film*, 3rd ed. (Englewood Cliffs, NJ: Prentice-Hall, 1990).

Arthur Knight, *The Liveliest Art: A Panoramic History of the Movies*, rev. ed. (New York: Macmillan, 1978; rpt. New York: New American Library, 1979).

Gerald Mast, *A Short History of the Movies*, 4th ed. (New York: Macmillan; and London: Collier Macmillan, 1986).

These are all useful as reference works for the teacher, and Knight and Ellis in particular are worthy of consideration as principal or supplementary texts on the Introduction to Film course.

Cook's *A History of Narrative Film* is the best and the most scholarly of the history texts, but generally too weighty for an introductory class. Every film teacher should own this book for its unparalleled combination of detail, careful scholarship, and original insight. Although the "Cook book" cannot be very enthusiastically recommended as a text in Introduction to Film, it is the best of all the history texts in providing historical—and aesthetic—material the teacher can use in lectures to fill in the blanks left by whatever text is used.

Ellis's *A History of Film* begins with a chapter about aesthetics and repeatedly returns to this subject throughout its very readable historical narrative. The chapters on Soviet film and Italian Neorealism, for example, are especially strong in identifying the aesthetic significance of these historical moments. Among the various history texts, Ellis is probably the one that could best stand on its own as the principal text in the Introduction to Film course.

Knight's *The Liveliest Art* is not really a textbook, since it is devoid of such scholarly trappings as footnotes and is available as a pocket-sized paperback. Nonetheless, it is a substantial book at a low price and has been in print so long that it is something of a classic. It is ideal as a supplementary history text to back up an aesthetically oriented text. Coverage of the 1960s and later is skimpy.

Mast's *A Short History of the Movies* is quirky in ways that will please some and infuriate others. Mast says practically nothing about documentary, for example, but devotes more than ample attention to some of the less familiar national cinemas and individual foreign directors. His approach is more auteurist[6] than most. In discussing aesthetics Mast is not systematic enough to be of much help in this important area of the Introduction to Film course.

The preceding discussion of history texts notwithstanding, it is more customary in the Introduction to Film course to select one of the aesthetically oriented textbooks. There are numerous such books, of which some of the best include:

David Bordwell and Kristin Thompson, *Film Art: An Introduction*, 3rd ed. (New York: McGraw-Hill, 1990).

Louis Giannetti, *Understanding Movies*, 5th ed. (Englewood Cliffs, NJ: Prentice-Hall, 1990).

Bruce F. Kawin, *How Movies Work* (New York: Macmillan; and London: Collier Macmillan, 1987).

James Monaco, *How to Read a Film: The Art, Technology, Language, History, and Theory of Film and Media*, rev. ed. (New York and Oxford: Oxford University Press, 1981).

Thomas Sobchack and Vivian C. Sobchack, *An Introduction to Film*, 2nd ed. (Boston: Little, Brown, 1987).

Giannetti and Bordwell/Thompson are probably the dominant texts, but not nearly to the degree that Head/Sterling dominates in Introduction to Broadcasting.[7]

Although nominally introductory, the five books mentioned above are all (with the probable exception of the Sobchacks) substantial texts—that is, they are serious, significant works of film criticism as well as surveys for the uninitiated. That these works succeed on both levels is remarkable and a testament to the high quality of teaching and scholarship prevalent in film studies.

Since the books listed are all of high quality, the best way to select one is probably to compare their organization and to look briefly at which films are selected for detailed analysis in each text. If the text devotes a great deal of space to a particular film, it may become almost obligatory to show that film in class. Given the desirability of in-depth coverage of individual films shown in class, textbook selection can easily come down to the question of how closely the films discussed in detail by the textbook author correspond to the films the teacher would like to show in class.

In any case, precise coordination of the screening schedule with textbook readings is difficult or impossible. This is one of the biggest problems a film teacher faces. It will almost always be necessary to assign chapters out of sequence and to develop extensive lecture notes to cover films screened in class but not discussed in the book.

The five Introduction to Film texts listed above differ significantly from each other and thus provide the teacher with distinct alternatives. All five books have glossaries, bibliographies, and indexes. Bordwell/Thompson and Kawin include suggested film screenings. Monaco includes a chronology.

Bordwell and Thompson's *Film Art* is the most formalistic of the five books, in keeping with the theoretical orientation associated with the authors. It is also the most scholarly book and includes an excellent "Notes and Queries" section at the end of each chapter, combining bibliographic citations with theoretical discussion. *Film Art* offers detailed discussion of numerous films, but many of these films are unusual choices and may not appeal to the teacher. The films include *Citizen Kane; Olympia, Part 2; The River; Ballet mécanique;* Bruce Conner's *A Movie; Our Hospitality; October; A Man Escaped; His Girl Friday; Stagecoach; North by Northwest; Hannah and Her Sisters; Day of Wrath; Last Year at Marienbad; Tokyo Story; Innocence Unprotected; High School; Man with a Movie Camera; Clock Cleaners* (a Disney cartoon from 1937); *Duck Amuck;* Robert Breer's *Fuji; Meet Me in St. Louis;* and *Tout va Bien.*

The Giannetti book is organized around aesthetic categories but still works well with film screenings organized primarily according to historical chronology. There are detailed discussions of *Citizen Kane, Persona,* and *North by Northwest* (the latter in an appendix that includes the "reading script" and "shooting script"—that is, a reconstructed storyboard—of the crop duster sequence, reprinted from Lehman's screenplay and LaValley's *Focus on Hitchcock*). The book is particularly strong in demonstrating the intimate relationship between film and the other arts (photography, theatre, literature).

Kawin's *How Movies Work* is strong in its discussion of equipment, production processes, and industrial structure. About one-third of the book is devoted to "The Film Artist and the Movie Business." This unusual emphasis cuts into the space available for the more customary aesthetic matters, and also for history. Because of this, Kawin is likely a problematic choice unless technical and industrial concerns figure prominently in the course. Films discussed in detail include *Citizen Kane; Close Encounters of the Third Kind; Sunrise; Vertigo; King Kong* (1933); *Hiroshima, mon amour; October; The Cabinet of Dr. Caligari; The Birds; Flashdance;* and *High Noon.*

Monaco's book is subtitled *The Art, Technology, Language, History, and Theory of Film and Media.* The author's attempt to be encyclopedic may well disqualify the book as an Introduction to Film text in the eyes of many teachers. "Media," while actually only a minor focus of the book, does include print, broadcasting, and records—which are unlikely to be included in most Introduction to Film courses. Not counting this principal aberration, the book is a solid Introduction to Film text. Another possible problem, however, is that the book has only six chapters (which are necessarily large), and one of these is "Media." Spreading readings across a fifteen-week semester in some logical way may be difficult. There are no detailed discussions of individual films.

The Sobchacks' *An Introduction to Film* attempts to meld the aesthetic and historical approaches by including seven "Historical Sketches" as interludes that interrupt the major chapters, which are derived mainly from aesthetic categories. The Historical Sketches cover the Image (i.e., cameras, film, etc.), Editing, Sound, Narrative Film (from Méliès to recent Australian film in fourteen pages!), Documentary Film, Experimental/Independent/Animated Film, and Film Reviewing/Criticism/Theory. The first chapter covers the film production process. The last chapter is a guide to "Writing College Papers About Film"—thus the decision whether to use the book will probably be based in part on whether one intends to assign papers and whether one believes students will need or benefit from the instruction provided in this chapter. Its inclusion, along with the overall tone and style of the book, makes this text more elementary than the other four titles reviewed. There are no detailed discussions of individual films.

In addition to the textbooks listed above, there are two reference sources I would recommend to every film teacher: Ephraim Katz's *The Film Encyclopedia* and Leonard Maltin's *TV Movies and Video Guide*.[8] The former is indispensable for its biographical entries, filmographies, and coverage of general topics such as national cinemas and film studios. The latter book lists thousands of films by title and gives, for each, such information as date of release, running time, alternate titles, director, stars, plot synopsis, and Maltin's critical rating. The book is accurate, fairly comprehensive, handy, and inexpensive.

CLASSROOM LOGISTICS

Concurrently with selecting a textbook, the teacher must decide which films to show, in what order, and in which of the various available film and video formats. This raises uncomfortable technical, aesthetic, and economic questions with which every film teacher must grapple. The wildfire diffusion of the VHS video format in the past few years has made it possible for schools, even fairly impoverished ones, to acquire large libraries of films on tape. For a one-time expenditure of a few hundred dollars, a school can acquire the fifteen or twenty videotapes it takes to show the equivalent of one feature film per week in a semester-long Introduction to Film course. This has the advantage of reducing or eliminating the 16 mm film rental fees, typically $1,000–3,000 per semester, which were once a fact of life in the course. An additional advantage is that the tapes, once purchased, remain available for additional viewing by students and faculty, whereas rented film prints must be returned to the distributor promptly after screening.

But VHS is no panacea. Even the economics of it are not as favorable as they might at first appear. In addition to the tapes themselves, the school must purchase playback and display apparatus. Playback is straightforward enough, but display of the video image is problematic. Two display choices are available—TV sets and video projectors. TV sets do not give the viewer a sense of watching a movie. Video projectors are highly variable in quality, convenience, mobility, and reliability, and cost several thousand dollars. They also exacerbate any technical problems in the videotape being shown. For example, many foreign films have subtitles that are hard enough to read in their 16 mm versions. Dubbing the film to VHS makes the titles more illegible, and projecting the tape on a video projector, especially a bad one, compounds the problem even further. An additional complication is that the quality of video copies available varies over a wide range and is almost totally unpredictable. There is one rule of thumb—be especially careful when buying videotapes of films that are old or foreign.[9]

Although the changeover to videotape in film courses seems inexorable, some teachers object on aesthetic grounds, maintaining that films should be shown as films, not as TV. Despite the surface validity of this argument, it is a position that is growing more and more difficult to maintain in the face of ever greater availability of film titles on videotape and a shrinking supply of 16 mm rental prints (which are also more expensive). Still, many schools own 16 mm prints purchased years ago (or continue to rent 16 mm prints, for whatever reason) and must therefore maintain 16 mm projection facilities as well as any VHS equipment they are using. Generally, the 16 mm equipment must be available in the same classroom along with the VHS equipment. This adds to a problem already existent at many schools, that of film classes being offered in classrooms not designed for that purpose.

For an Introduction to Film class taught using 16 mm prints exclusively, the ideal classroom would have a projection booth with two projectors, good sightlines, and a good sound system. For economic reasons, it would also be necessary in most cases for the room to hold a large number of students—several dozen to several hundred, depending on the specific case. If a video projector must also be available, several important issues arise: Will the projector be permanently mounted in the room? If so, will it be mounted on the ceiling, or elsewhere? How will this affect sightlines or the throw of the 16 mm projectors? Additional problems, too complicated to address here, include providing some apparatus to enable the teacher to play back excerpts of the film for discussion, preferably with controls located at the front of the room; and handling any other formats that may, for one reason or another, be needed in the course—slides, overhead, Beta, Umatic, video disc, 35 mm movies, and so forth.

The move to videotape may easily influence course content, since films not readily available on tape, or the taped versions of which are technically flawed, will tend to be used less. Thus the old and foreign will be de-emphasized, as will avant-garde and experimental films. Many recent experimental films one might want to show are not available on tape. Many of the older avant-garde films of interest are available, but only on compilation reels that also include films one might want to skip over—thus, using these reels at all is at best inconvenient.

A beginning teacher may very well inherit equipment and films selected by someone else, in which case the principal concern becomes that of trying to find the best fit between the existing inventory and one's aspirations for the course. On the other hand, the teacher may be faced with the necessity to specify which equipment and films will be purchased. This heavy and heady responsibility requires the teacher to make decisions on numerous matters previously discussed in this chapter. Outside of the aforementioned caveat concerning old and foreign films on videotape, perhaps the best advice that can be given at this point is that it is *possible* to obtain an acceptable picture on a portable video projector, using VHS tapes. The picture will not be as sharp as a projected film image, but it will be large and bright enough for a class of 100 to watch it comfortably. In order to obtain this salutary result, it is essential to get the right video projector (such as a Sony Super Bright VPH 1040Q, currently priced at about $2,500) and to operate it properly.

There are several other logistical concerns that make film courses rather difficult to fit into the standard way of doing things at colleges. The usual practice in a film course is to screen a feature film (or its equivalent in short films) every week. Because films vary in length, the screening period must be scheduled to last at least two hours, even though the majority of screenings will last only about ninety minutes. There must also be time for lectures and discussion—at least fifty minutes per week, and preferably seventy-five minutes or even longer, depending on the degree of scheduling flexibility possible at the institution. A typical and fairly satisfactory arrangement is a Tuesday-Thursday schedule with the film screening on Tuesday and lecture-discussion on Thursday. Generally there is much more to say about a film after it is shown than before, although occasionally the teacher will be obliged to warn the class in advance of things to watch for in the film.

Of course, a two-hour class period on Tuesday combined with a seventy-five-minute period on Thursday is difficult for university computers to understand and also plays havoc with students' attempts to fit other courses into their schedules on Tuesdays and Thursdays. This may significantly lower enrollment in the course unless it is required. Scheduling as late in the day as possible seems to ameliorate this problem slightly.

One method of scheduling that is generally not desirable is to hold class meetings only once a week, with discussion immediately following the film. This leads to two-and-a-half- to three-hour class periods that too heavily tax endurance. Another approach, impractical at commuter campuses and perhaps inconvenient for the teacher, is to hold the screenings at night, with lecture-discussion sessions in the day.

One last alternative is the "lab section" approach, with screenings scheduled at four or five different times for students' convenience. My experience with this method has convinced me that students unfortunately do not find that this helps them much in their scheduling of classes. Since class scheduling at colleges often adheres to a fairly rigid formula and since, increasingly, students seem to pick classes based on time of day rather than course content, it is probably best to try to conform to the school's prevailing scheduling system as much as possible. The lab section approach, while attractive in theory, seems to have mainly negative effects in practice—more wear on videotapes and students' anger upon being closed out of their preferred sections.

Film classes are often large, and Introduction to Film is normally the largest of all. With thousands of dollars being spent on film rentals, there was originally an economic incentive to recover that cost through tuition or "lab" fees. This may gradually change because of the conversion to video, but the course will probably continue to attract mass enrollments by majors, would-be majors, and students seeking whatever general education credit is available. Moreover, since the mass lecture approach seems somewhat more poetically just in a film course than in many other subjects, Introduction to Film will probably remain a mass lecture course at many colleges. This means that discussion is limited, papers are impractical, and "objective" tests are encouraged. This leaves much to be desired as a way to teach the humanities (or any subject), but such a course can still educate and inspire the student. The teacher must give a bravura performance as a lecturer and must work hard from year to year to adjust and update lectures and develop interesting handouts, slides, film excerpts, and so forth. Ultimately, one wants to make the student look forward to lecture day as much as to movie day.

CONCLUSION

This brief overview has covered at least some of the major problems and possibilities inherent in the Introduction to Film course. It is sometimes a frustrating course to teach, but, ultimately, the opportunity to put together a program of films, watch them for the dozenth time, and talk about them to a somewhat eager audience is a most rewarding classroom experience. This is an ideal place to begin to infect students both with a love of important films and with the desire to understand what makes them important.

NOTES

1. Charles Granade, Jr., ed., *The American Film Institute Guide to College Courses in Film and Television*, 7th ed. (Princeton, NJ: Peterson's Guides, 1980), 13. While some readers may take these figures as evidence that film has finally "arrived" in the college curriculum, it must also be remembered that film per se is losing ground on many fronts to video and television.

2. See, for example, Peter Lev and Barry Moore, "Introduction to Film—An Integrative Approach," *Journal of Film and Video* 38, no. 2 (Spring 1986): 81–87.

3. See the following "debate" in *Feedback* 27, no. 6 (Fall 1986): John David Viera, "Integrated Mediums: Converging Film and Video in Teaching Production," 14, 35–36; Gary Burns, "A Response to 'Integrated Mediums,'" 15, 36–39; and John David Viera, "Sharing Concepts: Viera's Rejoinder," 39–40. These articles also explore the differences between "video" and "television."

4. For two examples of the aesthetic approach, see Betsy A. McLane, "Introduction to Film, Approach I," *AFI Education Newsletter* (March-April 1981): 4–7; and David Bordwell, "Introduction to Film, Approach II," *AFI Education Newsletter* (March-April 1982): 4–7, 9.

5. "As the Critics Like It," *Sight and Sound* 22 (October-December 1952): 58–60; "Top Ten," *Sight and Sound* 31 (Winter 1961/62): 10–14; "Top Ten 72," *Sight and Sound* 41 (Winter 1971/72): 12–16; and "Top Ten 1982," *Sight and Sound* 51 (Autumn 1982): 242–46. See also Gavin Lambert, "As You Like It," *Sight and Sound* 22 (July-September 1952): 18–19 for a report on the "Brussels Referendum" of film directors that precipitated the critics' polls.

6. Auteurism is the study of master directors whose imprint on their films is as clear as that of book authors in their medium. For the etymology of "auteur," see Peter Wollen, "From Signs and Meaning in the Cinema" in Gerald Mast and Marshall Cohen, eds., *Film Theory and Criticism*, 2nd ed. (New York: Oxford University Press, 1985), 553–71.

7. This point is made by Douglas Gomery, "Radio, Television, and Film: The State of Study in the 1980s," *Feedback* 27, no. 2 (Fall 1985): 12–16.

8. Ephraim Katz, *The Film Encyclopedia* (New York: Putnam, 1979); and Leonard Maltin, ed., *Leonard Maltin's TV Movies and Video Guide, 1991 Edition* (New York: Signet, 1990).

9. For further guidance in selecting tapes and equipment, an outstanding source is John P. Smead, *Video Projection in the Film Curriculum*, paper presented to the University Film and Video Association, August 1987. Smead teaches in the department of communication, Central Missouri State University.

Chapter 5

INTERNSHIP PROGRAMS

S. Scott Whitlow

Internships—their practical value earns them a universal thumbs-up among professionals, students, and faculty. They permit students, for example, to step out of the academic cocoon and into a professional arena where they refine knowledge and skills and learn new perspectives and different ways of doing things. They also ensure that students get a taste of no-excuses-entertained deadlines. And they let students bump into the delicacies of maintaining healthy work relationships.

Yet these practical rewards are often not the only value of internships. On many campuses, there is a parallel value for students: academic credit. Academic hours and grades can be earned by students for successful completion of on-the-job training. This added value of academic credit transforms an internship. It's no longer just an opportunity for hands-on experience; it's a genuine course. While any program that champions internships among students ideally sustains a programmatic approach, it becomes imperative when internships achieve course status.

BACKGROUND

Our purpose here is to describe the structure of an internship "course"—the vehicle for academic credit in one school's internship program. Pinpointed in this overview are pivotal decision areas: administration of course; eligibility; policies; procedures; location and shaping of internship opportunities; program management.

The tasks characteristic to administration of a dynamic internship "course" of study are an alphabet soup assortment of responsibilities. Announcements about opportunities, deadlines, meetings, and so on, must be prepared. Student eligibility to embark on an internship must be verified. Orientation meetings must be scheduled. Contracts must be approved. New sponsors must be solicited. Site visits must be made. Interns' work must be reviewed and evaluated. Sponsors' evaluations of interns must be secured. Relations with current and past sponsors must be nurtured. These and a host of other tasks are on-going and frequently overlapping.

There is no one right way to administer these assorted tasks. The administration must fit the goals and resources of the parent unit. With that understanding, our faculty weighed the appropriateness for them of the two major approaches used in administering internships.

Administration by Staff

In some universities, a staff member works exclusively in an outreach position. The staffer oversees programs such as advising, job placement scholarships, recruitment, and internships. Alternately, a staff member with general responsibilities adds to his or her duties the administration of internships.

Administration Solely by a Faculty Internship Director

Full oversight of the myriad tasks associated with internships rests with one faculty member. This is a large load to shoulder along with continuing teaching and productivity expectations. A typical response in recognition of this overload—the ideal response—is assigning an assistant to the faculty member. For a set number of hours each week, a staff member, graduate student, or work-study student attends to details of the internship program.

Additionally, or alternately, the faculty member is granted release time in his or her teaching load. Depending on a school's particular situation, the faculty member may receive a one-course release annually, or a one-course release each term. The faculty's resources were slim in our situation. The current staff of two already bore a taxing workload. Further, there was no prospect of budget approval for a new staff member hired in an outreach capacity. Too, the faculty shared a desire to participate in the internship program. They preferred to have students confer with them during the internship about the links between classroom learning and on-the-job learning. The administrative approach the faculty opted for, consequently, is a hybrid one. One faculty member, serving as internship director, attends to all internship-related tasks with one exception: interns consult with and are evaluated by faculty members. The internship director receives a one-course release for the academic year.

Pertinent internship prerequisites nudge students into thinking ahead about internships, and eligibility becomes a central question. When will I be ready for one? What type of internship do I want? Who offers such an internship? This is the type of planning the faculty attempts to trigger among students with the eligibility criteria it established.

To participate in the internship program on a for-credit basis, students must have been granted major status in the unit. Among the requirements for achieving that status are completion of pre-major requirements and a minimum overall GPA of 2.6 on a 4.0 base. Students in each sequence must complete three of the required major courses prior to undertaking an internship. This ensures that they hold a reasonably informed understanding of the field, possess a beginner's array of skills, and consequently are better prepared to select an appropriate internship. Students in the advertising sequence, for example, must complete these coursework expectations:

1. Principles of Advertising
2. Two of the following required skills courses. (One of the courses is to relate to the projected internship.)
   - Advertising Media Planning
   - Advertising Research
   - Advertising Message Preparation

Grades are also a factor in students' preparation for an internship. The faculty sentiment is that internships should be undertaken by students whose academic records suggest they can balance their academic workload with the on-the-job time demands of an internship. Too, minimum grade standards help identify students who are better prepared and thus more likely to realize the benefits an internship offers. The minimum grade criteria, therefore, are:

- Maintaining the 2.6 overall GPA required for entrance to the major;
- Achieving a 3.0 GPA in major coursework.

The net effect of these criteria is that the earliest students are typically eligible for an internship is at the end of their junior year. Working toward an internship, they have paced themselves wisely in their course selections and are able to present themselves to internship sponsors as well-grounded, capable individuals.

A guiding set of policies and principles, nit-picky though they seem, benefit all. Everyone knows what's possible, what's impossible, and what's negotiable. Relatedly, it is prudent also to note the consequences that can be expected when a policy is profoundly bent.

The particular policies identified here flowed from the goals of the faculty and from their experience with interns. At that, the policies are primarily of the common sense variety and are therefore germane to almost any internship program. Each student's eligibility to undertake an internship for academic credit must be certified before he or she is permitted to register for the course. For this, there is a deadline at midterm; the specific date for a given term is publicized broadly each term. There is just so much students can help themselves to in the way of for-credit internships. School policy permits students to dedicate a maximum of three credit hours of internship toward their major coursework. The policy is one that is shaped by the minimum number of hours a student must earn to graduate (120) in our system, and the fact that the school is accredited by the Accrediting Council on Education in Journalism and Mass Communication (ACEJMC). The ratio of professional credit hours to liberal arts credit hours results in the requirement that students must complete ninety hours in liberal arts and thirty hours in professional coursework.

Realistically, however, these limits may unduly hamper some students' development. For example, unexpected local opportunities arise for students. Or, students apply for and are selected to participate in nationally competitive scholarships. Or, students find their career interests taking a new twist. These are situations which might evolve for students who have already reached the limit on internship credits. Consequently, flexibility is integral to our credit limit policy. It anticipates different students' needs in three ways:

1. In addition to three internship credits, students are free to participate in additional internships on a not-for-credit basis.
2. Qualified students who are willing to take more than the university's minimum graduation requirements of 120 hours may enroll for additional internship credits. Before approving this, the student's adviser confirms that the student has or is meeting the liberal arts requirement of 90 hours.

3. Credit can be earned by students for internships offered by other programs in the university system as long as they don't involve skills associated with the school's professional mission. Credit of this type applies to the student's coursework outside the major.

A fairly explicit policy for on-the-job hours guides students and their internship supervisors in structuring a work schedule. The policy takes into consideration two conditions: one is the number of credits for which the student is enrolled (one to three); the other is the length of the internship—the regular sixteen-week term, the eight-week summer term, or the four-week intersession.

For each credit hour, student schedules must meet these minimum expectations:

- 3 work hours per week in the 16-week term;
- 6 work hours per week in the 8-week summer term;
- 12 work hours per week in the 4-week intersession.

Often, of course, internship supervisors encourage students to exceed these minimum work hours. It is obviously advantageous to them and it broadens the intern's window of experience. Thus, the practice has faculty approval as long as the student's work hours do not exceed the minimum requirements by more than 20 percent.

Firms offering internships see the salary question from a variety of perspectives. Some have unions that dictate a policy on salary. Some feel a salary is essential for the internship to ring true as a work experience for the student. Still others feel the internship they offer is its own reward and offsets the need for a salary.

It is clear to the faculty that the salary question is often a pivotal one for students. All too often students who must work to meet their college expenses can't pursue an appropriate internship that offers no salary; they can't afford to cut back on paid hours to accommodate the internship hours. While the faculty endorses salaried internships, its salary policy notes an exception. Students are not permitted to earn internship credit for working in a job where they have previously earned a salary.

Students are permitted to seek provisional certification to enroll for internship credit during the term in which they are completing the coursework requirement. At the end of the term, assuming grades are maintained and all required coursework is complete, full certification is granted. However, in the unlikely event a student with provisional certification falls short of grade and/or course requirements at semester's end, the policy requires swift action. Provisional certification is withdrawn and the student is required to reapply in the next application cycle. If the student is enrolled for internship credit in the upcoming term, he or she is dropped from the course rolls with notice of the action conveyed to the internship supervisor and the student. The internship can be continued on a not-for-credit basis if the student and sponsoring firm agree to do so.

Internships that the school faculty considers to merit academic credit are listed in an internship registry. One volume of the registry presents nationally competitive internships and the other volume informs students of local and state internships. The registry is readily available for student reference in the college's on-site library. The school has a participatory role in the development of the local and state internships listed in the registry. The process ensures that the school can provide a helpful overview of each internship in the registry along with particulars of interest to students (salary prospects, interview expectations about portfolios, news clips, tapes, etc.).

A student who is eager to intern with a firm which has not received approval by the school is expected to initiate the screening process. To do this, the student provides the internship director with information about:

- Name of the firm where the internship is desired;
- Address of the firm;
- Name of the firm's president and phone number;
- Name, title, and phone number of the student's contact at the firm;
- Specification of the type of internship desired.

Armed with the necessary information, the internship director confirms the student's prospects with the contact person whom the student identified. If there seems to be potential for a well-structured, well-supervised internship, a registry listing form is then mailed to the contact as the first step in the internship development and screening process. Students are aware that approval of a firm's internship proposal is not automatic and, on occasion, may not be granted.

A list of students who have been certified to enroll for internship credit is given to advisers and staff members by the internship director at the beginning of the registration period for each upcoming term. Also identified on the list are students who have provisional certification. Both students and faculty know that the staff will give enrollment permits to the internship course only to students who are on the list. The name of a student who has received certification remains on the list until the student actually enrolls for an internship. That is, if a student decides not to enroll for internship credit in the upcoming term, the certification remains active as long as grade standards are maintained.

Eligibility Criteria—Policies and Procedures

Appeals can be filed by students concerning any policy or procedure. Students are advised, however, that the faculty considers the guidelines fair and reasonable and expects students to be responsible for meeting the varied expectations associated with earning credit for internship work. Appeals are reviewed by the school's director, the student's academic adviser, and the internship director.

Information about virtually every question a student might ask regarding internships is presented in a four-page document on Internship Procedures. Following is an overview of the procedures our students follow.

Come the third week of each term, mini-posters begin alerting students to apply for certification of internship eligibility. The publicizing builds as the deadline nears. All notices carry the specific midterm deadline date for that term. Application forms are available for students in the school's main office. On the forms, students report details of the GPA standing, their completed or current status on required coursework, where they wish to intern, and their personal internship goals. In addition, each applicant signs a pledge confirming that he or she has read, fully understands, and agrees to abide by the school's policies and procedures.

The day following the deadline, coursework and GPA information on each application is verified by the internship director. With that done, each student is classified as "eligibility certified," "provisionally certified," or "not certified/ineligible." Student names and addresses are coded on software to receive one of three standard letters that are printed and mailed promptly. Students who are fully certified and those who are provisionally certified learn in their letter that they are to attend an orientation meeting. The meeting is scheduled prior to the beginning of advisement and registration for the next term.

At the orientation meeting, the internship director steps through all the procedures with which interns must deal. These range from setting up an interview to preparing a learning contract to publishing a report on their internship. Students are reminded of the career preparation services available to them on campus and of the self-help materials on reserve for them in the college's library.

A final reminder to students is that their completed learning contracts must be on file by the next term's last "Add" deadline. Students enrolled for internship credit who have not filed a contract by that date are dropped from the class roll.

It is the goal of our faculty that students approach getting an internship just as they would approach getting their first job after graduation—the interview is critical. Thus, getting hired into an internship becomes a valuable grooming experience for the student. The realism is heightened since landing an internship is competitive. Students consult the internship program registry to identify the firm or firms best suited to their internship goals. Too, if there are reports available from past interns at the firm, they review these. Each student contacts his or her preferred firm(s) personally to arrange an interview.

Earlier, at the orientation meeting, students have been coached to think "job hunt": learn all they can about the firm before the interview; be candid at the interview about their abilities, interests, and goals; act and dress professionally; leave behind a resumé and any support materials specified in the firm's registry listing. The decision about accepting a student as an intern is entirely the firm's.

The faculty here, you'll recall, prefer to maintain their participation in the internship program as an intern's faculty instructor. In this capacity they meet with the student regularly to discuss the intern's activities, confer with the intern's site supervisor, oversee the writing and reading expected of the intern, and determine the intern's grade. Interns-to-be request the faculty member of their choice to work with them on their internship. The faculty vary in their approach to this role. Some will only work with students who have completed a class with them or whom they know in their role as an academic adviser.

An internship cannot begin until a learning contract is prepared and filed with the internship director. It is this contract that underscores for all involved—the student, the professionals offering the internship, and the faculty member—that the internship is an educational activity. A learning contract form is distributed to students at the orientation meeting. Its importance is emphasized, and students are told they must work closely with both their site supervisor and their faculty instructor in completing the contract.

The heart of the contract is the student's set of learning objectives. For this, students are urged to think about the changes and improvements they expect to see in themselves at the end of the internship.

These, they are told, are to be stated in the contract in a precise, readily observable way. In our packet of internship materials, this example is given students:

A poorly stated objective:

"I want to learn about the real world of advertising creativity."

Well-stated goal objectives are:

"To learn how advertising evolves within the agency—from the need voiced by clients to the actual ads placed in media."

"To improve my ability to read and interpret statistical data pertinent to a client's creative needs."

"To acquire skill in assessing budget capability and delivery of target in order to recommend appropriate media for the required creative needs."[1]

The contract calls for a variety of utilitarian items of information. Among these are the intern's as well as the supervisor's phone number and the specific days and times the intern is on the job. This finger-tip record enables the faculty instructor to make an occasional quick call to check on the intern. Relatedly, a for-instructor-use section of the contract provides space for the instructor to record notes about exchanges with the intern and with the professional supervisor. Another section of the contract lists the criteria for evaluation. Each criterion is identified by name, and the person is specified (the faculty instructor and/or the internship director) to whom the student is to submit it. Also, the standard deadline for each is listed; at the orientation meeting, each student receives a sheet listing the precise dates for those deadlines in the upcoming semester.

The internship director readies four photocopies of the completed contract which the student submits. The student, the internship supervisor, and the faculty instructor each receive a copy of the contract along with a note encouraging them to refer to it from time to time to ensure that the learning objectives are being realized. A copy is also placed in the student's academic file, with the original kept on file by the internship director.

There are four auxiliary performance tasks required of all interns and used for evaluation purposes. These include maintaining a journal; preparing a press release; writing a summary report; and writing and sending letters of thanks. Some faculty instructors add a fifth task, which is individualized to the student's interests.

At the end of each on-the-job week, interns record the salient details of the week's work. Their jottings note assignments they have handled, skills they have learned or refined working on the assignment, and the outcome of the assignment. They record remarks and critiques made about their work. They note the names of clients, suppliers, and others whom they have met during the week and what they have learned from them.

We ask that they list questions they want to ask their supervisor or instructor. We also ask that they reflect on each week's accomplishments and use them as a springboard for a specific goal to be accomplished in the upcoming week. Faculty instructors vary in their requirements about when journal entries are due. Some require that the intern submit the journal each Monday. Others have interns bring their journal to their regularly scheduled conference.

Press releases prepared by interns are mailed out to hometown newspapers at the midpoint of the term. For this, each intern prepares a release about the internship and types it up on a press release form provided by the internship director. The release is accompanied by a five-by-seven black and white photo of the intern and his or her supervisor and is clipped to a typed identification sheet. The intern is responsible for having the pictures taken and two copies printed; in some instances, this is handled through the firm where the intern works, through students in the school's photography classes, or by a friend of the intern. The second copy comes in handy for within-school displays and publications such as alumni newsletters.

Completing the press release packet which the intern submits to the internship director is a prepared mailing label, which is addressed personally to the business section editor of the student's hometown paper; if there is no business editor, the label is addressed to the managing editor. The internship director reviews all releases before sending them on. Where necessary, rewrites must be turned around promptly by interns.

Besides being another solid exercise in writing, this task helps students understand the value of releases to those preparing them—and the difficulty in actually having them printed. At the orientation meeting, interns-to-be learn that the press release provides visibility for the school and its students, and it helps the school show appreciation to firms which participate in the internship program. We can offer interns no guarantee that their hometown paper will use their release, but we do ask the intern to have hometown friends look for it and send clips along if it runs.

As the end of the term approaches, interns prepare a summary report. Each report includes four sections, starting with a job description summary. Here interns describe what they did, how they did it, with whom, and so forth. At this point, almost without fail, students realize the true value of the journal they have kept throughout the semester.

The second section is an evaluation of the internship. All interns are to assess the value of what they have learned and how they have developed professionally. In the third section, interns offer suggestions for improvement of their internship as well as the internship program itself. The final section of the summary report is an appendix in which students present samples of their internship work. For each sample, they include a brief note explaining the purpose of the work, the use to which it was put, supervisor remarks, and so forth. Once the organization of the exhibits is set, the student prepares a contents sheet to place at the start of the appendix section. Guidelines for the format of the summary report are specific. Reports are to be:

- Written to professional, error-free standards;
- A minimum of six typed, double-spaced pages with subheads used to flag each section;
- Spiral bound with a cover that includes the intern's name, the name of the firm, and the term during which the internship took place (for example, fall 1991).

Interns submit two copies of their summary report. One goes to the faculty instructor and is reviewed as part of the intern's overall evaluation. The other copy is archived by the internship director. (Interns are encouraged to make a couple of extra copies of their report to use on their first job hunt.)

The final end-of-term task for interns is a letter of thanks sent to their immediate supervisor and/or the president of the firm where they interned. As they learn at the orientation meeting, this is a simple act of courtesy. We ask that they mail their letter(s) the day following their last day on the job. Interns submit a copy of their letter(s) to the internship director along with their summary report.

Some faculty feel that the educational mission of the internship can be heightened by additional assignments. Others don't share that view. Thus, such assignments are an optional part of the learning contract. Typical instructor-specific tasks include the review of a book or set of articles relevant to the internship. When additional assignments are made, it is up to the faculty instructor and the intern to state them on the learning contract and to establish their deadline.

Two weeks before classes end for the term, the internship director mails each internship supervisor an evaluation form. The form invites the supervisor to critique the quality of the intern's work as well as the intern's professionalism and potential. To keep the form as simple and time-efficient as possible for the supervisor, a standardized check-list format is used with only a couple of open-ended questions. A postage-paid envelope returns the completed evaluation directly to the intern's faculty instructor.

CONCLUSION

There are internships. And then, there are internships! The latter is the kind we want for our students. To help foster such internships, we feel it helps to educate firms and their employees a bit about internships. We developed a printed four-page, one-fold internship overview to do just that. It begins by talking about benefits; specifically, it helps the firm see what it can get out of a well-structured, well-supervised internship. Then, with that train of thought set, the overview offers guidelines for structuring and supervising an internship. The guidelines address these topics: establishing the intern's role; selecting the intern; setting a work schedule; making assignments; advising interns; gaining cooperation of the firm's employees; working with the intern's faculty instructor; deciding on a salary.

Tucked into the internship overview is a sample of a registry listing. It shows firms how a well-structured internship might be described to students who are searching the registry for internship possibilities. Along with the sample listing are two blank listing forms and a prepaid return envelope.

Our internship overview kit is a hunting as well as a screening tool. We send our kit out whenever we learn of a new prospect or receive a call requesting an intern. When a completed listing form is returned, we also make a site visit; we decline any internship prospect that we feel does not (and cannot in the near future) offer our students the opportunities, structure, and/or supervision we require.

Special attention is paid to the evaluation of the internship and suggestions for improvements in each intern's summary report. Where it appears to be a genuine problem area, the internship director endeavors to work with the firm in resolving the problem. On occasion, when a problem can't be resolved, the firm's listing is withdrawn from the registry.

Finally, PCFile enables us to manage a data base consisting of firms that offer internships to our students and those we are currently exploring. In each file there is a field for the name of the firm, its address, its area code/phone number, the president of the firm, current supervisors (if any), and a classification code for the type of internship offered. For firms actively offering internships, there is also a historical field where a record of each intern is stored. This tool serves most of our list needs—for example: which active firms have not had an intern during the past two years? It also drives our letter writing and label preparation.

NOTE

1. Internship procedures, School of Journalism, College of Communications, University of Kentucky, 1989.

Part II

APPLIED COURSEWORK

The first two chapters in this part embrace two distinct journalistic forms: writing and reporting. Ellie Chapman and Michael Murray in chapter 6 suggest that student experience with news and news writing will have an impact on the way an instructor should teach the print or broadcast news course. Based on a significant number of semesters of experience teaching the course, they have found that the course is best taught if it focuses on the skills and techniques required for accuracy, brevity, and clarity in news. They offer two sets of objectives—one for print and one for broadcast news. An integral part of the broadcast course is an interview of a local news director or reporter. This assignment not only offers interview experience; it also offers a type of mentoring opportunity.

A good writing class clearly involves the instructor in terms of grading numerous writing assignments, and Chapman and Murray offer useful techniques to handle this aspect of the course. Also, they suggest that frequent writing practice under deadlines will lead to better quality work and ease problems that an instructor would have to contend with in poor quality writing.

David Bennett (chapter 7) sees reporting as an intellectual framework through which news persons plan and write stories. An important part of this course is the use of news "beats" in which students cover particular locales or areas like city hall, or broader beats or concerns like social services. He believes that students learn about the newsmakers from such beats. An interesting assignment he offers is the "story memo," in which students write a brief forecast about some story they intend to write.

Rather than simply giving students praise or criticism for their work, Bennett believes that students are best served by having the instructor involved in the process as the students are working. Thus, he suggests that the instructor should be watching over their shoulder while they are at the computers and should periodically ask them how it is going and what problems they are having. In this way Bennett offers a coaching format for the course, underscoring the applied nature of the material for student and instructor.

Jon Morris and Frank Pierce believe that those students furthest along in their academic career are best suited to take the advertising campaigns course. As outlined in chapter 8, the course includes the use of teams of five to seven students who prepare ad campaign plans for a real or fictionalized client selected by the instructor. An outline of a campaign plans book is included.

If the instructor chooses to use a real client for the course, then Morris and Pierce indicate the type of client that should be chosen. Using a real client can pose problems for instructor, student, and client if roles and expectations of student and client are not given or known. Morris and Pierce provide important and clearly delineated guidance in this area.

Few students who take an audio course will have a lifetime career in audio production, according to Robert Musburger in chapter 9. He believes that because students are audio users, their need and interest to know the audio production process will enable them to benefit from such a course. His course is process-centered in that it examines the preproduction, production, and postproduction aspects of audio production. The exercises used in the first half of the course are simple tasks that are necessary in the overall audio production process (e.g., cable-coiling-connecting; board operations; hand signals). The second half of the course includes open labs.

Musburger suggests that the exercises he offers "gently" ease the student through the production process since they each focus on a single aspect of the production course. He includes a clear, step-by-step description of how each production exercise is done. Evaluation in the course includes hands-on testing. For example, the course includes a midterm equipment review that allows the instructor to assess students' ability to use the equipment. As with the other exercises in the chapter, Musburger describes this midterm review clearly and fully.

Steve Craig (chapter 10) presents a rather broad-based approach to video production in that he includes critical thinking, aesthetic skill development, and video equipment skills. Acknowledging that video courses vary in the way they are taught at different institutions, Craig uses an empirical base to describe the "typical course." Using data from a survey of 142 Broadcast Education Association institutions, he outlines the typical or accepted structure of such a course.

Since this course is heavily oriented to lab work, Craig addresses such concerns as how laboratory sessions should be scheduled. He describes and illustrates clearly the practice of "rotation" in which students rotate through different production positions. He suggests that lab exercises should increase in complexity and should start with short exercises in order to ensure sufficient rotation early in the course. He includes descriptions and sample scripts for two short news exercises. He includes an evaluation of the relative problems and benefits of individual versus group projects. Finally, he describes and evaluates typical field production exercises.

In chapter 11 Kim Smith indicates that two important student perceptions must be taken into consideration for the research methods class. First, many students approach this course with some trepidation, and second, they may not see the need for such a course in their program. It is Smith's contention that most students will be required to be effective consumers of research rather than producers. Thus, the course is not designed to develop fully functioning experts in research methods—no one course can do this.

The course that Smith has developed focuses on the fundamentals of research including theory development, measuring variables, sampling, data gathering, data analysis, and presentation of results. Smith argues for a laboratory session to be added to the course to allow for focused, hands-on exercises with data collection and analysis. Frequent testing and evaluation are also considered to be an integral part of this course.

Chapter 6

WRITING NEWS FOR PRINT AND BROADCAST

Ellie Chapman and Michael D. Murray

Decisions about how and where to start this course will be based on assumptions about your students' experience with news and news writing, as well as their basic language skills. Some students in introductory news writing classes, it is safe to assume, will have limited experience with writing—or even reading—news. Some may even have serious problems with spelling, grammar, and usage, even at the college level.

Also to be considered are the writing classes already taken by the students. Typically students' classes are limited, for example, to one or two semesters of freshman composition, which may have instilled some composing habits—not necessarily bad—that need to be adjusted. Following current trends in the teaching of composition, instructors have approached writing as a process involving extensive prewriting, preediting, drafting, and revision stages. If your students have become accustomed to this unhurried process, you will need to build into your course, at the beginning, ways to help them revise the timing of their method to allow for meeting deadlines.

After projecting who your students will be and what they will know, you must settle on a starting point for the course. This choice is frustrating because you can't get to the main activity—writing—until students understand several important aspects of news writing that are new and sometimes difficult to master.

To address students' lack of familiarity with news and news writing in general, you'll probably have to begin with the basics: What is news and how does news writing differ from other kinds of writing, in both style and format? How does the writer decide which news elements are most important? For some students these concepts are easy to learn; other students take longer to grasp them. Regardless, the concepts must be mastered now, at the beginning, and you must schedule ample time for students to read, discuss, and become familiar with the new language and structure of news stories.

Before, during, or after the class works on these concepts, you'll need to introduce the new—sometimes confusing—journalistic stylebook guidelines for punctuation, capitalization, and word choice, along with use of standard copyediting marks. All this must be done while you constantly reinforce the importance of improving basic language skills and, perhaps, introduce students to the computer lab.[1]

Having decided where and how to begin, you'll discover, if you're a realist, that one semester is not long enough for all the material you'd hoped to teach. Although a carefully chosen textbook, workbook, and stylebook can be valuable instructional aids, don't count on them for guidance in how much you can cover in a one-semester course. Textbooks often include enough subject matter for several year-long courses. Chapters on journalistic issues, feature articles, freelance careers, and writing for public relations offer tempting, but time-consuming, side trips from the straight news routine. It's best to stick to the basics in this introductory course.

BACKGROUND

Floundering through several semesters of experiments with various combinations of class activities and textbooks, you eventually recognize a problem in attempts to do too much in a limited amount of time. We find the answer in our own experiences with news writing—first as beginning reporters learning journalistic writing and later as editors helping to train staff writers. Our pared-down syllabus now includes learning and practicing only those techniques and skills required for accuracy, brevity, and clarity in straight presentation of the news. And even within those limits, difficult choices remain.

When do the students finally start writing? After they understand this new style of writing, they can begin to practice making simple news judgments through experimenting with short news leads and then short, single-event news stories. Set high standards, but don't expect miracles early in the course.

With each new activity building on the previous one, your assignments can progress from writing simple inverted-pyramid stories for print—about fires, robberies, award winners, coming events, obituaries, and the like—to more complex reports of speeches, meetings, press conferences, and realistic, multiple-event happenings.

You should build into these writing assignments—also in increasing levels of difficulty—practice in attributing information to sources, using direct and indirect quotations, and localizing stories. Copyediting exercises and spelling-grammar-style quizzes are helpful in reviewing and reinforcing new skills and reviewing the basics (as well as identifying trouble spots).

You can control these increasing skill levels by varying the information from which the news stories will be written—a textbook, workbook, or your own handouts. The facts may appear, as they often do in real life, in random order of importance and in sketchy, ungrammatical, and inaccurate form. Writing from this kind of material helps students develop the ability to verify information, to organize according to news values, and to use their own words in correct journalistic style rather than depend on the language of the notes.

To help students improve their speed in organizing and writing, you will need to make daily writing assignments and allow for timed writing assignments in class as often as possible. It's important to set and strictly enforce deadlines from the first day of class and to increase your expectations for both quantity and quality of written work as the semester progresses and student skill levels improve.[2]

Every teacher knows that the only way to learn any kind of writing is by writing. Frequent writing practice under deadline pressure will help your students to overcome writer's block and the need for leisurely thinking and writing, as well as any bad habits of sloppy note taking and drafting they may have developed in their college work.

Although your paper-grading load will increase as the quantity of student output increases, it is reasonable to hope that the improvement in writing quality will lessen the time required for checking assignments.

Your class meetings should involve, from time to time, some combination of presentation of new skills, review of other news writing skills (along with basic language skills when relevant), discussion of writing assignments and, most important, writing. To balance the structured approach required for news writing, try for variety—and a light touch that encourages humor and fun along with the work—in your class activities.

It's important that everything the students write be marked and returned as soon as possible—while the questions involved in the process are still fresh in their minds. Although reading, copyediting, and commenting on the structure of each news story takes a large amount of time, it is the most important aspect of teaching this course. Correction time should be considered when you plan the frequency and kinds of your writing assignments.

You can save grading time by presenting a model story for discussion and editing after students have written their stories but not yet turned them in for correction. Class discussion and editing of these models, duplicated or displayed on an overhead projector, help students to improve their own work and also to clear up questions and misunderstandings.

Another way of cutting down on your correcting time is handing out edited student examples of well-written stories and problem stories (or these could be leads, quotations, chronological accounts, etc.) with your written comments. Students can then compare their own efforts with these examples. Small-group peer editing sessions can provide variety in class activity but little help with the paper-grading load. Some instructors find that small-group editing sessions lead to improved revisions that require less correction time.

You should consider one more dilemma that you may encounter as the course progresses: not what to include in the course but what to leave out. A "tentative" syllabus should always include more material than the class will be able to cover so that it can be adjusted as the semester progresses to meet the needs of the particular class. Since every class has its own pace, every syllabus is designed with flexibility in mind.

Although your expectations in the basic news writing course may appear to be demanding (to you and your students), most of them will consider the time and effort well spent. For those who plan to continue in journalism courses or careers, the ability to write a good news story is an obvious requirement. And even those who decide not to be news writers will discover that the same skills undergirding good news stories—the ability to write with clarity, brevity, and accuracy—are assets in any classroom or career. Who would argue the value of readable copy written to deadline?

TEXTS (PRINT)

Although you'll find that most news writing textbooks include far more material than you can use, some will fit better than others into your plan for the course. You'll want to be sure your selection covers all the material you plan to teach and provides practical writing exercises (your paper-correcting load will be too heavy to allow much time for creating extensive handouts). You'll also want to be sure that the text and exercises are presented on a level that matches that of your students. There is a wide discrepancy in expectations of students' experiences, aptitudes, and skills among writers of "college-level" news writing textbooks.

For beginning teachers of news writing, instructors' manuals can be extremely helpful. Ask the publisher or book representative to provide a copy of the manual before making your final decision on a textbook. Here are some suggestions that include textbooks and workbooks (note the ones with coordinating workbooks and those that combine text and practice exercises in one book):

Douglas A. Anderson and Bruce D. Itule, *Writing the News* and *Workbook for Writing the News* (New York: Random House, 1988).

Fred Fedler, *Reporting for the Print Media*, 4th ed. (New York: Harcourt Brace Jovanovich, 1988).

Evan Hill and John J. Breen, *Reporting and Writing the News* (Prospect Heights, IL: Waveland Press, 1988).

George Hough, *News Writing*, 4th ed. (Boston, MA: Houghton Mifflin, 1988).

Melvin Mencher, *Basic News Writing*, 5th ed. (Dubuque, IA: William C. Brown, 1991).

Melvin Mencher, *News Reporting and Writing*, 5th ed., and *Workbook: News Reporting and Writing* (Dubuque, IA: William C. Brown, 1991).

Ken Metzler, *Newswriting Exercises*, 2nd ed. (Englewood Cliffs, NJ: Prentice-Hall, 1986).

The Missouri Group Staff et al., *News Reporting and Writing*, 3rd ed., and *Workbook for News Writing and Reporting* (New York: St. Martin's Press, 1988).

Mitchell Stephens and Gerald Lanson, *Writing and Reporting the News* (New York: Holt, Rinehart & Winston, 1986).

To supplement the text and workbook, you will probably want to require students to use as a reference either the Associated Press or United Press International stylebook. A helpful style workbook is *Programmed News Style* by Blanche G. Prejean and Wayne A. Danielson (Englewood Cliffs, NJ: Prentice-Hall, 1988).

ORGANIZATION

The introductory news writing course is designed to teach students to write for newspapers. However, the writing skills it emphasizes—

accuracy, brevity, and clarity—are basic to successful writing for radio and television, as well as for public relations and advertising.

At the end of the course, students should be able to:

1. Use news style and handle news copy:
   - Learn basic rules of news style and use them in writing all news copy;
   - Learn standard copyediting symbols and practice;
   - Follow accepted standards of spelling, grammar, punctuation, and usage in contemporary American English;
   - Meet deadlines.

2. Follow newsroom practice in:
   - Identifying people, places, and events;
   - Attributing facts to sources;
   - Referring to hours, days, months, and other time;
   - Using direct and indirect quotations;
   - Verifying information through use of reference materials.

3. Compose simple news stories:
   - Identify and weigh news values;
   - Write concise single-incident, inverted-pyramid reports;
   - Write summary leads;
   - Write blind or delayed-identification leads.

4. Develop various kinds of news stories:
   - Write about coming events;
   - Recognize and emphasize local angles;
   - Use chronological material;
   - Write routine obituaries;
   - Update news stories;
   - Write round-up stories.

5. Use quoted material:
   - Write about speeches, meetings, or interviews, making effective use of summary and paraphrase;
   - Use and attribute direct and indirect quotations.

Following in the footsteps of the first course in News Writing, many students elect to enroll in Broadcast Writing, or at other schools—Broadcast Writing and Reporting. Some courses combine both print and broadcast news writing. Most institutions with a developed curriculum, however, require News Writing with a print orientation as a prerequisite to the first course in broadcast writing. This assures the broadcasting instructor that students have knowledge of the basic elements of news, story construction, and newsgathering techniques. Ironically, the skill associated with high quality broadcast writing requires the student to rethink format and story makeup, beginning with the construction of a good lead—focusing on ability to attract viewer or listener attention. Students also need to work on simplifying and synthesizing information and coming across in a conversational way. The News Writing prerequisite frequently assists in providing a foundation in spite of differences in the way stories are constructed and in writing style.

You may want to begin the Broadcast Writing course or section where many instructors end—with an overview of career prospects and what could best be described as a focus on lifestyle concerns, a description of the process of building a career in broadcast news, and an overview of newsroom operations focusing on who does what. These considerations are critical because of the popular myths and major misconceptions about the field of broadcasting, beginning with the most basic facts of life—issues such as levels of compensation, job security, and, of course, the importance of writing ability. These concerns are more than justified, given the level of interest in the field and the unusual demands required of broadcast writers and reporters.[3]

Once you are reasonably sure that students have their feet on the ground with respect to the profession and its demands, you can proceed with important content considerations. These include format and usage guidelines available in most specialized texts in the field—how to present copy ideas, rules for editing, sources of information, newsgathering techniques, and types of specialized reporting, as well as some production considerations. Specific content topics include libel and privacy concerns, ethical questions, and the role of the Federal Communications Commission—usually a reinforcement of concepts presented in introductory survey courses.

TEXTS (BROADCAST)

Copy basics and practical information on current practices are contained in these textbooks:

Roy Gibson, *Workbook for Radio and Television Reporting* (Boston: Allyn & Bacon, 1990).

R. H. MacDonald, *A Broadcast News Manual of Style* (New York: Longman, 1987).

Peter E. Mayeux, *Broadcast News: Writing and Reporting* (Dubuque, IA: William C. Brown, 1991).

Milan D. Meeske and R.C. Norris, *Copywriting for the Electronic Media: A Practical Guide* (Belmont, CA: Wadsworth, 1987).

Roger L. Walters, *Broadcast Writing: Principles and Practice* (New York: Random House, 1988).

Also useful for interview preparation are:

Shirley Biagi, *Interviews that Work: A Practical Guide for Journalists* (Belmont, CA: Wadsworth, 1986).

Akiba A. Cohen, *The Television News Interview* (Newbury Park, CA: Sage Publications, 1987).

George M. Killenberg and Rob Anderson, *Before the Story: Interviewing and Communication Skills for Journalists* (New York: St. Martin's Press, 1989).

Ken Metzler, *Creative Interviewing* (Englewood Cliffs, NJ: Prentice-Hall, 1989).

Some of these texts take a purely professional approach. Students are treated to a liberal dose of both in-class writing and field assignments in which story construction and editing are emphasized. Just as in the beginning course in News Writing, each in-class writing assignment focuses on a particular copy objective. Beginning assignments, for example, stress the preparation of a good lead with emphasis on information stated in a conversational broadcast tone. Concerns about meeting time restrictions also come into play in the preliminary class meetings and throughout the course. As a means of encouraging improvement, it is explained at the start that for grading purposes, only the top five graded stories written for in-class review will count, grading on a scale from 1–5, with 5 being the best possible grade. Since the class is supplemented with current events quizzes and a good number of in-class writing opportunities, good attendance is ensured in spite of what some might view as a liberal grading policy.

This approach provides students with latitude at the start of the course and lets them know that irreparable damage to the overall grade is not being done at the outset, while they are only beginning to master the basics of good broadcast writing. This is a process that usually takes us through the first half of the term, for those who have had a good first course in News Writing. In addition to regular writing and some field reporting assignments, we also have required our broadcast news students to conduct studio interviews for television with both prominent newsmakers and news professionals from the community. Newsmaker guests, selected by the students, usually turn out to be local mayors, police chiefs, prosecutors, or professional athletes. They offer perspective on the newsgathering process and local reporting from the vantage point of regular press contact from a consumer perspective. As a follow-up to this assignment, while we were on the faculty of another university, students who enrolled in Broadcast Writing and Reporting conducted videotaped interviews with local reporters and news directors for use on a public affairs television program.[4] This interview assignment has now become an integral part of our beginning broadcast writing course, conducted in our studios. Students are responsible for lining up reporters who are ostensibly doing the same kind of work to which some of the best of our students aspire.

Students completing this assignment have interviewed news professionals from all three network affiliate stations locally, the independents, and the public television station—every outlet with a competitive newscast or public affairs component. Guests have included general assignment reporters, investigative reporters, news directors, and specialists in politics, consumer affairs, health—virtually anyone and everyone in the newsroom including both sportscasters and weather people. The subject of the interview is the field itself along with a profile of the person and background on their experiences—daily routine, working conditions—usually concluding with advice to students considering a career in the field. Students are discouraged from interviewing anchor people on grounds that they are less likely, in a good-sized market, to always be able to convey the rigors of the beginning reporting experience.

The students are required to obtain a biographical sketch of the reporter and prepare a list of possible questions for the interview. They are graded on the basis of their preparation, use of questions, providing perspective, organization, and their choice of guest. We have found that this assignment, above any other, forces students to face up to the realities of the field.

Almost all of the guests discuss, for example, the importance of being willing and able to move in their beginning positions every few years. Since most of our students were born and raised in the metropolitan area or suburbs surrounding our area, they tend not to want to acknowledge mobility as a factor in their future prospects. A talk with a reporter new to the city tends to reinforce the fact that relocation is a given in landing that all-important first job.

Unlike the guest lecture format, this assignment also forces the student to gain something of an understanding of the working conditions of the particular reporter they intend to interview since they are often invited to accompany the reporter on assignment or meet them at a location and observe their newsgathering methods. Even the process of gaining consent for the interview offers the student some insight into the demands of the field although we have yet to be disappointed by a reporter or news director for their unwillingness to participate. After making contact, reviewing biographical information, and explaining the nature of the assignment, the students must provide directions on how to get to our studios and what guests can expect when they get there.

In spite of competitive tendencies and the potential awkwardness of appearing on-camera in an alien setting, the reporters and news directors we have talked to—and there have been nearly one hundred to date—show a genuine interest in the students and go out of their way to provide an in-depth understanding of their work. We have found that students are effective at gaining information and perspective from reporters because these professionals acknowledge the wide gap in public understanding between what they do and the popular perception of their work. They react favorably to an opportunity to set students straight about the rigors of the field. Beyond this, the assignment can help to break down professional barriers for small but competitive institutions laboring in the shadows of the large, established schools of journalism.

This mini-mentoring program has been an asset in that, like an internship, it gives students a perspective they may not have gotten after working in a small market for a year or two; they have conveyed to them the demands of big city journalism directly from a working reporter. So much of what we stress in the early part of the course about meeting deadlines and the importance of writing skills is reinforced again and again through this exercise. On many occasions, in the course of interviews, students off-camera will look over and smile knowingly when a guest reinforces a point frequently made in the classroom—such as the need to write well.

Another added benefit of the professional interview assignment is that it has allowed us to develop a considerable library of interviews—so extensive that we can offer an individual student with a particular interest in an area the views of two or three of the most respected specialists in the community on that beat. They have an opportunity to hear a very candid assessment of what the local experts have to say about their work. Let's face it, most broadcast academics are faced with the periodic challenge of clueing in a campus beauty queen or jock with limited writing or editing skills who is set on an anchor job. It's great to let local news pros share in the opportunity to set them straight with respect to professional requirements and expectations.

In addition to the other benefits—learning about the demands of the field, gaining some on-camera experience, and making an important contact—this assignment demonstrates to local professionals that we care as educators about their newsroom, their station, and the kind of job they are doing for the community. In short, it dramatically shows that we are not operating in a professional vacuum. We can say that at one time or other, because of this assignment, we have met most of the working reporters at competitive local media outlets. They appreciate the opportunity to visit a campus and impart some specialized wisdom about their work. In this way, both students and the school benefit.

NOTES

1. See Paul Adams, "Personal Computer, VDT Use Increases in Journalism Classes," *Journalism Educator* 42 (Spring 1987): 24, 57.

2. Gerald Stone, "Measurement of Excellence in Newspaper Writing Classes," *Journalism Educator* 44 (Winter 1990): 4–19.

3. One of the best and most up-to-date sources of information on job prospects and career development concerns is a pamphlet: Vernon Stone, *Careers in Radio and Television*, prepared for the Radio-Television News Directors Association, and available from their national office, 1717 K Street, N.W., Washington, DC 20006.

4. See Michael D. Murray, "TV Public Affairs Series Gives Class Professional Outlet," *Journalism Educator* (Spring 1982): 15–17.

Chapter 7

REPORTING

David Bennett

Filing into my reporting class, students find a familiar liturgy—
WHO? WHAT? WHERE? WHEN? WHY?—scrawled across the
blackboard. "You know all about this 5W stuff from beginning news
writing, correct?" Heads nod; a few students smile smugly. "Well, I
certainly hope so. But just to make sure, let's apply the formula to our
own situation." We go down the list, quickly establishing that they
are the WHO, learning to report is the WHAT, here is WHERE, and
now is WHEN. The WHY, however, usually prompts some dead air
time.

The point is that my students, and most likely yours, don't really
know *why* they are taking reporting, other than that it may be
required. They have only the foggiest notion that this journalistic
act we call "reporting" has something to do with the First Amendment, which in turn somehow helps keep the Old Republic creaking
along.

I use the WHY of reporting as a philosophical springboard for a
plunge into that inseparable trinity of free expression, democratic
government, and the press.[1] Of course, this never fails to reveal my
own bias as a First Amendment zealot. Students need to know that,
too. At the end of the first class session, I hand out this value statement
and ask that students consider it as a context for reporting:

A free society can survive only through a free exchange of ideas among its
citizenry. This unfettered marketplace of ideas is the essence of the American
political experiment, the "bedrock" into which we have carved such concepts as shared governance.

Since answers to the WHY of reporting form the rationale for western journalism, I see no point in going on to the HOW of reporting until students have thought about, and talked about, the philosophical underpinnings of their profession. Reporting, at least as I teach it, is much more pragmatic than philosophical, despite my opening tactic. Simply put, the class goal is for students to learn to report. (Note the emphasis on students learning rather than teachers teaching. A body of knowledge can be taught; skills can be learned. Reporting is a little of one and a lot more of the other.)

Reporting is a process of gathering, selecting, organizing, and sharing information with readers or viewers that they need or want. The process becomes more complex when one insists that to be effective, any communication must not only be clear but as complete and comprehensive as the situation dictates.

BACKGROUND

Some schools combine news writing and reporting in a single course. This can be a bad idea. Many college journalism students, even after general education English courses, do not write well. Their problems with spelling, grammar, structure, and syntax become apparent as they attempt to master news writing and its clear, concise forms. If at the same time they are also struggling to learn the basics of reporting, some students may feel overwhelmed and simply give up.

Ideally, people taking reporting should already be adept at such basics as recognizing news; applying news values; writing leads; structuring a news story; attributing information; and using direct and indirect quotes.

ORGANIZATION

From the instructor's point of view it may be useful to think of reporting as an intellectual framework. Within this structure things such as planning, news values, and knowledge of audience are used to guide the actual gathering of information and, finally, the writing of a news story. Obviously, some stages of the process are more cognitive than "hands-on," yet all are essential to good reporting.

Consider designing your reporting course, first of all, to maximize the probability that students will learn to report. By the end of the term they should be able to plan, research, and write acceptable news stories of some complexity. (I define "acceptable" as publication quality, with some editing and minor rewriting. More on this later.) I've found it helpful to clearly indicate, at the beginning of the course, some basic competencies students can expect to develop. These include recognizing news; planning and researching stories; locating appropriate sources of information; conducting interviews and taking effective notes; deciding what to include or exclude in a story; deciding how to structure or organize a story; writing and rewriting a story; and meeting a deadline.

One way to help students learn is to organize your course around these competencies in increments that build upon each other as new parts of the reporting process are introduced. Additional increments might include specialty reporting areas such as city and county government, criminal justice (police and courts), the environment, science and medicine, education, business and economy, and legal issues and ethics.

Before you begin to do this, however, allow me to suggest that you give some thought as to what your students will bring with them into the classroom. Have they all taken a course in news writing? Are they familiar with the structure and workings of local and state government? Will most be traditional students (late teens, early 20s) or will some be older returning students? In short, speculate a little about their general level of knowledge as well as their probable life experiences.[2]

Obviously, if your students don't know what news is and can't write a news story, it is folly on your part to begin the course with the essentials of reporting. You'll have to teach them news writing first. Even more startling is the discovery, when your students do their first story on the city council, that they don't have a clue about how government works. Most likely this will be the case, even if they have taken a government course or two. That's why I schedule an increment, early in the course, on the structure of state and local government.

There are probably as many possible ways to organize a reporting course as there are professors. One way to begin is to decide what specific experiences you think are important for your students. In my course, for example, during the first half of the term each student must report on meetings of the city council, county supervisors, and school board, and cover a hearing in federal or district court. They also research and write about a continuing local or regional environmental issue. In the last half of the term, they switch to the "beat system" and are expected to generate a weekly hard news story from the beat they have chosen. This mix ensures that students develop at least a surface understanding of several government agencies and also gain the deeper experience of covering a specific beat for a period of time.

TEXTS

Selecting a text for a reporting class is seldom easy. You will want to pursue a number of possibilities to see how each fits into the general "game plan" you've decided upon for the course. Keep in mind the probability that you will want to assign outside readings as well. Thus a text satisfactory in most areas but weak in one or two can likely be supplemented.

Some textbooks attempt to combine news writing and reporting. If news writing is not a prerequisite for reporting, you may need the all-purpose text. Ideally students will have taken news writing and you can select a text that concentrates on reporting. Textbooks you may want to examine include the latest editions of:

Gary Atkins and William Rivers, *Reporting with Understanding* (Ames, IA: Iowa State University Press, 1987).

Edward J. Friedlander, Harry Marsh, and Mike Masterson, *Excellence in Reporting* (Saint Paul, MN: West Publishing Co., 1987).

Bruce D. Itule and Douglas A. Anderson, *Contemporary News Reporting* (New York: Random House, 1984).

Curtis D. MacDougal and Robert D. Reid, *Interpretive Reporting*, 9th ed. (New York: Macmillan Publishing Co., 1987).

Melvin Mencher, *News Reporting and Writing*, 5th ed. (Dubuque, IA: William C. Brown, 1991).

If you plan to work in a block on local government, you may be fortunate enough to find a book that specifically addresses the structure of state, county, and city government in your state. It should detail such things as elections, recalls, and referendums (if your state has provisions for these), as well as the legal forms of government (general law and charter cities, for example).

To further supplement a primary reporting text, you may also want to adopt one or more of the following books. Most are available in relatively inexpensive paperback editions:

Shirley Biagi, *Interviews that Work: A Practical Guide for Journalists* (Belmont, CA: Wadsworth Publishing Co., 1986).

John Brady, *The Craft of Interviewing* (Cincinnati, OH: Writer's Digest, 1977).

Lauren Kessler and Duncan McDonald, *Uncovering the News: A Journalist's Search for Information* (Belmont, CA: Wadsworth Publishing Co., 1987).

Ken Metzler, *Creative Interviewing*, 2nd ed. (New York: Prentice-Hall, 1989).

John Ullman and Jan Colbert, eds., *The Reporter's Handbook: An Investigator's Guide to Documents and Techniques*, 2nd ed. (New York: St. Martin's Press, 1991).

Either the *Reporter's Handbook*, which was prepared by Investigative Reporters and Editors Inc. (IRE), or *Uncovering the News* would be valuable to students in learning to follow the paper trail of government and legal documents.

The face-to-face interview is probably the most important tool that reporters use to gather information. It is also the most difficult for many students to master. They certainly need all the help we can provide in learning interview techniques. As a beginning reporter, I would have welcomed the tips any of the primers offer, along with those offering examples of exemplary writing and tips on writing well. Any one would be a fine reference for student journalists serious about mastering their craft.

Don Fry, ed., *Best Newspaper Writing 1987*, Annual (The Poynter Institute for Media Studies, 1987).

Peter Jacobi, *Writing with Style: The News Story and the Feature* (Chicago, IL: Lawrence Ragan Communications, Inc., 1982).

Christopher Scanlan, *How I Wrote the Story*, rev. ed. (Providence, RI: Providence Journal Company, 1986).

William Zinsser, *On Writing Well: An Informal Guide to Writing Nonfiction*, 4th ed. (New York: Harper & Row, 1990).

There is no substitute for reading good writing. Reading is perhaps the only thing a reporter can do—aside from writing itself—to develop the depth necessary for a personal style to emerge. Thus it follows that student journalists need to read good writing. A lot of it. Daily. They should read a local newspaper and an elite national newspaper. The local read keeps them abreast of developments in their community; the national newspaper provides a broader universe of news and good writing as well. Best bets include the *Wall Street Journal*, the *New York Times*, the *Los Angeles Times*, and the *Christian Science Monitor*.

Occasional reading assignments from general interest magazines are also valuable. News magazines often run national overviews on education, the environment, courts, the economy, etc., which can be tied in as background for local reporting on those issues. (For example, *Insight* magazine's January 1987 cover story examined the plight of American education.) *Columbia Journalism Review*, *Washington Journalism Review*, the ASNE *Bulletin*, *Presstime*, and other trade-specific publications regularly run stories examining journalism problems and issues. Biographies of prominent journalists can also be assigned. Those such as Edna Buchanan's *The Corpse Had a Familiar Face* and Linda Davis's *Onward and Upward: A Biography of Catherine S. White* offer unique insights into the personal nature of news work.[3]

Imagination is the only limit to the kinds of writing your class will do. An occasional creative assignment can be a breath of fresh air in a reporting class. Writing about an historic local cemetery, for example, can produce unexpectedly lively stories. Ask for three pages on such a subject and suggest that both research and personal observation be used to gather information. Some students will find out who owns the cemetery, what it costs annually to maintain it, how many folks are buried there, and so forth. Others will stroll through the graveyard at sunset to gather its sights, smells, and sounds. A few may notice more curious facts, such as the pioneer family whose grave markers tell the story, year after year, of infant mortality. When students share their writing, they'll be amazed at the variety of approaches to a story. This itself is a lesson worth learning.

Even if students think city council members are, collectively, ready for interment in that historic cemetery, council actions are nevertheless news. Students covering city council, for example, can be urged to view the meeting they will report as part of a process rather than a solitary event. Prior to the meeting, they should go to city hall for an agenda, then research the major agenda items and write a short (one-page) advance. This ensures that they don't go to the meeting unprepared. Then they cover the meeting, select the major issue or council action, seek any additional information they may need, and write the story. (If the meeting is at night, you might set a deadline on the story of 5 PM the following day. If they miss the deadline, have them cover another meeting.) In addition, they can write a second story from the meeting as a follow-up, perhaps a "wrap" of the less important council business. This approach is quite useful during the first part of the term, especially if you have broken the course into content increments and you liken the reporting assignments to those increments.

About midway in the term, my students choose individual "beats" to cover. Thereafter, each student writes at least one each week from his or her beat. Although these stories should generally be hard-news treatments, an occasional feature story may be acceptable if a student's beat has run dry temporarily. Covering beats has distinct advantages. First, it allows each student to pick a reporting area of personal interest and develop a little expertise in that area. Second, it makes each student responsible not only for writing news stories but also recognizing them. Third, student reporters develop longer-term relationships with their news sources. The initial step in setting up beat reporting is the development of specific beats. Here again there are several possibilities. You may want students to cover on-campus beats, with the idea that their stories will then be more appropriate for possible publication in the campus newspaper. Or you may choose to have them report on the community. The following is an introduction and beat list created for community coverage:

BEATS FOR REPORTING BLOCK—A significant part of your time during the reporting block will be spent developing and covering news and features on a specific beat. You will be expected to report one hard news story a week from your beat (no meeting stories) and, over the term, several features. Do yourself a favor by choosing a beat that is personally interesting and has the potential to readily generate news. Some beats are inherently "newsmakers"; others will require more initiative on your part to come up with stories. This list includes the active beats one finds at most newspapers. If, however, you have a burning desire to cover a more specialized beat, see me and make your pitch. The number beside each beat is the maximum number of students who will be allowed to work it.

ARTS AND PERFORMING ARTS (no reviews) 1
CITY COUNCIL 1
COUNTY COMMISSION 1
ECONOMIC DEVELOPMENT (local economy, etc.) 1
ENVIRONMENT (effects of humankind on environment and vice versa) 3
FEDERAL COURTS 1
HEALTH CARE (hospitals and public health)... 2
HIGHER EDUCATION (public and private)... 3
HOUSING AND COMMUNITY DEVELOPMENT 1
LAND USE (city and county) 1
LOCAL MEDIA (changes, competition, etc.)... 1
MILITARY (local bases, national guard, ROTC) 1
MINORITIES 1
POLITICS AND VOTERS (local and state) 2
PUBLIC SAFETY (police and fire departments) 2
REGIONAL BUSINESS/INDUSTRY (includes unions) 2
RELIGION (hard news, not sermons)... 1
SCHOOLS (K-12).. 2
SOCIAL SERVICES 1
SPORTS (issues/sports as business. No game stories).. 2
SUPERIOR COURT 4
TRANSPORTATION (highways, rail, air).. 1

Pass out the beat list. A day or two later, have students sign up for a beat on a first-come, first-served basis. (I flip a coin. Heads and the list starts at the back of the room; tails, the front.)

Once beats are selected, a good first assignment is researching and writing a "beat report." Included should be such things as the appropriate regulatory agencies on a particular beat; the names, titles, and phone numbers of potential sources; an overview of major news from the beat in the past year; and delineation of any continuing problems, trends, or issues. Producing a beat report forces students to become familiar with the "shakers and makers" on their beat, while also giving them the historical context they need to begin to nose out news. You can use the beat reports and occasionally call a source to confirm quotes and information in stories and chat about how the student is handling his or her beat.

Story memos are brief forecasts of stories students intend to write. They can give an instructor the opportunity to offer insight and advice before the reporting process begins. Their purpose is to convince the editor (instructor) that the writer (student) has a story worth doing; one that won't cost an arm and leg in money, time, energy, and legal fees. A story memo should include a clear statement of the central idea and focus of the proposed story, the news peg or angle, and sources the reporter expects to use.

Since students cannot assume approval, their typed memos should be submitted well in advance of the target deadline of their story. Although the reporter must collect some information prior to writing the memo, no actual interviews should be conducted. A major strength of the approach is that it prompts a formulation of pre-story strategy that is easily modified and fine-tuned in a brief meeting with the instructor. A danger is that students, armed with approved memos, may be too inflexible to handle field situations that differ considerably from their original expectations. They should view story memos as simply tools for planning, and understand that the best plan often changes as more becomes known about a situation.

Brief writing assignments can be used to ensure that students do their assigned reading. One workable method is to require a "reaction/response" paper (one page) on each week's assigned (nontext) readings. Keeping free-form journals, in which students record a short daily entry, can also be quite interesting. Students can recount what they've read, experienced, agonized over, and so forth—so long as the entries relate to their work and growth as journalists. Have the journals submitted each Friday; they'll offer much insight into your students as people, as well as reporters.

Make time, even during lecture and discussion sessions, for a little writing. Bring in common objects for the class to look at, feel, smell, and maybe even taste—then have them spend five minutes jotting down descriptive impressions. Pass around a magazine photo of a rock star. After everyone has had a close look, ask them to describe what the person was wearing, the hairstyle, the facial expression, or the background in the photo. Little writings like this break the monotony of a classroom and tune the senses.

Research is the foundation for some news stories, especially those that are process-centered rather than event-centered.[4] Consider working a few research assignments early in the term to give students practice following a paper trail. Such assignments work well when linked with specific content areas of a course, such as politics and local government. Students can select an elected city or county official and use public records (property tax rolls, conflict of interest statements, campaign disclosure statements) to find out what the person earns and owns. Then they write a short report of research. For part two of this assignment, students can take the same official and research (again through public records) that person's campaign spending the last time he or she stood for election.[5] Who contributed? How much? Where was it spent? Combine with information from part one of the assignment for a news story.

Each student can also select the environment: a major housing project, subdivision, shopping center, or industrial complex. Then they must locate the Environmental Impact Report (EIR) or development plan that local government required to be filed before the project was built. The assignment: write a detailed advance story, using the EIR material, as if the project was coming before the city or county next week for approval. Other assignments focus on criminal justice. Each student can go through back issues of the local newspaper to find coverage of an arrest in which local police used a search warrant. Noting the evidence that was seized, they then check court documents filed by police before the arrest to secure the search warrant. The assignment: write a story comparing what police thought they would find and what they actually found.

Most reporting courses combine lectures, discussions, and lab work. Classroom sessions can be used to lecture, share experiences and problems encountered in the field, critique stories, plan coverage, and offer writing tips to the class as a whole. But there is no substitute for lab sessions where students are coached individually as they write. Even though most writing will be done on the students' own time, reserve the writing lab for at least one extended block of time each week. Be available at the lab then to consult with students on developing stories and coach them through rough spots in their writing.

Students need more feedback on their reporting and writing than any of us can possibly offer. Instructor response to student writing completes the feedback loop that is essential to learning and change. Nevertheless, there is simply never enough time, a fact that becomes more problematic in direct proportion to the number of students in a reporting class. Reporting students deserve much more than a letter grade and a "good job" scrawled across their stories. They need to know what went wrong, what went right, what was missing or misplaced or awkwardly worded. But just as important, they need to know how to improve what they wrote.

CONCLUSION

Good editors coach more than they critique and praise more often than scold. So do good teachers of writing and reporting.[6] I like to work with students while they are actually writing. I peer over their shoulders at the VDT screen and ask, "How's it going?" or "What are you having problems with?" Once writers have identified problem areas, I ask how they think they can work through or fix them. Often they will be near solutions and just need a little nudge or reinforcement. If a writer is really stuck, I sometimes pose a series of "what if?" questions. "What if you used a transition to introduce the quote? Would that work better? What if you fleshed out this idea more completely before working in the next main point?"

Occasionally I'll ask a student writer to look at me and not at the VDT and tell me—in a few short sentences—what the readers need to know first. This works especially well when writers are hung up on leads. Once they collect and verbalize their thoughts, the log jam is broken. This sort of one-on-one coaching, while writers are writing, is the most valuable form of response you can offer. But written critiques are necessary as well.

Also consider developing a written checklist to help you evaluate and critique stories. I use a sheet with nearly forty numbered items that include common errors in leads, sentence structure, grammar, and style. Run-of-the-mill story problems are simply circled and numbered. The time you save in noting common errors can be used to write detailed comments regarding content, form, and possible ways to address serious deficiencies. To finish off a critique, I pop the checklist into my printer and, at the bottom in a comments section, dash off a brief note about what worked and what didn't.

Every week or so, students can be instructed to come to class on a particular day (usually when a story is due) with copies of their latest effort. The class can be divided into three-person critique groups. Students exchange stories and offer comments and suggestions to their peers, which then form the basis for rewriting stories. Of course, all writers rewrite when time allows. This fact comes as a shock to many students, who naturally assume that "professionals" produce perfect copy on the first draft. Students need to be encouraged to write, rewrite—and rewrite again when time permits. This can be made an essential part of the learning process: reporting and writing a news story (doing), receiving instructor or peer response (feedback), improving performance (rewriting story). Fine. But doesn't that double the number of stories or assignments that must be critiqued and graded? Certainly, if you critique and grade each one. Ideally, the grades for each story and matching rewrite could be averaged, thus clearly rewarding improvement. But again, do you have time?

One alternative is to only critique the original story and only grade the rewrite. Another is to critique and grade only the original, but require a rewrite before recording the grade. Criteria for critiques or grades can be divided into two areas: content and mechanics. The first includes accuracy, degree of difficulty of story, completeness, newsworthiness and significance of information, and fairness and balance. The second weighs such attributes as clarity, conciseness, readability, precision of language, grammar, spelling, and style.

Knowing that a story will be published also adds spice to the life of a journalist. Often editors at local daily newspapers, and especially community weeklies which traditionally are understaffed, will be happy to consider well-written stories by students. You will probably want to exercise some control over which stories are offered for consideration. Other avenues for publication include local or regional magazines, specialized newsletters and, of course, the college or university's student newspaper. In this regard, student reporters need to learn about open meeting and public records laws, which vary considerably by state. In 1989, the Reporters Committee for Freedom of the Press published *Tapping Officials' Secrets: A State Open Government Compendium*. Copies of individual state booklets can be ordered from the committee, P.O. Box 33756, Washington, DC 20033–0756.

As a research tool, the Poynter Institute for Media Studies has compiled a number of useful bibliographies, including "Reference Sources for Student Journalists," "Government and the Press," and

"Best Newspaper Writing." Direct inquiries to Jo Cates, chief librarian, the Poynter Institute, 801 Third Street South, St. Petersburg, FL 33701. There is also a series of thirty-one videotaped interviews, each running thirty minutes, available from the Poynter Institute. Among the journalists interviewed were Ben Bradlee, John Chancellor, Meg Greenfield, Katherine Graham, Al Neuharth, James Reston, and Eric Sevareid.

NOTES

1. For a discussion of the relationships between the press, free expression, and democratic government, see Maurice R. Cullen, Jr., *Mass Media and the First Amendment* (Dubuque, IA: William C. Brown, 1981).

2. For reporters to write meaningful stories, they must know how society operates. They must be knowledgeable about a broad range of human activity that extends from sports to business to science. Too often, however, today's students lack so-called cultural literacy. For a full discussion, see E. D. Hirsch, Jr., *Cultural Literacy: What Every American Needs to Know* (Boston, MA: Houghton Mifflin, 1987).

3. Sources for biographies include *Journalist Biographies Master Index*, Alan E. Abrams, ed. (Detroit, MI: Gale Research, 1979); *American Newspaper Journalists*, Perry J. Ashley, ed. (Detroit, MI: Gale Research, 1984, 4 vols.); *Great Lives from History* (American series), Frank N. Magill, ed. (Englewood Cliffs, NJ: Salem Press, 1987).

4. See Todd Hunt, "Beyond the Journalistic Event: The Changing Concept of News," in *Enduring Issues in Mass Communication*, Everette E. Dennis, ed. (St. Paul, MN: West Publishing, 1978), 139–46.

5. In most states, the Secretary of State's Office oversees campaign spending as well as local elections and can provide information regarding access to information candidates have filed.

6. For those not familiar with the coaching process, see Roy Peter Clark, *Free to Write: A Journalist Teaches Young Writers* (Portsmouth, NH: Heinemann, 1987).

Chapter 8

ADVERTISING CAMPAIGNS

Jon D. Morris and Frank N. Pierce

Theoretically, this course is intended to assist students in acquiring the intellectual skills needed in the development of well-planned and effective advertising strategies. In practice, this course is designed to focus on application. Teams of five to seven students prepare advertising campaign plans for a client who has been selected by the instructor. The client selection will be discussed in another section; however, the product or service may be actual or fictitious. Actual clients seem to give the students more realistic, challenging, and rewarding experiences, although there are some benefits to the case study approach. The purpose of this course is to provide students with a hands-on opportunity to develop an advertising campaign. The objectives of the course are:

1. To review the procedures used in creating print and broadcast advertising (and to a lesser degree related sales promotion);
2. To expose students to the terminology and techniques used in the business of advertising;
3. To provide the students with an actual advertising problem and guide them through the development of a campaign.

BACKGROUND

The requirements for the course have been designed to provide the students with concepts and experiences needed to meet the above-stated objectives and to measure the amount of success toward reaching these objectives. Students are required to:

1. Attend class meetings, first as a unified group, then as part of a competing team;

2. Read the suggested text and other supplemental material;

3. Take one exam over the reading material (optional). The test is used more to ensure that the students read the material than to determine a course grade. The value that is usually assigned to the test is 15 percent of the final grade;

4. As part of a team, complete one campaign—a strategic plan designed to recommend advertising techniques that will be used for the promotion of a product or service;

5. Provide the instructor with weekly call reports—a record of individual and team activities for the week;

6. Prepare and participate in a verbal and visual presentation of the team's advertising recommendations;

7. Complete one peer evaluation.

TEXTS

One text is usually required for this class. Additional material may be assigned from other texts and placed on reserve in the library or given to students in the form of handouts. The text usually purchased is:

Don E. Schultz, *Strategic Advertising Campaigns*, 3rd ed. (Lincolnwood, IL: NTC Business Books, 1990).

Additional texts which may be of value either to students in the class or the instructor include the following:

Philip Ward Burton and Scott C. Purvis, *Which Ad Pulled Best?* (Lincolnwood, IL: NTC Business Books, 1986).

A. Jerome Jewler, *Creative Strategy in Advertising* (Belmont, CA: Wadsworth, 1989).

Sandra Moriarity and Tom Duncan, *How to Create and Deliver Winning Advertising Presentations* (Lincolnwood, IL: NTC Business Books, 1989).

Hanley Norins, *The Compleat Copywriter* (New York: McGraw-Hill, 1966).

David Ogilvy, *Ogilvy on Advertising* (New York: Vintage Books, 1985).

Kenneth Roman and Jane Maas, *How to Advertise* (New York: St. Martin's Press, 1977).

Don E. Schultz and Stanley I. Tannenbaum, *Essentials of Advertising Strategy*, 2nd ed. (Lincolnwood, IL: NTC Business Books, 1988).

James Webb Young, *A Technique for Producing Ideas* (Chicago, IL: Crain Communications, Inc., 1975).

ORGANIZATION

The campaign plans are developed using the "agency team" approach. Students are divided into a number of competing teams, with five to seven persons per team. Students may be allowed to select their own colleagues with some guidance from the instructor, or the instructor may assemble the teams. No "totally correct" way has been established; however, the best method seems to be to allow the students themselves to be responsible for the final selection of colleagues on their team.

Students should be encouraged to choose colleagues who would like to earn similar grades in the course. This will assist in matching students with similar ambitions. Moreover, students should be chosen by matching complementary skills and interest. Best results occur when students are matched with others who have interest and experience, both classroom and practical, in each of the following areas: media planning; creative strategy/copywriting; creative strategy/art direction; advertising research; management/marketing.

One (or two) students should be responsible for each of the above areas; however, all students on the team should be involved in the preparation of each area, at least to some degree. The responsible person (or persons) should direct the development of the material, edit or rewrite a good proportion of the team's plans book, and be responsible for at least one section of the presentation. Having someone on the team with an art proficiency is most helpful; however, teams are permitted to purchase finished art. The team should develop the visual concepts and rough layouts, but the finished or comprehensive artwork may be done by someone outside the team.

To give the students time to become acquainted with each other as co-workers on an extensive project, teams should be selected as early in the school term as possible. The instructor should keep a careful record of the persons on each team and their local telephone numbers. This will assist in disseminating information on short notice. Once the basic lectures in the course have been completed, each agency team should meet regularly at least once a week with the instructor. These team meetings serve to involve the instructor in the development of the campaign plans. Although the instructor must remain somewhat removed from the process, it is appropriate for him or her to offer suggestions, correct errors of fact or grammar, assist students in finding strategies for solving the problem that has been presented, or check the teams' progress at completing the exercise.

The client may be fictitious or real. Experience has shown that actual clients seem to give the students more realistic, challenging, and rewarding experiences, although they also may be more troublesome for the instructor to manage effectively. It requires more time to secure and work effectively with a company that has an advertising problem compared to a case study that has been created for simulation. If an actual "real world" client is desired, the following protocol may be helpful.

Look for a client who might benefit from an association with a class or school. The client should be matched to the school and class by contacting those businesses that appear to be large enough to provide a sizable advertising problem and small enough so as not to over-power the course. One suggestion is to start small and work up after some experience with this exercise.

Try to obtain a client with an assignment that is large enough to allow the students real choices in the selection of media and perhaps even in geographic segmentation. The "lowest possible budget" that we are willing to work with is $50,000 in proposed media expenditures. We would much prefer significantly larger possibilities, however. From a geographical standpoint, a regional account is better than a national one, because more attention must be paid to individual cities and media scheduling possibilities. Recent clients working with us have given us advertising budgets in the $100,000 to $1,000,000 range for three months to one year.

Your greatest difficulty may well come from determining current rates in the broadcast area. Standard Rate and Data Service (SRDS) often does not carry any rates at all for many radio or TV stations. If the creative aspect of your assignment requires the use of broadcast media, you probably will need to get in touch with each station to learn what current rates are. As an example, if your student teams are working within a single state and there are 100 radio and TV stations which might possibly be used, you may need to start a letter-writing campaign for information. Two other methods of obtaining broadcast information are telephone calls (somewhat time-consuming) and faxes. Of course, you can ask the teams themselves to try to obtain the proper information from any station they finally propose using for the campaign.

On the other hand, if your client will allow you to specify broadcast Gross Rating Points (GRPs)[1] generally (and you're working with larger cities), there are some brochures available that give such information. One example is the *Leo Burnett 1989 Media Costs and Coverage* brochure. It may be ordered from the Media Department, Leo Burnett U.S.A., Prudential Plaza, Chicago, IL 60601.

Print rates are less likely to be negotiable than broadcast rates, although that is changing somewhat today. However, we have always allowed our students to use whatever rates SRDS printed for magazines and newspapers. For outdoor rates, the "Buyer's Guide to Outdoor Advertising" is usable.

Additional reference materials would include the Simmons Report on TV audience demographics (Simmons Market Research Bureau, 42nd Street, New York, NY 10017), and the television and radio rating data from Arbitron (Arbitron Ratings Company, 1350 Avenue of the Americas, New York, NY 10019). Their reports are available for purchase at the above addresses.

Don't hesitate to charge a fee for the assignment. This is helpful to defray some of the costs for conducting the course and other school expenses. (It is not personal money paid the instructor on the side.) A portion of the fee may be awarded to the students at the end of the campaign to help cover some of their costs. Often student teams are awarded varying amounts depending on how the client evaluates their plans book and final presentation. The fee may be used as added incentive to spur students to do the best possible work.

The client should travel to the school sometime during the first three weeks of the term in order to make the official assignment to the class and to answer questions. During this visit, each student team should be prepared to ask questions about the product or service to be advertised. The client should provide the class with information about the product or service before the meeting; however, students will need to prepare themselves by conducting additional secondary (library) research.

The client should be available to answer questions throughout the term. Student teams should be required either to select one member to initiate all team/client contact or all questions should be presented to the instructor, who will make the contact. Regardless of the method that is chosen, contact should be limited to once or twice a week in order to minimize interruption of the client's normal business activity.

In some cases, visits to the client's business may be helpful. If students would benefit from seeing the manufacturing process, the service, or any aspect of the business assigned, then the instructor should arrange a group trip. Some products or services cannot be portrayed clearly without some observation by those preparing the advertisements. Amusement parks or housing developments are good examples of the need for on-site visits.

The client should be prepared for at least one more visit to the class. Although it may be helpful for the client to return midway through the course to evaluate progress or answer questions, it is essential that the client return at the end of the course to view the students' final presentations. Although each team should present the client with an advertising plans book, the campaign cannot be clearly understood by the client without a verbal and visual presentation. This also gives the client an opportunity to ask questions and to question rationale.

Campaign Plans Book. A great deal of time and effort is needed to prepare a well-thought-out, eclectic campaign. Each team should prepare a campaign plans book, which is a permanent record of the analyses and proposed solutions to the assigned advertising problem. There is no prescribed length for these campaign books; however, recent books produced for this class at the University of Florida have ranged between 80 and 150 pages in length. Once the course is established, it is helpful to place copies of previous campaign books on reserve in the library. Initially, instructors may locate copies of actual campaign plans or use case studies (such as the one found in Schultz) or contact the American Advertising Federation for copies of winning books from the annual NSAC (National Student Advertising Competition). Whichever method is used, the instructor should locate more than one example, since there are differing approaches to developing a campaign plans book. Instructors should monitor carefully the manner in which these books are handled and used. Students should be discouraged from abusing the books or from copying directly from them.

The Schultz book contains a general outline for preparing an advertising campaign. Few campaigns follow this outline to the letter. Moreover, each campaign plan has its strengths and weaknesses. The students' task is to determine the good and bad points of each preceding campaign and apply the good ones in the preparation of their own plans book. Students should bring any questions to the team/instructor meetings. Students should help each other improve by continually reviewing and critiquing each other's work.

The following table (see Table 8.1) is an outline of a typical advertising campaign book. This outline will vary somewhat from case to case depending on the needs of the client.

Table 8.1
Outline of Plans Book

Item	Required	# of Pages
1. Title Page	Yes	1
2. Table of Contents	Yes	1+
3. Agency Philosophy	Optional	1–2
4. Executive Summary	Yes	1–2
5. Situation Analysis		
Relevant History of Organization	Yes	1+
Product/Service Evaluation	Yes	1+
Consumer Evaluation	Yes	1+
Competition Analysis	Yes	1+
6. Marketing Objective(s) and Goal(s)	Yes	½
7. Advertising Objective(s) and Goal(s)	Yes	½
8. Budget	Yes	1
9. Advertising Recommendations		
Target Market	Yes	¼–½
Advertising Communication Objective(s) and Goal(s)	Yes	½–1
Creative Strategy	Yes	½–2
Executions	Yes	Whatever
10. Media Recommendations		
Key Media Problem	Yes	¼–1
Media Objective(s) and Goal(s)	Yes	½–1
Media Strategy	Yes	1–2
Media Plan	Yes	Whatever
11. Sales Promotion Recommendations (if any)		
Sales Promotion Objective(s) and Goal(s)	Yes	¼–1
Sales Promotion Strategy	Yes	1–2
Sales Promotion Execution(s)	Yes	Whatever
Sales Promotion Plan	Yes	Whatever
12. Public Relations Recommendations (if any)		
Public Relations Objective(s) and Goal(s)	Yes	¼–1
Public Relations Strategy	Yes	1–2
Public Relations Execution(s)	Yes	Whatever
Public Relations Plan	Yes	Whatever
13. Evaluation of All Plans	Yes	1–2
14. Additional Recommendations	Optional	1–3
15. Appendix	If applicable	Whatever

If a "real world" client is used, each team should prepare a minimum of two complete, identical plans books. One book should be given to the client personnel to use at their discretion. All recommendations there should become the property of the client, unless otherwise specified, and students should be informed of this arrangement in writing early in the course. The second plans book will become the property of the instructor and serve as a record of the team's work. The best books may be used as guidelines for future campaigns classes.

Absolute due dates should be assigned in the first week of class. Completing a project on time is an essential component of advertising planning; students should be informed that the plans books must be handed in on time. The date for handing in the books should be approximately two weeks before the date of the presentation. This will allow the instructor and client personnel adequate time to review the plans prior to viewing the final presentations.

Presentation. Each team should make a verbal and visual presentation of the essential elements, particularly their recommendations, to the instructor and the client. The best time to schedule the presentation is as close to the end of the term as possible. Each team member should participate in the presentation, although it is not essential that the amount of time allocated to each student be the same. Immediately following the presentation to the client, a question/answer and critique (or discussion) session should be held. The session should last from ten to thirty minutes. The first portion (Q&A) is for the benefit of the client to clarify any ambiguities and to discuss rationale. The second portion (critique or discussion) is held for the benefit of the students and should be handled appropriately. Students often learn the most if the client is candid but supportive.

Students should view their team's individual presentation as an opportunity to present their proposal in a favorable light. It is a time to convince the client that they have the best solution to the problem. The approach should include a significant amount of rationale to help persuade the client to select their team's proposal. It is an excellent opportunity for the team to present its ideas to a group of interested, knowledgeable persons who make their livelihood by working for the client's organization.

Weekly Call Report. As soon as individual agency teams begin meeting with the instructor, each person should turn in a weekly call report. These reports assist the instructor in determining how the team and the individual are progressing. In addition, these reports serve as a valuable tool in evaluating the student's work by a) offering a tool for determining what the student contributed to the team's campaign; and b) serving as other graded assignments. Failure to produce well-written call reports following the guidelines listed below should be an indication of the students' inability to write business reports effectively and to follow directions.

Here are guidelines for students for writing call reports.

1. Each call report must be typed on plain white paper. Use 8½ x 11 typing paper. No onion skin or erasable bond, please. Double-space your report. You may correct errors neatly on the page, but a report with more than three uncorrected errors per page will cause you to lose points.

2. Each full report must be a minimum of one full page in length. This is loosely defined as 250 words. A page and one-half is the maximum.

3. Each report should be divided into two sections: team activities and individual activities. Please report all significant activities that have been undertaken by your team and by yourself. This information assists the instructor in guiding and evaluating your work. Please be somewhat detailed in your descriptions. If you worked on some aspect, describe and report a brief summary of your findings or accomplishments. Also, you should indicate some future plans and the target dates.

4. Each call report must begin with five pieces of information at the top right-hand side of the page. These are, in order: (A) your name, (B) call report number, (C) the date of the meeting with the instructor, (D) agency team name, and (E) agency team number. Single-space this information.

5. Call reports are due on, for example, Friday morning at 9:30 AM. In a space in the office, there will be either an envelope with your team's name and number on it, or a special box. Whichever receptacle is used by the instructor, please seal your call report in a letter-sized envelope and place it in your team's receptacle.

6. All call reports should be prepared as professionally as possible. They are designed to give you some experience in organizing a report of activities. Recalling actions you and your team have undertaken should be helpful in deciding on your next steps. Additionally, it helps the instructor enormously in keeping track of your team's activities. Call reports are an individual activity and should not be done as a group.

The following is an example of a call report.

Susan Spiegal
Call Report #4
November 13, 1991
Krystal Advertisers
Team #5

Team's Activities. As a group we discussed our creative plans and media allocations in detail. We are going to have three thirty-second TV spots and two print advertisements aimed toward our primary target audience. We are going to develop one print ad geared toward our secondary target audience. We also talked about a trade ad to get the professional portrait photographers more involved. Promotions will be another consideration for our campaign. We are planning on finishing all of our written material by this week and will begin typing the final portion of our project (as well as including charts and graphs).

Individual Activities. Media has been a big project of mine this week. My associate Gina Rothman and I have established several different media packages. We have received a great deal of information from Hearst Publications in order to use the Women's Super Plus media package. We feel that it is to our advantage to use a group package because it will in turn reach our target audience of female homemakers with a great impact. We were trying to fit a sixty-second commercial in but it was *impossible* with our budget. Researching through the 1991 Media Guide has been a terrific aid and has allowed our campaign to focus on using a heavier amount of magazine. . . .

Peer Evaluation. The performance of a team may be difficult to separate from the performance of the several individuals on that team. For this reason, some instructors have attempted to become more knowledgeable about each person's contribution to the group effort by asking for confidential peer evaluations on a regular basis. The final peer evaluation, on the other hand, is a major component of all students' final grades.

The evaluation is a four-part confidential procedure in which the student first rates everyone else in the group according to their order of contribution, with first being highest (i.e., first, second, third). There can be ties. Secondly, the student assigns a letter grade for each member's performance including himself or herself. Third, the student is asked to write a brief description of each group member's performance. Finally, the student is asked to write about his or her own performance.

The instructor will average the several scores received for each student and apply them to the overall grade sheet.

One instructor we know uses both a midterm and a final peer evaluation. The midterm format is used to learn if any student seems to be shirking his or her responsibilities as far as the other team members are concerned. If one or more are doing so, a reminder that the instructor knows of the possible lack of effort often can right the situation before any further damage is done to the overall group effort. The instructor who uses this system tells each student beforehand that nothing from this evaluation will ever be written down in a grade book. It is advisory only.

Grading Policy. Although the client may determine which team(s) have done the best job of solving the advertising problem, the instructor should assign the grades. The instructor may take into account the client's judgments; however, the grades should be assigned independent of these findings. Below is an example of a typical campaigns class grading policy.

One Exam	15% by number of correct responses
Plans Book	35% based on each student's portion of the book
Presentation	20%; all team members receive the same score
Call Reports	15% based on quality and quantity
Peer Evaluations	15%
Total	100%

CONCLUSION

The discussion in this chapter has been concerned solely with an Advertising Campaigns class. This is not meant to exclude the possibility of using a similar program with public relations students. Our particular university runs the same type of program with its public relations students as it does with its advertising students.

NOTE

1. A Gross Rating Point is the rating a program or commercial gets multiplied by the number of times the program or commercial is played.

Chapter 9

AUDIO PRODUCTION

Robert Musburger

The teaching of audio production can be an exhilarating yet frustrating experience for both the faculty member and the student. Audio production provides the student with immediate creative personal feedback with a minimum of knowledge, experience, and equipment operation ability. For the instructor, the simplicity and relative low cost of the equipment allows the production process to be taught quickly, without lengthy technical explanations. On the other hand, all production courses share the common impediment of equipment and material costs and teaching students to synchronize mental concepts with eye/hand coordination.

Besides the joy of actually completing a media project, there are rational reasons for teaching students audio production. To begin with, audio production is the basis for all other productions. Neither film, nor video, nor audio-visual productions are complete without quality audio. If audio is taught first in the production sequence, then when the students go on to other production courses they will have learned (one hopes) how to create with the three-step production process (preproduction, production, postproduction). They also should have a grasp of how to solve audio problems and how to operate audio equipment, so they may concentrate on learning the video and/or film equipment operation processes.

BACKGROUND

Students learn audio production easily since they have to contend with only one medium and essentially only one channel of communication. That one channel is quite familiar to most students since they seem to be born with earphones on their heads and loudspeakers in their modes of transportation. Audio constantly surrounds them in one form or another, and although they may have a very distorted concept of how audio and/or radio production is carried out, they deal, at the very least, with a medium that envelops them daily.

The possibility of creating as an individual, rather than as a member of a crew, provides each student the opportunity to feel rewarded for doing his or her own work and accomplishing it as he or she originally conceptualized the project. Although teamwork on crews should not be ignored in audio production courses, the majority of projects at the introductory level generally are individual projects.

For the instructor, an audio production class provides the opportunity to use audio media to increase the student's awareness of the importance of the research, writing, planning, and operational skills necessary for a successful audio production. The student can be taught to become a much better, more critical listener, not only to radio, but to recordings and sound tracks of both film and television programs. This increased awareness of media is as important as training a student for a career in media production. Few, if any, of your students will have a lifelong career in audio production, but every one of them will be consumers of audio, and if the class is well taught, they will become educated, critical consumers, not just funnel-shaped ears.

A well-taught audio production course is an excellent prerequisite for all other media production courses, especially for video and film production courses.

ORGANIZATION

The goals of an audio production course will be achieved if students are able to:

1. Clearly think through the concept of a production design;
2. Design projects using the three-step production process:
    • Preproduction
    • Production
    • Postproduction;
3. Create copy that is well written and in proper format;
4. Understand the functions of all the equipment in the control room;
5. Operate satisfactorily all basic audio equipment;
6. Take and give direction;

7. Use standard hand cues;
8. Choose and place microphones properly;
9. Physically edit audio tape.

The lecture/lab sessions may be organized in a variety of ways, but the most popular is a single two-hour lecture session each week and a single three-hour lab session.

In this method a full-time faculty member delivers the lecture in one large section with students assigned to individual lab sections of no more than twenty students each. If graduate assistants are available, they may supervise the labs while the full-time faculty delivers the lectures and supervises the graduate assistants.

Some open lab time should be made available for students to rehearse and to work on individual projects. Some exercises are performed with the instructor in the control room observing, and others are performed without supervision. More about the individual exercises later.

During the first half of the semester, the lecture period is utilized for lectures, discussions, and examinations over the textbook. During this time, the laboratory time is used to perform the six introductory exercises. After the text has been covered, both the lecture and lab periods may be used for in-class exercises and practical examinations on the equipment.

TEXTS

Several years ago there were very few suitable texts for classroom use. Today several publishers have released excellent books and, as the audio industry changes, more texts will be published. The following is a list of relatively new general production texts suitable for classroom or reference use.

Stanley R. Alten, *Audio in Media*, 3rd ed. (Belmont, CA: Wadsworth, 1990). The standard for middle and upper level audio production courses. Comprehensive, but organized so that not all material must be used.

Linda Busby and Donald Parker, *The Art and Science of Radio* (Newton, MA: Allyn & Bacon, 1984). Restricted to radio only, but also covers history, regulation, writing, management, and programming.

Lynne Gross and David E. Reese, *Radio Production Worktext: Studio and Equipment* (Stoneham, MA: Focal Press, 1990). A combined workbook and text, with self-guiding exercises for students. Excellent, especially for an instructor without professional experience.

Michael C. Keith, *Radio Production: Art and Science* (Stoneham, MA: Focal Press, 1990). Good for teaching strictly radio production; also contains excellent chapters on programming.

Robert McLeish, *The Technique of Radio Production*, 2nd ed. (London: Focal Press, 1988). Another text that concentrates on radio only. Spends only two chapters on audio characteristics and operations, the rest on formats. Includes some British terminology.

Lewis B. O'Donnell, Philip Benoit, and Carl Hausman, *Modern Radio Production*, 2nd ed. (Belmont, CA: Wadsworth, 1986). An excellent, easy-to-use text, well illustrated; concentrates on radio.

Robert S. Oringel, *Audio Control Handbook*, 6th ed. (Stoneham, MA: Focal Press, 1989). At one time the standard text, has now been updated. Spends much space describing specific models of certain brand name equipment.

Beyond these, there are at least twenty specialized texts in areas such as recording, microphones/speakers, technology, and digital audio, available for consideration.

No production course ought to be taught without at least one copy of Herbert Zettl, *Sight Sound Motion: Applied Aesthetic*, 2nd ed. (Belmont, CA: Wadsworth, 1990) on hand. For audio production, chapters 1, 12, 16, and 17 are invaluable sources of applied aesthetic information.

EQUIPMENT

The minimum equipment for teaching an audio production course consists of a control room containing an electronic timer, a large clock with a sweep second hand, a multiple input control console, two turntables, one open reel one-quarter-inch tape deck, an audio cassette recorder/player, and a broadcast cartridge recorder/player, a control room mike, and a studio or announce booth with at least one microphone.

More realistic training may be accomplished if the control room is equipped with the above plus a second open reel deck, cart machine, cassette deck, CD player, patch panel, and several microphone inputs from the studio. Headphones for the operator are optional.

One of the lessons learned by students is the proper care and treatment of equipment. It is important that students understand that even though the equipment is made for professional use, it is expensive to repair and/or replace. Some schools charge a lab fee to cover these costs or require students to sign an agreement that they will pay for any equipment they damage or lose.

HANDOUTS

In addition to formal textbooks, most instructors of production courses assemble two types of handouts. The first are self-generated forms, instructions, and sample scripts and/or formats, and the second are the manufacturer's instructions for the equipment students will be using. The most efficient manner of handling handouts is to take master copies of the handouts to a reproduction business and let them assemble them into a bound booklet for which the students will pay the appropriate fee. This system saves the department time and money, and presents each student with their own set of handouts, which they have paid for and might take care not to lose. This system also means every student gets exactly the same project and equipment instructions and forms.

If larger departments and schools publish their own production manuals, all of this material may be included in the packet.

EXERCISES

A series of relatively simple exercises, each designed to teach one aspect of the production process, gently moves the students through the process until they have acquired the technique of each individual step and finally discover they have mastered the entire procedure.

To form the basis of good operational procedures, as well as to introduce the student to professional terminology, a two-part exercise, "Cable Coiling-Connector Identification," is performed in the lab. The first part teaches the students how to properly coil a cable; the second teaches how to identify all of the plugs and jacks used in audio production. On the surface these seem like petty operations, but in the long run they remind students that the most common equipment failures are from cables and their plugs. In addition, these provide a nontechnical lab exercise for use early in the semester.

The "over-under" method of cable coiling is demonstrated, and then each student attempts to coil a microphone cable until he or she performs the operation correctly. At the same time (especially if an assistant is available), each student is shown a variety of cable plugs, adapters, and jacks and asked to identify them by name, sex, and use.

The plugs used should include XLR, mini, DIN, RCA (phono), one-quarter-inch (phone), and patch bay cable. A discussion of balanced versus unbalanced mic lines and low and high impedance would be appropriate at this time. These two operations should take less than a two-hour lab with twenty students.

A second exercise designed to ease the students into the production process tests their ability to communicate through a window using standard media hand cues. Students receive in their handout packets a list and description of standard hand cues. On the day of the exercise, one student at a time is sent into the control room or announce booth with a chalkboard. The rest of the class stays in the studio and a second student is chosen to "throw" the cues. As the instructor calls out a cue, the student in the studio must perform the cue until the student in the control room "catches" the cue and writes it down on the board. The students are rotated through both positions until each student has thrown and caught five to six different cues. This process can be completed easily in one two-hour period.

Part of this exercise includes an important demonstration that the students observe. Depending on the size of the control room or studio, the class gathers in one room with the instructor or assistant in the other. A microphone on a floor stand is placed in the middle of the room, a normal level is set on the mike, and then the instructor or assistant walks toward and away from the mike without changing vocal levels. If the room is large enough, students clearly will hear the difference between "on mike" and "off mike" acoustics.

The mike is then placed next to and pointed at a sound-absorbing surface. The instructor starts talking about three feet away and continues talking at the same level until he or she is close to the mike. The same procedure is repeated, only this time the mike is placed facing and next to a hard sound-reflecting surface. The same demonstration may be repeated if the two types of surfaces can be placed adjacent to each other with the microphone pointed at the intersecting point of the two surfaces. The instructor then speaks toward the hard surface and without changing volume moves his or her head until he or she is speaking toward the sound-absorbing surface. A chalkboard on wheels, or one light enough to move easily, placed at right angles to the studio wall, works very well in this exercise if the studio has dead walls for the absorbing surface.

The second part of this exercise consists of the instructor or assistant explaining and demonstrating the operation of a patch panel. One method requires a sound source, such as a record, to be fed through the audio board (as long as that source passes through the patch panel). A patch cord is plugged into that source's jack, lifting the sound and breaking the normal connection. The other end of the patch cord is then patched into another board input, and the pot is brought up so the sound can be heard and controlled by a second pot.[1] Once there is recognition that the students understand the process, each is required to patch a cord into the panel and move the signal to another pot. These two exercises can consume up to three lab hours with twenty students.

This board operation exercise is what most students have been waiting for—the chance to get their hands on the control equipment. The instructor demonstrates each of the functions of the board by first threading playback tapes and records on all sources. Then each control is explained: monitor control, delegation switches, pots, channel switches, cue controls, level indicators. Using the available sound sources, each of these functions can be demonstrated so the students can see the operation and hear the results. At this time, it is appropriate to demonstrate the differences between a cross-fade, a segue, and a cut, with brief explanations on the reasons for using each transition. This is also a good time to demonstrate proper setting and maintaining of levels, smooth operation of controls, and general operational procedures.

One by one each student operates the board following the commands of the instructor. The exercise should include at least one fade-in, one cross-fade, one segue, one cut, and one mix of two sources. During this time, the student should be instructed to change monitor level, listen to a source on cue, and if available, switch to a "B" or audition channel. As each command is given, the instructor must check to make certain level is reached quickly and maintained within proper limits.

With twenty students, this exercise may take more than a three-hour lab period, especially if the control room is small enough to force the instructor to split the class and repeat the lecture and demonstration a second time.

Depending on the number and type of tape decks, a tape decks exercise may take more than one lab period, due to the amount of equipment needing explanation and demonstration.

Assuming the control room contains at least one each cassette, reel-to-reel, and broadcast cart deck, each deck should be demonstrated individually but following a parallel pattern so that students will see that all decks are basically the same, with just different labels and position of controls.

After each machine is loaded, a recording is made and then played back. Each student is instructed to bulk erase the tape stock, load each of the decks, and make a recording on each deck from a source fed through the board by the instructor. After each recording is made, the student must rewind the tape, cue it, and then feed the playback through the board at proper levels, rewind the tape stock, and unload the decks.

It is important at this stage that the student appreciates the necessity of bulk erasing tape stock, setting levels with a tone, accurate and proper threading of machines, and understanding the power presented by a tape deck in full fast forward or rewind speed.

The last of the demonstration exercises is relatively simple and can be accomplished easily in a three-hour lab period. Extra time should be used to answer some of the many questions students now should have about all of the equipment they are now responsible for operating.

The turntable is demonstrated, especially the proper techniques of handling the tone arm and cuing techniques. CD instruction will vary with the type of deck in use, but as with tape decks, each function should be explained and demonstrated, especially accurate cuing of a particular cut on the disc. As with the other exercises, each student is required to operate each piece of equipment in a professional manner. If time allows, a simple exercise involving all of the control room equipment could be assigned at this time, with students allowed to sign up for a specified amount of facilities time to practice and perform such an exercise.

By this time the textbook material and written tests should have been completed in the lecture sessions, and the semester should be about at the halfway point. It is time for a comprehensive review of all equipment operations. This can be accomplished by an exercise that requires the student to perform a set number of procedures in a precise amount of time.

Such an exercise would require the student to thread a tape on a reel-to-reel deck (after properly bulk erasing), setting a level with a tone through the board, cuing a 45 rpm record on one of the turntables, a 33 rpm record on the other, and a thirty-second commercial cart in a cart deck. The student then starts the recording deck rolling, opens the mike, and with his or her first word of introduction of the 45 record, starts the electronic clock and plays the 45. As soon as a level has been set on the 45, a segue is performed to the commercial in the cart deck. At the end of the commercial, the student must open the mike, introduce the 33, and play it. While it is playing, a second 45 must be cued (if it wasn't cued during the commercial) and back-timed, ready to dead-pot[2] it so it will end at exactly 4:30. During this same time, a commercial must be cued on a reel-to-reel deck.

At the proper timing point, the second 45 will be rolled with the pot down and the reel-to-reel will be played before the 33 ends. At the end of the commercial, the pot is brought up on the 45 and the instructor stands by the clock to stop it on the last sound of the record.

Scoring on this exercise is done on the basis of how well each piece of equipment was operated, how well levels were maintained, how operational procedures were followed, and how close to the exact 4:30 time the last record ended.

Obviously, this is a challenging exercise, and students should have the instruction in hand well before they are expected to perform the review. They also should be motivated to rehearse the exercise as often as possible before they must perform it with the instructor watching in the control room. This process may take as many as three three-hour lab periods to complete. Each exercise should take about fifteen minutes, plus some time for each student to set up and strike.

Students spend the last half of the semester performing two types of exercises: those accomplished by the student unsupervised on his or her own during "open lab" times, and exercise-tests performed during class periods with the instructor watching and grading while the student is "on the air."

The first unsupervised exercise is designed to teach students appreciation for and techniques of physically editing tape. Each student is provided with a roll of original session material consisting of several takes of a thirty-second spot. Each of the takes contains errors or is for some reason unusable in total. The student is provided precise instructions on the finished length, labeling of the box, reel, head and tail leaders, and a copy of how the finished spot should read, and is allowed an hour in the control room to complete the project. The student provides his or her own editing block, splicing tape, and marking pen. Included in the student's handout packet are instructions and hints on editing tape. The instructor also delivers a lecture and demonstration on tape editing techniques at the time of the assignment. The students are graded on the basis of accurate timing, quality of edits, number of edits, labeling, and meeting assigned deadlines for turning in the finished product. If several tape decks with head phones can be set up in a room aside from the studio and control room, students can finish the project more quickly and with fewer interruptions to the studio use.

In the meantime, during class periods, students are given the opportunity to prove and to improve their operational ability with two similar exercises. Following a preset schedule, students individually are given a "log" which calls for a series of audio functions to be performed. The exercise is similar to a radio station's log, but is intended to reinforce all audio operational techniques, not just those used in a radio station situation. A student is handed a copy of the log and has about fifteen minutes to "pull" the material from a library containing many more tapes, records, carts, cassettes, and discs than called for on the log. The student then enters the control room and has a set amount of time to complete the entire operation, including setting up a tape deck to record and then playing the recording back at the end of the log.

Each log requires the student to look and plan ahead, keep something going to avoid dead-air, maintain levels, and properly operate all of the equipment. The emphasis is on equipment operation, not performance, but for those students who want some announcing experience, the opportunity is present.

The difference between the simple and complex log is a matter of shorter intervals to complete operations during the complex log; instead of 60- and 30-second spots, only 30-, 20-, and 10-second spots are used in the complex log. Tape commercials are not the first cut on the reel, nor are any of the record cuts the first on the disc in the complex log. A live newscast is scheduled in the middle of the complex log, requiring students to set up and cue the newscast through the window using hand cues. A commercial is scheduled in the middle of the newscast and the newscaster must be cued off to meet a specified time.

These two log exercises fill all of the class time to the end of the semester with the exception of the time used to hand out critiques, discuss problems, and make verbal assignments. Students not performing on any particular day are invited to sit in the studio, providing an audience for the student being tested, and also giving the students the opportunity to learn from others' mistakes. The log exercises are graded on the same order as the midterm, only more critically and precisely.

During the class time period consumed by the logs, two exercises are assigned to be completed during open lab periods. The first gives the students an opportunity to actually produce a spot. The copy is in their handout packet, and they are responsible for casting (it requires two voices), producing sound effects (three are required; one must be done live, the other two may be played back from disc or tape), and scheduling a one-hour recording session in the studio. The exercise must be done live, without any editing except for adding head and tail leaders. The grading is based on the same values as the editing exercise, except the producer is also graded on the delivery of the spot and the appropriateness and timing of the sound effects.

The final open lab exercise is designed to give the students an enjoyable and creative opportunity with as much freedom built in as possible. The music mix requires the student to use three cuts from three separate records, recorded so that they time out at exactly one minute. This requires the student to choose three related cuts (part of the grading is on the appropriateness of their choices), cuing the first two, segueing or cross-fading between them in enough time to cue, and accurately rolling the last cut so it will end at one minute. There are no restrictions on content, but the recording must be accomplished without editing except for the head and tail leaders. Each student has a one-hour block of time to complete the project. Grading is based on the relationship of the three music pieces, levels, transitions at appropriate times in the music, and proper labeling.

FINAL EXAMINATION

A final examination for an audio production course should include both written and practical aspects. I recommend that students be allowed to conceptualize, write, and produce their own final project. A specific amount of studio time (twenty to thirty minutes) is scheduled and the student may create any audio production he or she wishes within that time block while being observed by the instructor. Students should be aware that the heavily weighted final project will be graded on their written scripts, evidence of research, amount of materials used, and skill shown in the operation of the equipment. The actual grading is accomplished on the same basis as the logs and midterm, with the instructor sitting in the control room watching and taking notes on the student's operational procedure.

Since most schools schedule very specific final examination times, the additional time required to allow this type of final exam must be taken out of class time. Final exams may start a day or so after completion of the complex log exercise. Students must be given equal time to prepare for their final, so the final schedule must be announced well in advance.

OTHER COURSE CONSIDERATIONS

One of the major problems in teaching a production course is that of grading the student's work. In an entry level course, such as the one described in this chapter, it is more important that the student learn the process of audio production rather than spend time producing a creative gem. The grading should, therefore, reward those who learn the process and show it by their work. This grading procedure is not easy for some students to accept since their reason for taking the course may not agree with the stated course objective. Students who spend the greater portion of their time creating that one marvelous production, but who ignore the procedures set up to teach the process of audio production, should not receive a high grade. A balance must be reached, but it is better to err on the side of rewarding a less-than-professional end product gained through diligently following process than rewarding great creativity gained through sloppy process.

The key to this class is to motivate students to grow and excel by learning how to produce audio in class as preparation for the day after leaving school when they have the time and equipment to really do their creative work. This course offers students the chance to show their instructor and themselves how much they have grown and stretched during the time of this course.

It is impossible for the instructor to teach this course without learning something new about media production. Even if there is no concerted effort (and there should be) to read the trades and follow the progress of the audio industry, students will force faculty to respond to their inquiring minds and questions. The new technologies of digital audio, electronic editing, multitrack recording, stereo miking, and tapeless production are here now and, although most of those techniques should be covered in an advanced second semester, they all impact on this course.

Besides reading the trades, faculty should interact with the industry through personal contacts at stations and studios, by belonging to or attending meetings of such organizations as the Society of Broadcast Engineers (SBE), the Society of Motion Picture and Television Engineers (SMPTE), the International Television Association (ITVA), the Audio Engineering Society (AES), the National Sound & Communications Association (NSCA), and the academic organizations of the University Film and Video Association (UFVA) and the Broadcast Education Association (BEA), as well as other recording and audio-producing organizations. Students should be motivated to take part in an active and well-organized internship program that offers the qualified student the opportunity to spend time at a professional studio observing how the real world actually operates.

CONCLUSION

After surviving a semester of teaching audio production, an instructor should be able to take great pride in the growth and accomplishments of his or her students. In this course, an instructor will watch as young people who have had little or no contact with tools or equipment, who panic over the thought of having to push buttons, turn knobs, and physically move parts of electronic equipment, change dramatically. By the end of the semester, these same students will be doing all of the required operations not only easily, using both hands, but with confidence and eagerness to improve their skills and techniques.

The instructor also will see a change in attitude about audio and radio production—an appreciation by the students for those who have learned how to use the skills of audio production and an understanding of the complexity of utilizing media production equipment to create. Students also should leave this course eager and prepared to take the next step in learning the more complex and complicated processes involved in producing with video and/or film equipment, knowing that they already have acquired half of the skills and knowledge to do so.

NOTES

1. The "pot" is the potentiometer or fader.
2. To "dead-pot" is to fade out the sound all the way. To pot "up" or "down" is to fade sound up or down in volume.

Chapter 10

VIDEO PRODUCTION

Steve Craig

The teaching of a production course can be one of the most rewarding in the mass communication curriculum. Students are excited about the opportunity for hands-on work, and many whose performance in traditional lecture classes is only adequate will display exceptional talent and energy in a production class. At its best, the production course encourages creativity and self-expression, fosters teamwork, and builds self-confidence. Certainly every production course strives to teach students to communicate with their audiences. But in attaining this goal, the well-taught production course should accomplish broader goals as well. These may be divided into four related areas: (1) development of the aesthetic sense, (2) encouragement of critical thinking, (3) management of resources, and (4) mastery of equipment skills and techniques.

BACKGROUND

Unfortunately, few courses in the typical American high school or college student's academic career deal with nonverbal expression, and few students have developed visualization skills before their first production class. In short, most students suffer from visual illiteracy. Although the astronomical number of hours Americans spend watching movies and television or listening to radio and recordings has been well documented, few students have been exposed to works that express the electronic media's full aesthetic potential. For example, most first-year college students have never seen an art film or a work of experimental video. However, most have at least seen music videos, which, for all their shortcomings as an art form, do serve to demonstrate the potential of television to break from the traditional formulas of network and local production.

Production requires the expression of ideas visually and aurally rather than in writing (but, of course, written scripts are an important precursor). Visual and aural composition and the effective use of color and light, music and sound must be introduced. If the course involves single-camera production, students must be taught the basics of editing and shooting out of sequence. Both require the ability to visualize the finished product before production begins and as it is being shot.

Hand in hand with becoming visually literate is the development of critical thinking. Students must become good judges of their productions. Traditional forms and techniques should be questioned and evaluated rather than blindly emulated. The answer "Well, that's the way they do it on Channel 3!" should become an anathema.

Critical thinking also means that every production is carefully planned, with as little as possible left to happenstance. The production course is, therefore, an ideal place to teach the necessity of proper management of resources. Although smaller projects can be completed by individuals working alone, video is more commonly a team effort, requiring complex planning and careful management of time, equipment, and people. At first, students almost always grossly underestimate the time and effort required to complete even a simple production. One of the major goals of the course must be to emphasize the necessity for organization, leadership, timely completion of projects, and making do with the resources available.

Like music, painting, and drama, audio and video production are forms of creative expression that require mastery of some basic tools. An understanding of camera and recorder operation, editing, lighting, and sound is essential to the crafting of the message, whether it be a news show, a commercial, or a music video. On the other hand, learning equipment operation must not become the exclusive end of the course. Sometimes students (and even instructors) become so involved with hardware that the ultimate goal of communicating with an audience is forgotten.

Within the parameters of these goals, there are several successful approaches to the teaching of basic production. Some colleges and universities offer courses with a professional orientation, having as a major goal the training of students who hope to apply their skills in conjunction with a media career. These courses emphasize the mastery of existing standardized formats and procedures of the industry. Commercial production is promoted as a model, and students are rewarded for successfully emulating industry practices. Some professionally oriented schools offer even more specialized training in instructional or corporate media.

However, Eastman and Adams (1986) reported that of the nearly 150 Broadcast Education Association (BEA) member schools responding to a survey, less than one-fourth considered themselves professional programs, while over two-thirds said they were liberal arts programs.[1] Following the liberal arts philosophy, substantial numbers of instructors de-emphasize production as it is practiced in industry, instead stressing the creative and aesthetic aspects of production as a form of expression and encouraging innovation and exploration. Other instructors find a combination of the professional and liberal arts approaches to be successful; students are taught some basic industry techniques and formats, but are also encouraged to originate their own styles.

ORGANIZATION

In many schools, production instruction goes beyond a single introductory course to a series of courses, or even to a full-fledged production curriculum leading to a production degree. Clearly, the content of an introductory course such as that described in this chapter depends largely on its place within the curriculum, and many acceptable approaches and course modifications can be used.

Even with a diversity of approaches, a consensus of what constitutes the "typical" introductory production course does seem to exist, at least at the college level. Grant and Leebron surveyed introductory production course structure and practices at 147 BEA member schools.[2] From this research emerged a picture of a course offered at the sophomore or junior level, small in size (between ten and twenty students), concentrating heavily on hands-on experience (90 percent included a lab).

The study also found that an average of about 26 percent of course time was dedicated to preproduction planning, 65 percent to production itself, and the remainder to postproduction. There was also remarkable uniformity in book selection, with over 70 percent of the schools using one of the following texts.

TEXTS

T. Burrows and D. Wood, *Television Production: Disciplines and Techniques,* 4th ed. (Dubuque, IA: William C. Brown, 1988).

Herbert Zettl, *Television Production Handbook,* 4th ed. (Belmont, CA: Wadsworth, 1984). A new edition is forthcoming.

These two books cover much the same subjects and give a good idea of the areas covered in a typical course: cameras (including lenses), lighting, audio, videotape, video switching, on-camera talent and performance, directing (including control room techniques, staging, and blocking), set and graphic design, production planning (including budgeting), single-camera field production, and editing.

The Grant and Leebron study also reported that over 40 percent of the schools surveyed teach no field production in their introductory course, while 6 percent teach only field production. The remainder teach both studio and field production, but with about 75 percent of class time spent on studio topics. This weighting is doubtlessly influenced by a reluctance to give up the traditional approach to the course developed in the days when technology dictated that virtually all television production was multicamera and carried out inside a studio. Today, a more balanced approach is appropriate in the introductory course, especially if substantial numbers of the students do not go on to an advanced course in field production.

Many instructors schedule one or two classroom sessions each week to give lectures, demonstrations, and examinations on course topics, but plan for most of the class's time to be spent in the actual hands-on experience essential to the students' full understanding of the topics. A single, long lab session each week is generally preferable to two or three shorter labs since the time and effort to set up and take down equipment can be considerable. The longer lab also allows time for more complex productions and simplifies equipment and studio scheduling.

One ratio that seems to work well is to have two one-hour lecture sessions during the week with one three- or four-hour lab session. Lab sessions can be scheduled in the early morning or evening hours, when the studio is in less demand for other uses. For courses where enrollment warrants, multiple sections of labs can be offered with all students attending common lecture sessions. A lab size of twelve to fourteen students is ideal, with fifteen being the maximum recommended size for a single instructor. Larger labs are possible if they are divided into smaller groups working under the supervision of a competent teaching assistant. The major pitfall is having labs so big or poorly organized that students spend large amounts of time standing around watching, rather than doing.

Many instructors use some variation of the rotation method for at least some of their lab sessions. This method consists of rotating students through different production positions according to a preset schedule (see Table 10.1). The rotation schedule lists production positions down the left side and show numbers along the top. Each student is assigned a number to be used throughout the rotation, so that for show number 1, student 1 is the director, student 2 is the switcher, and so on. After each production, students rotate to the next position according to the schedule. For show number 2, student 2 becomes the director, student 3 the switcher, and so on. The rotation method can also be adapted to field production situations.

Table 10.1
Sample Lab Rotation

SHOW NR:	1	2	3	4	5	6	7	8	9	10	11	12	13	14	15
DIRECTOR	1	2	3	4	5	6	7	8	9	10	11	12	13	14	15
SWITCHER	2	3	4	5	6	7	8	9	10	11	12	13	14	15	1
TIMER	3	4	5	6	7	8	9	10	11	12	13	14	15	1	2
CHAR GEN	4	5	6	7	8	9	10	11	12	13	14	15	1	2	3
AUDIO	5	6	7	8	9	10	11	12	13	14	15	1	2	3	4
ASST AUDIO	6	7	8	9	10	11	12	13	14	15	1	2	3	4	5
FLOOR MGR	7	8	9	10	11	12	13	14	15	1	2	3	4	5	6
CAM 1	8	9	10	11	12	13	14	15	1	2	3	4	5	6	7
CAM 2	9	10	11	12	13	14	15	1	2	3	4	5	6	7	8
CAM 3	10	11	12	13	14	15	1	2	3	4	5	6	7	8	9
ANNCR	11	12	13	14	15	1	2	3	4	5	6	7	8	9	10
HOST/ESS	12	13	14	15	1	2	3	4	5	6	7	8	9	10	11
GUEST 2	13	14	15	1	2	3	4	5	6	7	8	9	10	11	12
GUEST 3	14	15	1	2	3	4	5	6	7	8	9	10	11	12	13
OBSERVER	15	1	2	3	4	5	6	7	8	9	10	11	12	13	14

The rotation positions will vary with the type of production, number of students, and equipment available, but should be arranged so that each student has a task assigned for each production, even if some of the positions would not generally be found in an actual production situation. Students usually take their assigned tasks seriously and learn to watch what is also going on in the next position to which they will rotate. Upon changing positions, they frequently volunteer to offer assistance and advice to the person rotating into their old position.

Lab productions should be simple at first, increasing in complexity as the term progresses. It is useful for the instructor or some other skilled person to work the director's position at first, allowing close control over the exercise and quick correction of mistakes. Few beginning students have ever observed a television director at work, and they need to emulate a good model of assertiveness, leadership, and directorial style. For the first few studio lab sessions, the use of very short productions repeated over and over while students rotate positions makes the lab fast-paced, adds excitement, and gives students the opportunity to try several different jobs in a relatively brief time. Five-minute mini-shows, patterned after formats the students will encounter in local stations, are ideal. If five-minute shows are used and five minutes or so is allowed after each rotation for students to familiarize themselves with their new responsibilities, a ten-minute rotation pattern is established. A class of fifteen students can then rotate through all production positions in a single lab period.

This method can be modified by pairing students and having them work each position as a team. In this case, each production is repeated twice, so that both partners have the opportunity to do all essential tasks. The partnership strategy has the advantage of encouraging peer tutoring, and the instructor can even discreetly pair stronger students with weaker ones. Another modification is for students to repeat every position before rotating, so that each has the opportunity to perform in one "rehearsal" and one "production." This allows students to correct the inevitable first-time-through mistakes and gives them a heightened sense of satisfaction at their improvement.

The news show and the interview show are especially effective studio exercises. Not only are they fairly simple to produce, but they also represent the two most common studio production situations students will encounter at the local station. Formats such as those in Tables 10.2 and 10.3 can be used. The addition of timing columns gives students a feel for the concept of program backtiming, aids in giving time cues to the floor, and emphasizes the necessity for precise

Table 10.2
Five-Minute News Show Format

Elapsed Time	Remaining Time	Event Time	Video	Audio
0:00	5:00	0:15	MCU of Anchor	ANCHOR: (Teases)
0:15	4:45	0:15	WS Set	MUSIC: In, EST, and Under for . . . ANNCR: This is the Evening News, a report of the day's events from around the world and here at home. Now, here is (anchor name).
0:30	4:30	1:30	MCU Anchor	ANCHOR: Reads for 1:30, then cues commercial.
2:00	3:00	0:30	Commercial	Commercial
2:30	2:30	0:05	MCU Anchor	ANCHOR: Intros sports
2:35	2:25	0:55	MCU Sports	SPORTS: Reads for :55, then swings back to anchor.
3:30	1:30	1:00	MCU Anchor	ANCHOR: Reads for 1:00, then wraps.
4:30	0:30	0:30	WS Set, Key Credits	MUSIC: Sneak in during wrap, then up full to end.
5:00	0:00		Fade to Black	MUSIC: Out.

timing required in studio productions. The news show tends to be simpler for beginning students since camera shots and timing are tightly formatted. After a few rotations, the news show virtually directs itself. The interview show allows the director more choice of shots and introduces the concept of calling shots in response to the unrehearsed action on the set. All productions in the rotation should be slated and videotaped. The audio from the intercom line can be recorded onto one channel of the videotape and program audio onto the other. This allows later review not only of the show itself, but also of the director's commands.

Table 10.3
Five-Minute Interview Show Format

Elapsed Time	Remaining Time	Event Time	Video	Audio
0:00	5:00	0:30	WS of Set	MUSIC: In, EST, and Under for . . .
			Key Title	ANNCR: This is "Insight," an interview program probing the burning issues of today. . .
			2S Guests	Our guests today are (reads guest 1 & 2 names and titles).
			MCU Host	Now here is your "Insight" host (host name).
				MUSIC: Out.
0:30	4:30	1:30	MCU Host alternates with MCU Guests.	HOST: Asks questions for 1:30, then cues commercial.
2:00	3:00	0:30	Commercial	Commercial
2:30	2:30	2:00	MCU Host alternates with MCU Guests.	HOST: Asks questions for 2:00, wraps on cue.
4:30	0:30	0:30	WS Set	MUSIC: Sneak in under wrap, then up full.
			Key Credits	
5:00	0:00		Black	

Watching and critiquing all the lab productions during class is a time-consuming exercise that quickly becomes repetitious, so the instructor may wish to select only a representative few shows to review. However, students will want to see the productions in which they were talent since, for most, this is their first time on-camera. One solution is to assign each student the out-of-class task of reviewing his or her performance as talent, switcher, and director and writing a short self-critique. (Visual slating before each show allows students to easily locate the appropriate productions.) This assignment is made easier at schools that have video viewing areas at the library or at other locations on campus.

Both the news and interview formats can be modified as time, skills, and facilities dictate. The thirty-second commercial in the middle of the shows can be rolled in from an external film or tape machine—a reel of old PSA's can be assembled for this purpose—or if such support is not available, thirty seconds of black can be used. Wire service news and sports copy can be obtained for the news show. The interviews can be based on ad-libbed questions on a topic agreed upon by host and guests, or prepared ahead in response to an out-of-class assignment. Other embellishments such as sets, visuals, and props can also be added, but avoid getting too complex too soon. Beginning students are often overwhelmed with the equipment and complexity of even the simplest studio production. The repetition of a simple production early in the course gives them the confidence needed for more complex shows later.

A major drawback of using these easily produced preset formats is that they de-emphasize the need for careful preproduction planning. Beginning mini-productions are necessarily structured so that little preparation time is necessary, but later productions should emphasize the need for planning and teamwork before the actual production begins. One frequently used way to do this is to assign group projects.

Group productions have the advantage of involving more students in the preproduction process, but suffer the seemingly unavoidable flaws of group projects in all academic areas—the benefits and workload are uneven for the members of the group. Invariably, one or two students enjoy key positions of responsibility while the remainder are relegated to more mundane tasks. In a real-world situation, the production team has a clear hierarchy of authority, based on the ability of those in charge to hire and fire. In group projects, however, students are equals, with the willingness of group members to accomplish their assigned tasks based on voluntary cooperation. Because of this, the group project does not function as an accurate representation of a real-world production experience. Understandably, the students given less interesting assignments learn less and are often unwilling to put forth the amount of effort demanded by peers who are more ego-involved. If a substantial amount of course time is dedicated to such group projects, the learning experiences of some students will invariably suffer.

Instructors should be especially alert for sex-role bias in student groups. Left to their own devices, student production teams will almost invariably elect to have all male directors and all female production assistants. Men are frequently expected to climb ladders and carry and lift equipment, while the women are relegated to carrying papers and clipboards. Instructors should discourage such sex-based divisions of labor, and the class should be informed from the beginning of the course (perhaps in the syllabus) that positions and duties are to be shared equally among all students.

Despite their potential problems, closely monitored group projects can be successful and productive, especially if the instructor is careful to rotate positions of responsibility. At least one textbook (Burrows & Wood, 1986) contains ideas, scripts, and visuals for group lab productions.

An alternative that solves some of the problems of the group project is to combine individual projects with group rotation. One such assignment is the production of a thirty-second commercial, which has the advantage of being preproduction intensive but, because of its short length, requires relatively little actual studio time. In this way, sufficient lab time can be made available for each student to produce a project. Each student is assigned a different sponsor's product or service, for which he or she must produce a single thirty-second spot. Students must write the script (or scripts can be obtained from a writing course), plan the production, recruit talent, and obtain music, props, and visuals. The instructor schedules a certain amount of studio time during lab and makes a student crew available for the production. (Crew positions should be rotated for each commercial.) Enough studio time should be set aside to allow for set-up, rehearsals, and two or three takes. Studio time allocations must be the same for all students and scrupulously adhered to.

A variation is to split a large lab into two or more production crews, with one crew working in the studio producing a commercial while the others meet with a producer in a preproduction meeting or rehearsal. Another strategy is to pair each producer with a director from the beginning. The director is then expected to participate in the preproduction planning from an early stage. In this way, every student serves as producer on one project and director on another.

Students frequently become quite ego-involved with their commercials and must learn to confront the problems associated with translating one's personal vision into a product produced by a group. The instructor must be sensitive in overseeing and grading such projects, since emotions often run high.

With individual and group projects, good preproduction planning must be stressed. It should be made clear to the student producers that, like professionals, one of their most important tasks is to produce the project within the limitations of time, talent, and equipment available to them. Beginners almost always grossly underestimate the amount of time and planning required for their projects, and frequently want to bite off more than they can chew. The instructor must provide gentle but firm oversight so that an inordinate and unfair amount of production time is not spent on one project simply because of poor planning.

The Grant and Leebron study (1988) revealed that about 60 percent of the schools surveyed taught some field production in their introductory course. However, methods used in field production are fundamentally different from those used in the studio. While most studio productions are shot in sequence and edited "live," single-camera field productions are shot out of sequence and edited during a postproduction session. The production course must address not only these differences in technique and equipment, but also the need for a fundamental difference in conceptualizing and planning the production.

For those courses that do include some field production lab work, some of the projects and strategies discussed in the studio lab section can be modified and used in the field. Rotation and mini-productions can be used for team assignments but, by its nature, field production generally requires a smaller crew than studio work. Without careful planning, group labs in the field can easily result in 25 percent of the class doing something while the other 75 percent are watching. While this may be appropriate in the lecture or demonstration, it should not be the rule during hands-on lab time.

Depending on the amount of equipment available and its replacement cost, the instructor may or may not be in the position to check out production equipment to individuals or small groups. This strategy has been employed in film production courses for years and is not without certain pitfalls: equipment being lost, damaged, stolen, abused, or simply not returned on time. On the other hand, extending equipment access to periods outside lab time allows the assignment of more complex and time-consuming projects, giving each student more time with the equipment. Access to editing equipment is somewhat simpler. Editing suites can be installed in a fixed location, with students given access to them on a regular schedule. Ideally, the site will be accessible after hours and on weekends, but still secure enough so equipment is safe from theft and vandalism.

Assuming equipment is available, a typical field production assignment is made like this: Cameras and recorders are checked out to groups of three or four students, with a fairly specific shooting assignment. Once shooting is completed, each member of the group independently edits the raw footage. This not only requires each student to learn editing techniques but also makes the point that there may well be several acceptable ways to edit the same raw footage. Additionally, students who have edited the footage themselves become more interested in how others have accomplished the task. If equipment cannot be checked out, raw footage can be shot as a team effort during lab sessions, or perhaps with the supervision of a trusted student assistant. Another alternative is to divide the class into groups with one (or more) working in the studio and one (or more) working on field projects nearby. If the groups are kept in proximity, the lab instructor can move from one to the other to supervise and answer questions. (An inexpensive walkie-talkie system can even be used to keep tabs on groups.)

Field production assignments can range from a simple "Get Acquainted with the Equipment" tape, which would include a series of specific shot variations (e.g., LS, MS, CU, pan, tilt, outdoor, indoor, a simple sequence, etc.), to more complex stories or interviews. Here are some fairly basic field assignments that seem to work well:

The Silent Movie. In this exercise, a small group is assigned the task of producing a three- or four-minute "silent movie." The movie should follow the model of an early silent film—tell a simple story and have at least one chase scene.

The Music Video. In this assignment, the group must create a music video, similar to that most have seen on MTV. A piece of music is selected, and video must be shot and edited to it.

The News Feature. After watching some typical television news feature stories in class, student groups are assigned to produce their own. An emphasis in this project is sound. The feature should include some interview footage with live sound, some voice-over, and mixing of narration and wild track.

Regardless of the topics covered and the assignments made, every production course is complicated by the need for a minimum of good, well-maintained equipment. The Grant and Leebron survey (1988) reported that 94 percent of the schools responding had at least one television studio use for their course, and over half used editing equipment. The minimum recommended equipment requirements for a course intending to teach a studio laboratory are as follows:

- A basic TV studio with a lighting grid and enough instruments to properly light a basic set. A riser and some basic furniture pieces should be available for simple sets.
- Two (preferably three) professional studio cameras mounted on mobile tripods or pedestals.

- A separate control room with a video switcher, monitors, audio board, and character generator.
- A video tape recorder. (This could be something as simple as a consumer model VCR in the control room.)
- Miscellaneous other items such as studio monitors, microphones, intercommunication headsets, audio and video tape, prerecorded music, etc.

With a well-maintained complement of the above items, a good, basic studio course can be offered. If other equipment is available, it can be integrated into the course. Especially helpful is the addition of a telecine and/or source video tape machines, allowing for the integration of outside video materials into the productions. Equipment need not be state-of-the-art or even broadcast quality. In fact, beginners are less intimidated by basic audio boards, video switchers, and character generators which are simple to operate and easily mastered. If more complex equipment is all that is available, the instructor should not ask students to master all its capabilities in the introductory course.

Some schools have had success using relatively inexpensive half-inch consumer model camcorders for the introductory level course. These cameras are lightweight and generally easy to operate. Along with a couple of editing suites, a few of these units can supply all the equipment needed to teach the basics of field production. Although the professionally oriented purist may find the use of less-than-broadcast-quality equipment to be objectionable, the fact remains that few departments have sufficient funding to purchase enough broadcast-quality equipment to allow it to be checked out and used without supervision.

Every beginning production course should at least introduce the concept of postproduction editing. Good quality half-inch editing equipment is now available with automatic editing controllers that work on the same principles as those used with the more professional tape formats, and the purchase price can be a fraction of that for three-quarter-inch equipment. If three-quarter-inch editing is already available, raw footage from half-inch camcorders can be dubbed up for editing with acceptable results. Conversely, half-inch editing equipment can be used to edit dubbed-down field footage from three-quarter-inch recorders. A cuts-only system is adequate for teaching editing, especially at the introductory level, but the addition of a low-end character generator, an audio cassette player, and a microphone for voice-overs enhances the production potential of the editing suite considerably.

Administrators should be reminded that equipment costs are not one-time-only costs. Annual budgets should reflect the need for routine maintenance, tools, parts, repair, and replacement. Instructors should not be expected to take on the extra duties of a technician simply because they teach a production course. Trained technicians should be available (perhaps on a part-time, contract basis) to carry out routine maintenance and make minor repairs. Instructors should work out a maintenance schedule with the technical staff to ensure that all equipment is serviced regularly and is available and in top condition when needed. School holiday periods should be used to conduct routine cleaning and preventive maintenance. Wherever possible, sufficient back-up should be available in case of midterm equipment failure. This is especially easy to do with vital but relatively inexpensive items such as headsets, microphones, cables, batteries, and tripods.

For the new production instructor, a good source of additional information about teaching is available from the Broadcast Education Association (BEA), especially members of its production committee. This committee, comprised mostly of college production teachers, carries out projects dedicated to improving production instruction, and committee members are generally receptive to mail or telephone requests for advice from new teachers. Articles on production teaching and curriculum are frequently published in *Feedback*, one of the BEA's quarterly journals. Several production-oriented sessions are presented each year at the annual BEA convention, which is held concurrently with the National Association of Broadcasters (NAB) convention. (The NAB convention also represents the nation's largest annual display of radio and television equipment and new technologies.) Information about the BEA (including the name of the current production committee chair) can be obtained by contacting BEA, at 1771 N Street NW, Washington, DC 20036 [(202) 429–5355].

CONCLUSION

The advent of relatively low cost consumer television equipment has now made video production available to the casual user as well as the professional. The novelty of the new technology has attracted more and more nonprofessionals, and now video seems to be supplanting film as the preferred format for the hobbyist. Several amateur video production magazines can be found on the newsstand, and there is an increasing demand for instruction at the amateur level.

Some secondary schools have begun to use low cost production equipment to teach art, drama, and journalism. While this level of production teaching is still in its infancy, it promises to continue growing. At least one book (Utz, 1987)[3] is geared toward such courses, and many of the projects and strategies described above can be adapted for secondary school use.

NOTES

1. Susan Eastman and B. Adams, "A Radio-TV Program Profile," *Feedback* 27 (5) (Summer 1986): 11.

2. A. Grant and Elizabeth Leebron, "Introductory Video Production Courses: A Field Survey," *Feedback* 29 (4) (Fall 1988): 27–34.

3. Peter Utz, *The Video Users Handbook: Completely Revised and Expanded* (Englewood Cliffs, NJ: Prentice-Hall, 1987).

Chapter 11

TEACHING RESEARCH METHODS TO UNDERGRADUATES

Kim A. Smith

No other mass communication course raises more apprehension in undergraduate students than the basic research methods course. Many students pursuing mass communication degrees have an aversion to any course involving, as they put it, "numbers." Despite this challenge, the research methods course can, if properly designed, prove to be a rewarding experience for both students and the instructor.

BACKGROUND

As Wilbur Schramm has noted, as the scholarly study of the mass communication process began to grow in the late 1950s, departments of journalism, broadcasting, and speech began to add courses emphasizing theory and methodology to their predominantly skills-oriented curricula.[1] At first, research methods courses were taught primarily at the graduate level. Today, however, the ability to understand and interpret research results is necessary to succeed in a variety of mass communication fields. As a result, an increasing number of departments and schools are requiring undergraduate students to take a research methods course.

Yet, many students need to be convinced of the importance of understanding research methods. As we all know, students don't always readily accept their professors' wisdom about "what's good for them." Early in the course, then, it is useful to face the issue head-on by holding a discussion about the importance of research in today's society. To get the discussion going, try raising these issues:

Should newspaper content be determined from marketing surveys?

Is ratings research the best way to determine the television programming tastes of the American public?

Should the networks broadcast election results based on exit interviews before the polls close?

Does empirical research dehumanize people?

You might also augment the discussion by assigning the students to clip or videotape stories containing research results from media over a one- or two-day period. They usually are impressed by the amount of news coverage that is generated by research results. Guest speakers from mass communication fields who can testify to their use of research can also be effective in convincing skeptical students of the importance of understanding research methods.

ORGANIZATION

Given their enthusiasm for the topic, rookie instructors frequently attempt to cover too much in the research methods course. However, you should take into account the limited preparation most mass communication students are likely to have for the subject matter. Unless the course has restrictive prerequisites, students are likely to have little or no knowledge of even the most basic concepts taught in the course. Thus it is important to focus the course on the most fundamental aspects of the research process.

As with any course, setting reasonable goals is the first step in focusing the research methods course. There are two major limitations. First, it is impossible to produce competent researchers in one semester. Second, the future careers of most students will require them to be competent consumers rather than producers of research. Accordingly, two reasonable goals for the research methods course are (1) to provide a base of knowledge that will allow interested students to take more advanced-level courses; and (2) to develop the ability to detect good and bad research.

The research methods course is easier to teach if students have had some preparation in statistics or research methodology. At the undergraduate level, however, such requirements would, in most cases, greatly limit the number of students taking the course, especially if it is an elective. More realistically, the course usually will need to be designed for students with little or no background in research methodology. A well-taught course will, however, encourage interested students to take advanced-level methodology and statistics courses.

With goals set, the instructor can then begin to decide on the specific topics to be included in the course. At a minimum, each of the basic steps in the research process should receive attention, including (1) theory development and hypothesis construction; (2) measurement of variables; (3) sampling procedures; (4) data-gathering methods; (5) analysis of data; and (6) presentation of results. Additionally, units on ethics, secondary analysis of archival data, and the politics of research are also included in many research methods course. A separate course could be taught on each of these topics. Although your decision on what material to cover will be influenced by individual circumstances, here are a few thoughts.

The preeminent importance of theory and hypothesis construction should be emphasized. Early sessions of the course should be devoted to an extensive discussion of how theory and hypotheses are constructed and tested by the use of research methods, using mass communication examples.[2] Thereafter, the instructor should continue to emphasize the link between theory and methods in each unit in the course. At the end of the course, students should have a clear understanding that research methods are merely "tools" in theory building. It is also useful to discuss the nature of causation in this section.

The research process first involves the specification of abstract concepts (conceptual definitions of variables), and then the creation of specific operations by which observations can be classified (operational definitions of variables). As such, these conceptual and operational definitions are the basic links between theory and methodology, a basic point which should be stressed throughout this section. Time should also be devoted to introducing the concepts of reliability and validity as measures of the quality of conceptualization and operationalization of variables. Heavy use of examples is necessary to make reliability and validity understandable. As with theory and hypothesis construction, these basic concepts should be discussed throughout the course.

Both probability and nonprobability sampling procedures should be discussed in this unit. Most textbooks contain a number of exercises to illustrate various sampling procedures. Emphasis should be placed on the implications of deviating from simple random sampling procedures, as is frequently the case in the "real world" of research. Students should be given exercises in the calculation and interpretation of sampling errors and confidence intervals. Mastering the sampling unit builds student confidence as they face the dreaded statistics unit.

Until recently, many research methods courses covered only quantitative methods—surveys, experiments, and content analyses—to the exclusion of qualitative methods—textual analyses, participant observation, historical, and legal. As a result, the impression left with students—sometimes purposely by the instructor—was that quantitative methods were, in general, superior to qualitative ones.[3] A less methodologically chauvinistic approach is to expose students to both types of methods, while emphasizing the tradeoffs between reliability and validity inherent in each. As noted below, recently published texts contain sections on both quantitative and qualitative methods. Students should gain a basic understanding of the factors that influence the selection of an appropriate data-gathering method. Discussion of the advantages of combining methods is useful.

Because the statistics section of the course causes considerable apprehension and grumbling among the students, the instructor may be inclined to trim it. However, even students with the poorest math backgrounds can learn to calculate and interpret measures of central tendency, correlations, and basic inferential statistics. More complex techniques, such as multiple regression, usually are beyond the grasp of the student in the basic research methods course.

The key to teaching this section is to start at the most basic level, usually how to calculate measures of central tendency, and then slowly and carefully work up to more sophisticated statistics. Using the same data set to calculate the statistics discussed in the lectures provides continuity in this section. Although many experienced research methods instructors disagree with this point, students should be given exercises requiring them to calculate statistics through the level of bivariate correlations.

Time constraints usually prevent students from doing extensive writing projects in a basic research methods course. Nonetheless, students can be lectured on the basic principles of writing research results. An important emphasis in this section should be on interpreting results. Students can be given tables containing various types of statistical analyses from published studies and asked to interpret the findings. They can then compare their interpretations with those of the actual author. For a rousing discussion, ask the students' opinions about the quality of journal articles they have been asked to read in other classes.

A variety of suggestions were given above for hands-on exercises to supplement lectures. Veteran research methods instructors would probably agree that it is difficult, if not impossible, to cover even the basic material adequately through lectures alone. Thus, a one- or two-hour laboratory period per week in the methods course is strongly suggested. The instructor manuals for most methods texts contain a program of exercises that can be used in these laboratory sessions.

You might also give consideration to using the laboratory sessions to design and execute a class research project. The development of this project can be cued to parallel the progression of the lectures through the research process. If a class research project is undertaken, the instructor should guide the students to a project that interests them and can be completed without undue stress by the end of the course. Projects requiring extensive in-person or telephone interviews are difficult to supervise and complete. Experiments and content analysis projects tend to be more manageable. (A warning: if you desire poor course evaluations, have your students gather data for your personal research project.)

Time and money constraints used to make it impractical to have students actually do data analysis exercises on the mainframe computers. If your students have access to a microcomputer laboratory, however, it is now possible for them to get experience in data analysis inexpensively and with much less hassle—for them and for you. For a reasonable price, students can purchase the SPSS/PC+ Studentware data analysis program, which includes a scaled-down version of the SPSS analysis programs, as well as a guide to installing and using the various programs.[4] A variety of other software programs of statistical and data analysis exercises are also available.[5]

Students much prefer analyzing data sets that include mass communication variables. At the beginning of the course, they can be provided with data sets from a content analysis, an experiment, and a survey. If you don't have a certain type of data set from your own research, your colleagues will likely have one they have "wrung dry" and will let your students use. Smaller data sets, no greater than 100 observations, work best for student exercises on a microcomputer. These can be created by drawing a smaller subset from a larger survey conducted by the instructor. Laboratory exercises using these data sets can then be assigned, illustrating concepts discussed in class. Lecture examples can also be drawn from them.

TEXTS

Students tend to evaluate poorly even the better written research methods texts. Student dissatisfaction with methods texts often can be traced to their impatience with not being able to grasp the material easily by skimming through the chapters a couple of times. Students need to be cautioned that reading and understanding a research methods text takes effort.

Despite student opinion, there are currently a number of excellent research methods texts available. They all cover the basic research methods topics, but each also has unique aspects that might make it especially suitable for your particular approach to the course. Some texts worth considering:

Neil M. Agnew and Sandra W. Pyke, *The Science Game: An Introduction to Research in the Behavioral Sciences* (Englewood Cliffs, NJ: Prentice-Hall, 1982). A well-written introduction to behavioral research, although not specifically oriented for a mass communication course. Useful if accompanied by a supplementary reader (see below) on mass communication research methods.

Earl Babbie, *The Practice of Social Research*, 6th ed. (Belmont, CA: Wadsworth, 1992). Widely used text is not specifically intended for mass communication research methods courses, but readable and even entertaining. Instructor's handbook and computerized exercises are helpful.

Philip Meyer, *Precision Journalism* (Bloomington, IN: Indiana University Press, 1973). Used as a supplementary source, Meyer's essays, now dated, on social science methods for the working press are still among the clearest explanations available.

Nancy Weatherly Sharp, ed., *Communication Research, The Challenge of the Information Age* (Syracuse, NY: Syracuse University Press, 1988). This text contains a series of essays written by well-known mass communication researchers on the role of research in mass communication. These sometimes provocative essays can help stimulate class discussion on various research issues.

Mary John Smith, *Contemporary Communication Research Methods* (Belmont, CA: Wadsworth, 1988). Covers the standard topics on empirical research methods, but also includes interesting chapters on the analysis of interactive and narrative discourse. Well suited for students who have a speech communication orientation.

Guido H. Stempel and Bruce H. Westley, eds., *Research Methods in Mass Communication* (Englewood Cliffs, NJ: Prentice-Hall, Inc., 1981). Contains a series of articles by prominent mass communication researchers on various aspects of the research process. They will challenge the students.

Roger D. Wimmer and Joseph R. Dominick, *Mass Media Research: An Introduction*, 3rd ed. (Belmont, CA: Wadsworth, 1991). A strength of this text is that it emphasizes the relationship between theory and methodology. Both quantitative and qualitative methods are discussed.

CONCLUSION

Given the nature of the course, students should be tested at frequent intervals to ensure they are understanding the material. Students can be tested on each unit or given two major tests along with frequent quizzes. A test format of multiple choice and short-answer essay questions fits well with the course subject matter. In addition to the examinations, all exercises assigned in class or the lab should be graded to ensure that the students put sufficient effort into them. If a class project is assigned, having students grade each other's work on the project will ensure full participation.

Overall, the research methods course is difficult and time consuming to teach. Because students tend to be anxious and even hostile toward the subject matter, you will be especially challenged to teach well. However, if you can convey your sense of excitement about the research process, you will succeed.

NOTES

1. Wilbur Schramm, "The Unique Perspective of Communication: A Retrospective View," *Journal of Communication* 33 (Summer 1983).

2. It is useful at this point in the course to trace the history of a particular theory in mass communication research, such as agenda-setting or cultivation analysis.

3. Methodological chauvinism can result in serious consequences. Stories abound in the mass communication field of researchers who have been disparaged and even shunned by their colleagues because of their methodological orientation. Intelligent researchers respect the rich variety of methods used to study the mass communication process.

4. For information about Studentware, SPSS/PC+, contact the Marketing Department, SPSS, Inc., 444 North Michigan Avenue, Chicago, IL 60614.

5. For example, Professor Jerry Nelson at Iowa State University has developed some interesting software programs of exercises on measurement and statistics. For more information on them, he can be contacted in the Department of Journalism and Mass Communication, Iowa State University, Ames, IA 50010.

Part III

ADVANCED COURSEWORK

In chapter 12, Roy Moore discusses the position of media law courses in the curriculum and presents a historical overview of the development and the importance assigned to this course by both practitioner and students. Widely regarded as one of the more demanding courses in the curriculum, this is one that requires constant vigilance on the part of the instructor and a greater degree of specialization. Moore surveys all of the professional subgroups in the area and gauges their interest in and support for the study of media law. The author is particularly enthusiastic about the importance of legal study by students in fields such as advertising and public relations, and he advises instructors to consider the needs of these students in course design.

As testimony to its changing nature, Moore points out that the first text in the field, published twenty years ago, is already in its sixth edition and now has a host of competitors. He also cautions of the complexities of the area and the need for instructors to pursue wide-ranging sources to support their study, especially in those cases in which no legal coursework has been completed. He also suggests that in organizing this course, a thorough evaluation of student needs must be completed. Consideration should be given to the types of coursework students have had prior to enrolling in the media law course. A complex discussion of libel may be much less complicated to a student who has been introduced to the topic in an earlier course such as news writing.

Moore also insists that the instructor decide on realistic parameters for study—a topical outline to account for how much information can be reasonably covered in one course. His very detailed outline can be amended to take institutional differences into consideration, as in cases in which a broadcast or advertising regulation class exists as part of the curriculum. The author discusses the use of the Socratic method and advises against a straight lecture format because of the nature of the course. He advocates a very detailed course outline and offers a listing of eight texts, supplementary sources, and advice on evaluation procedures.

Using a systems analysis approach, John De Mott considers management coursework in chapter 13 of this section, beginning with the placement of the course in the broader context of curriculum. De Mott offers a very specific statement of purpose for the course and four course objectives before turning attention to a series of questions that need to be answered regarding students' status in school and resources available within the academic unit in which studying takes place. These are very pointed, serious issues that institutions must address in progressing with a course beneficial to media management students.

Once fundamental topics are addressed, assuming they are adequately answered, a list of concepts used in systems analysis is treated as another preliminary step in implementing the process advocated on a session-to-session basis. This is done to draw out students' special interests in order to make comparisons that might best illustrate principles of management. Each of six management functions constitutes a unit in the course of study presented by De Mott, and included as well is a list of assigned readings, seminar discussions, presentation of findings on local mass communication organizations, and a special project with instructions on how to complete examples. The instructor is encouraged to involve resource persons representing a wide variety of management areas, with managers from advertising, public relations, broadcast, and print invited to serve on panels set up in conjunction with the course.

As far as texts are concerned, De Mott uses *Managing Media Organizations* by John Lavine and Daniel Wackman, but advises against letting the text dictate course content or scheduling, advocating a systems flow and analysis approach. A formula is presented for grading purposes, and a recommendation is made to utilize the Media Management and Economic Resource Center at Northwestern University, as well as trade publications of various subfields. A wide variety of general interest publications offered by De Mott concludes this section.

In addition to her overview of teaching the media history course, Maurine Beasley provides a review of the reasons why media history should be of special concern as an important but sometimes undervalued part of the curriculum. In chapter 14 she discusses the steps taken over the past decade to offset a strange stepsister status which developed on some campuses for the media history course and offers the reader a cogent argument for recent revitalization, concluding this section of her chapter with a review of two surveys containing information on the current status of courses being offered today. She gives a persuasive argument as to why this course needs to be taught by a trained historian—a history enthusiast and one with a diverse outlook and sensitivity, pointing out that areas such as advertising, public relations, and broadcasting have sometimes been given short shrift in a traditional journalism school context.

Similarly, Professor Beasley argues that the role women and minorities have played in the development of the American mass media has been largely overlooked. The author's objective—to give students an acquaintance with the origins of contemporary practice in the field while introducing major figures—is offered with the acknowledgement that past oversights be taken into account. Her detailed course outline follows the progression of media development in the United States and leads to a broader discussion of the media history course as a requirement in the curriculum. Beyond this, she offers the reader a listing of specialized media history courses currently being taught on college campuses and a review of some prominent texts in the field. Finally, she reviews some strategies and special assignments for the course as well as some sources of additional information.

Dan Nimmo begins chapter 15 by pointing out that the study of mass media and politics within the context of political communication is a relatively recent phenomenon owing to the development of a wide variety of coursework addressing both skills and theory type orientations. For this reason, mass media and politics coursework, as outlined by Nimmo, must concentrate on specialized areas of study and avoid confusing goals and objectives, for example, with survey courses in areas such as political campaigning with a skills orientation.

Nimmo offers what he feels is a minimum set of topics for the course, with an essay on each section and an outline of suggested topics. The opening section is the place where broad definitions of concepts of power, politics, and media are offered, using exercises in which each area is related to everyday life. He goes on to offer the reader a vast selection of recommendations on topics central to this course as well as collateral readings from sources such as Walter Lippmann and Murray Edelman. Classroom exercises, including student preparation and presentation of brief "political media autobiographies," are introduced to spark discussion and expand the application to student interests and knowledge. He also offers discussion and lecture ideas on the role of the mass media in electoral politics, primary coverage, debates, consultants, political advertising, and election night coverage.

In the summary section, he looks at the variety of effects research in media and politics and discusses how these might be addressed in the course. This is a prelude to offering the reader a review of controversies in the field. This last section deals with philosophical differences of opinion with regard to the nature and variety of research in the field, interpretation of data, and the role of the government in ethical and economic contexts. His assessment of five texts for possible adoption begins with Doris Graber's topical approach and ends with one of the author's own works (with James Combs) designed as a supplementary reader. All in all, this chapter provides a very thorough and balanced orientation to the course.

The emphasis on media criticism in chapter 16 may be a bit deceiving in that the focus of the chapter is almost exclusively on the television and film area. In what is perhaps the least developed academic area of mass communication, Michael Russo offers the instructor a highly specialized look at a course in its developing stages—one which uses a California base-and-field experience to enhance appreciation of film and television in a critical context. Russo, a veteran producer of CBS Television, relies on his many contacts to bring students face-to-face with the Hollywood film industry from the inside. In doing so, he exposes the many myths associated with the "dream factory" with opportunities for students to reflect on their experiences and interact with those in the field.

Russo demands that students view films as artistic forms and presents a very detailed reading list in conjunction with film screenings, the viewing of television productions, and talks by both directors and professional critics. Class sessions often include a lecture related to readings for the day and class discussion revolving around the previous day's screening. Students are also expected to survey what other critics have said about the work under study. In attempting to match student interests with available film and video, the author acknowledges a number of pitfalls concerning scheduling and acquisition. In this regard, he relies heavily on his college media resource center, since class presentations based on critical essays prepared by members of the class are supplemented by video examples.

Inevitably, as Russo points out, students use the experiences and exposure of the class to help weigh personal ambitions and decide whether they are suited for the field—an unintended by-product of the approach. Beyond this consideration, Russo emphasizes the importance of the planning process for anyone ambitious enough to invade Hollywood as part of a course in media criticism. Although specialized and unique, his case study with topics such as scriptwriting, the social responsibility of the mass media, and the legal and business side of Hollywood, demands a great deal of planning and a willingness on the part of the instructor to heavily research available facilities—both production houses and specialized academic institutions such as University of Southern California, University of California–Los Angeles, and the American Film Institute. For the instructor with that kind of commitment, this approach is worthwhile. For others, the resources and approach outlined here are exemplary.

In the final chapter of this book, Jay Black suggests that a course in media ethics should consist of material on the thinking of ethics and should not moralize or give advice. Black describes five instructional goals recommended by the Hastings Center that he says are appropriate for any ethics course. These include recognizing moral issues, developing analytical skills, tolerating disagreement and ambiguity, stimulating moral imagination, and eliciting a moral obligation. One interesting technique he offers for stimulating moral imagination is the use of specific movies and novels like *Citizen Kane*, *Broadcast News*, and *All the President's Men* for critical viewing and discussion.

Black next offers different approaches to the instruction of values. These approaches range from the growth orientation of Carl Jung and Carl Rogers to the classical approaches of Plato. And finally, he describes fifteen major topic areas or units that can be used to organize the ethics course. These units include concepts to be discussed, topics, and how to involve students. Black offers a list of contemporary ethics texts along with an evaluation of these texts.

Chapter 12

MASS COMMUNICATION LAW

Roy L. Moore

The initial reaction of journalism and mass communication instructors when they are assigned to teach the basic media law course is usually a mixture of excitement and trepidation. The excitement can be traced to the fact that, while this course keeps both teacher and students on their toes, the material can be quite stimulating. The trepidation stems from the realization that, like many mass communication instructors, he or she may have, at best, an extremely limited knowledge of communication law.

Almost without exception, students dread this course and inevitably postpone enrollment until their last semester because probably no other course in the mass communication curriculum is as demanding and time-consuming. Once the course has begun, however, the students and the professor typically find the material both thought-provoking and sobering. One of the most exciting aspects of mass communication law is that the principles can change from day to day as new statutes are enacted and new court decisions are handed down, often foretelling dramatic shifts in the law. Because the content changes so readily, especially from semester to semester, the instructor must constantly update the material and eschew traditional teaching techniques for more innovative strategies.

BACKGROUND

Regardless of the title (Mass Communication Law, Law of the Press, Mass Media Law and Regulations, Journalism Law and Ethics, etc.), all media law courses share two common goals: (1) to introduce students to the American legal system, including the types and sources of American law and the civil and criminal judicial processes, and (2) to teach the basic principles of communication law, such as censorship, prior restraint, defamation, privacy, copyright, advertising rules and regulations, telecommunications law, access to news sources, and obscenity. Most mass communication and journalism programs include the course as part of the required core curriculum, while nearly all of the remaining programs either strongly recommend the course or offer it as a general elective. Very few programs have opted to exclude the course from the curriculum or to simply integrate the material into other courses. However, it is not unusual for the course to formally include ethics in the content or to be allied with a separate but sequential course in media ethics.

In 1989 an Association for Education in Journalism and Mass Communication (AEJMC) Task Force on the Future of Journalism and Mass Communication noted in its comprehensive report on the challenges and opportunities:

We seek to prepare students by putting them through skills courses; by requiring a broad array of supporting courses with an emphasis on the liberal arts; by providing a context in which to make decisions (history, *law*, *ethics*, economics of the media, etc.); and by helping them see how these things fit together in a pattern (albeit a shifting one) that will be useful in the "real world." [emphasis mine][1]

Part two of the report, which dealt with the advertising curriculum, noted that in a survey for AEJMC and the American Advertising Federation, advertising educators ranked the study of communication ethics and law ninth, while advertising practitioners ranked the area twelfth in importance as specific areas of study in the advertising curriculum. Many schools now offer a course in advertising rules and regulations, but the vast majority of mass communication programs with advertising majors continue to rely on the basic media law course to build the appropriate foundation in communication law for these majors. All media law instructors, but especially those in programs with an advertising sequence, should include advertising law as a topic in the basic media law course when no separate advertising law course is offered on a regular basis. Advertisers also face a rising tide of litigation in areas such as misappropriation (one of the four torts of privacy) and copyright infringement. The laws regarding professional advertising (by lawyers, physicians, pharmacists, etc.) have also been altered significantly since the last decade, especially with the expansion of First Amendment protection, thanks to a series of U.S. Supreme Court rulings. The task force also included broadcast, magazine, news-editorial, public relations, and visual communication curricula. No direct reference to law is made in the broadcast section of the report, although broadcast majors, like advertising majors, should certainly not be excluded from learning media law. The magazine section of the report noted that a mail survey of magazine editors, educators, and graduates found that respondents as a whole were not enthusiastic about law, and the news-editorial section only peripherally mentions law.

The Public Relations Committee of the task force endorsed in its section a so-called Design for Public Relations Education proposed in 1987 by the Commission on Undergraduate Public Relations Education. Under this plan, 25 percent of the curriculum prescribed by the Accrediting Council on Education in Journalism and Mass Communication for Professional Studies would be about equally divided between general communications and specific public relations studies. General communications would include communication law and ethics (under historical/institutional studies).

Finally, the general curriculum proposed for visual communication was divided into five major areas, including law and ethics as separate areas. Law would focus on "principles of visual communication law" and "press access rights, e.g., open meeting laws, invasion of privacy, copyright, libel, model releases," while ethics would deal with "appropriate representation of data in infographics and facts in photo illustrations," manner of coverage, and photo editing.

A careful reading of the task force report reveals two trends likely to affect the teaching of mass media law. First, communication law, in spite of its specialized nature, will continue to be a major concern of both educators and practitioners. This concern is likely to lead to a significant increase in the number of mass communication programs requiring the more general course for all students and those offering more specialized courses such as advanced media law, advertising law, cable regulation, and broadcast rules and regulations. Second, following on the heels of the first trend will be a much greater demand for instructors, especially those with media law backgrounds, qualified to teach the media law course in its many variations. Already there are several attorneys, including the author of this chapter, who teach media law and related courses full time, plus dozens of lawyers who are part-time instructors in mass communication law.

Although the primary focus of the media law course is on basic media law principles, the judicial system, and the legal process, the course is usually also geared to teach future communication practitioners how to cover civil and judicial proceedings (pretrial, trial, and post-trial) and to arm them with sufficient knowledge to avoid legal actions against them (contempt of court, libel, invasion of privacy, intentional infliction of emotional distress, and other torts), as well as the ability to adequately defend themselves, with the assistance of counsel, against such actions if they are filed. Students in the course should also learn how to gain access to public documents and other news sources with the support of open meetings and open records statutes.

ORGANIZATION

Traditional teaching techniques alone will not suffice in the mass media law course. The instructor must be innovative, flexible, well-organized, and well-prepared. Fortunately, for neophytes, there are some tried and true strategies that have proven valuable over the years for their predecessors, but before these techniques are tested, the new instructor should (1) carefully review the discussion that follows to ascertain with which approaches he or she is most comfortable, and (2) consult colleagues who have taught the course for their advice. Be forewarned: tackling mass media law without thorough preparation is risking a colossal faux pas.

Before discussing teaching strategies further, however, let's deal with course structure. A convenient but often unproductive approach to organizing the course is to rely on the outline in the textbook. A serious weakness of this choice is that the instructor may be stuck with an outline that may not work well with the particular type of students in the program. For example, while some media law textbooks immediately jump to a complex area such as libel after a historical overview of the First Amendment, students in some programs may find the transition too abrupt, because they lack a basic understanding of the judicial process and the court systems. On the other hand, students in other programs may have absorbed this information in previous courses, such as advanced news writing or even in the introduction to mass communication class. The instructor should be thoroughly familiar with the background of the students before the course begins; thus the organizational scheme can be geared to suit student needs.

A second step in organizing the media law course is to decide realistically how much material can be reasonably covered in the given time frame. There is a world of difference in the amount of information that can be imparted in a three-hour course in a quarter system versus a three-hour semester class. In the quarter system, the instructor will be forced to focus only on essential topics such as libel, invasion of privacy, prior restraint, access, copyright, and obscenity at the likely expense of important areas such as advertising regulations, telecommunications law, media ownership, and First Amendment history. The ideal time frame is either the three-hour semester or the five-hour quarter, because a broader range of topics can be handled.

Once a viable list of topics has been chosen, the instructor should review the major texts available (discussed below) and select one that appears to cover the topics best.

Here is a good working draft of an outline, developed by the author during twelve years of teaching the course:

I.   The American Legal System and the Judicial Process
   A.   Sources and Types of American Law
      1.   Constitutional law, including the Bill of Rights
      2.   Statutory law
      3.   Administrative law
      4.   Common law
      5.   Equity
      6.   Civil vs. criminal law
      7.   Torts vs. contracts
   B.   The American Legal System
      1.   Federal court system
      2.   State court system (including own state)
   C.   The Judicial Process
      1.   Civil lawsuit
      2.   Civil trial
      3.   Criminal lawsuit
      4.   Criminal trial
      5.   Appellate process
      6.   Alternative dispute resolution
II. Governmental Restraints
   A.   Prior Restraint

1. Civil vs. criminal contempt of court
2. *Near v. Minnesota*
3. Sedition
4. Justification
5. Time, place, and manner restrictions
6. Injunctions

B. Commercial Speech
   1. Advertising
   2. Federal Trade Commission and other federal agencies
   3. Federal and state antitrust laws
   4. Joint operating agreements and other monopolistic practices
   5. Other state regulations

C. Broadcasting and Telecommunications
   1. Rationales
   2. Federal Communications Commission
   3. Fairness Doctrine
   4. Equal opportunities law
   5. Public access
   6. Deregulation
   7. Cable
   8. New technologies
   9. Recent developments

III. Infringement on Individual Rights
   A. Libel
      1. Libel vs. slander
      2. Libel *per se* vs. libel *per quod*
      3. Typical libel case
      4. Elements of libel
      5. Damages
      6. Defenses
      7. Constitutionalization (*New York Times v. Sullivan* and *Gertz v. Welch* and progeny)
      8. Mitigation, including retraction
      9. Neutral reportage
      10. Insurance
      11. Criminal defamation

B. Privacy
  1. Constitutionalization
  2. Intrusion
  3. Public disclosure
  4. Appropriation and right of publicity
  5. False light
  6. Privacy Act of 1974

IV. Press and Public Access
  A. Public Right to Know
    1. Freedom of Information laws (state and federal)
    2. Sunshine laws (state and federal)
  B. Press and Public Access to Places
    1. Private property
    2. Prisons and prisoners
    3. Legislative process
    4. Courtrooms and other public buildings
  C. Press and Public Access to the Judicial Process
    1. Cameras in the courtrooms (state and federal)
    2. Free press vs. fair trial
  D. Protection of Sources and Information
    1. Journalistic privilege in general
    2. Shield laws
    3. Subpoenas vs. search warrants, including *Zurcher v. Stanford Daily* and the Privacy Protection Act of 1980

V. Other Media Concerns
  A. Intellectual Property
    1. Copyright, including Copyright Act of 1976, fair use, and registration
    2. Patents
  B. Obscenity and Pornography
    1. U.S. Supreme Court decisions, including *Miller v. California*
    2. State and federal controls
    3. Recent developments, including U.S. attorney general's commission

The neophyte instructor should find this scheme useful as a working outline that can be modified with teaching experience. Any of the major textbooks can be reorganized to fit the scheme, especially with additional resources, as noted.

An alternative is to organize the course around the traditional major topics but organize the content for specific topics with a flow chart or similar scheme. Flow charts not only add visual appeal but serve as productive learning tools. Most media law topics can be illustrated with a flow chart, with libel and invasion of privacy especially amenable. One of the most useful flow charts on libel was first proposed by Albert Skaggs in 1982.[2] Evan Smith recently updated and expanded the chart to include invasion of privacy.[3] Court cases can be readily inserted into the chart with new decisions simply tacked onto the chart at the appropriate juncture. For other topics such as obscenity and access, the instructor can develop an individual flow chart by following the basic set-ups of Skaggs and Smith.

Two of the most important determinants of the amount of time the instructor can devote to individual topics are the number of students in the course and length of the class term. Regardless of class size or term length, the agenda should be set in advance on at least a week-to-week basis. That is, the syllabus should clearly indicate which topics and readings are assigned each week, and the instructor should deviate from the schedule only when absolutely necessary such as when a new state or federal statute is enacted or the U.S. Supreme Court or the state's highest court issues a major decision. Seasoned media law teachers can ardently attest that significant deviations, which inevitably mean extra time on a topic, can play holy havoc with the schedule. Given the tremendous amount of material to cover, it is unfair to the students for topics to be shortchanged simply because they were scheduled during the latter part of the course but were bumped when an earlier topic received significantly more than its scheduled share of time.

Many media law instructors use the Socratic method, patterned after the teaching techniques of the Greek philosopher Socrates (470–399 BC). This method uses a series of questions and answers and emphasizes learning *how* to think rather than *what* to think. Every major law school in the country liberally uses this technique, especially in the required first and second year courses. The problem is that this method, like any other approach to teaching, can be improperly used and even overused. During the centuries since Socrates, teachers in virtually every discipline have employed this method, even though it is not appropriate in every circumstance nor for every type of student.

One of the rewards of successfully using Socratic dialogue comes with observing students being stimulated to think and thereby to learn how to critically analyze a complex situation, to derive a common principle that was not obvious before the series of agonizing questions began. The jury deciding the effectiveness of the Socratic method in teaching mass communication law is still deliberating. Indeed, the ultimate outcome may be a hung jury. A sizable group of instructors swears its allegiance to the technique, but another fairly large group has taken a vow of abstinence. The rest of the media law professors dabble with the method occasionally but not at the exclusion of other approaches.

A new instructor contemplating use of the Socratic method should, at the very least, audit a first year law course such as criminal law or torts to acquire the subtleties and intricacies of the process. Never try this technique unless you have seen it in action.

One effective variation of the Socratic method is the case study approach in which the students focus on a series of court decisions in a given area such as the "actual malice" rule in libel or "newsworthiness" as a defense to invasion of privacy. The approach involves assigning the class longer excerpts from major state and federal court decisions to determine the legal principles laid down by the courts, including their evolution. Clearly, the students must play a major role in the process. This can be done by having individual students "brief" (that is, summarize major points) cases and by encouraging them to ask relevant questions as the cases progress. The essential key to success with the case study approach is preparation by the students. Some instructors "force" students to prepare by calling on them at random to brief. This step usually works because most students do not want to be embarrassed by having to say "I haven't read the case" or by providing a weak answer. Calling on a few "confederates" (students who have been surreptitiously told in advance to be prepared for a particular case) during the first week or two of classes can set a positive tone for the rest of the term.

A serious weakness of the case study method lies in the fact that it will not work for all media law topics, since some areas such as open meetings/open records and copyright are grounded in statutory law rather than case law. However, there are usually a few cases, especially those interpreting the statutes, to give the topic a case law flavor in the class discussion. The key to success is flexibility. The instructor must vary the teaching techniques as appropriate to a given area of study.

One method is surely doomed to failure if used exclusively in the media law course—the traditional lecture format. A subject as complex as mass communication law does not lend itself well to being principally taught via lectures. The students will be bored, the instructor frustrated, and learning will be minimal. Lectures are certainly germane in some circumstances, but they should be used only sparingly. Class size will particularly dictate the extent to which lectures will work. If the class has approximately forty or fewer students, lectures should be kept to a minimum because direct instructor-student interaction is feasible. The classroom should be kept competitive but in a way that stimulates students to respond rather than encouraging them to keep quiet. One instructor, for example, has created "Journalism Jeopardy" (patterned after the popular TV game) for midterm and final exam sessions.[4] Variations of other television shows (not just game shows) such as "Sixty Minutes," "People's Court," "Superior Court," "L.A. Law," and so forth, could be used to stimulate interest in discussion and thereby make learning interesting, if not fun.

There are at least three excellent sources for tips on teaching media law. *Media Law Notes* (the newsletter of the AEJMC Law Division), the *AEJMC Newspaper Division Newsletter*, and *Journalism Educator* (also published by AEJMC) feature occasional pieces on innovative teaching, sometimes dealing specifically with the media law course. The instructor's manuals accompanying most of the major texts on media law also offer teaching tips but, unfortunately, their advice can often be rather generic. The manuals are still quite valuable, however, for their suggestions on organizing the course and evaluation procedures.

Finally, a learning aid most students will particularly appreciate is an advance, detailed outline of the course. This should not be simply a cursory list of major topics but instead should be a comprehensive review of every major concept in the course. On the first day of class, the author provides his students with a ten-to-twelve-page, single-spaced outline listing each concept, legal principle, case, and statute with the exact page on which it is covered in the reading materials. No pretense is made that every item will be discussed in class, but the student is promised that only those items in the outline and any others announced in class (such as new Supreme Court decisions) will actually be tested on the exams. The outline is stored in a computer so that it can be updated each semester. Enterprising students use the outline as a study guide, and even less enterprising individuals at least know when they have gaps in knowledge and how much effort is needed to fill those gaps. During the last dozen years the outline has been distributed, not one class member has complained about it, and many students have indicated the outline was their most valuable tool for exam preparation. As the outline is distributed, the class is told: "There are no secrets in this course. Everything you need to know is in this outline."

TEXTS

The list of mass communication law texts is still relatively short, although it is expanding each year. No one book is perfect for every situation, but they are all generally well written and comprehensive. The choice will depend upon several factors: duration of the class term, size of class, level (beginning, intermediate, or advanced) of the course, background of the students, and whether the instructor takes the case study or traditional (non–case study) approach. Current books include:

T. Barton Carter, Marc A. Franklin, and Jay B. Wright, *The First Amendment and the Fourth Estate*, 5th ed. (Mineola, NY: Foundation Press, 1991).

T. Barton Carter, Marc A. Franklin, and Jay B. Wright, *First Amendment and the Fifth Estate*, 2nd ed. (Mineola, NY: Foundation Press, 1989)

William Francois, *Mass Media Law and Regulation*, 5th ed. (Ames: Iowa State University, 1990).

Marc Franklin and David A. Anderson, *Mass Media Law: Cases and Materials*, 4th ed. (Mineola, NY: Foundation Press, 1990). (casebook)

Don Gillmor, Jerome A. Barron, Todd F. Simon, and Herbert A. Terry, *Mass Media Law: Cases and Comments*, 5th ed. (St. Paul, MN: West, 1990). (casebook)

Douglas A. Ginsbury, Michael H. Botein, and Mark D. Director, *Regulation of the Electronic Media*, 2nd ed. (St. Paul, MN: West, 1991). (casebook)

Ralph Holsinger, *Media Law*, 2nd ed. (New York: McGraw-Hill, 1991).

Kent Middleton and Bill Chamberlain, *Law of Public Communication*, 2nd ed. (New York: Longman, 1991).

Harold Nelson, Dwight Teeter, and Don LeDuc, *Law of Mass Communication*, 6th ed. (Mineola, NY: Foundation Press, 1989).

Don Pember, *Mass Media Law*, 5th ed. (Dubuque, IA: William C. Brown, 1990).

William W. Van Alstyne, *First Amendment: Cases and Materials* (Mineola, NY: Foundation Press, 1991). (casebook)

Harvey L. Zuchman, Martin L. Gaynes, T. Barton Carter, and Juliet Lushbough Dee, *Mass Communications Law (in a nutshell)*, 3rd ed. (St. Paul, MN: West, 1988).

Each text has its strengths and weaknesses and should be carefully reviewed before being adopted. Nelson, Teeter, and LeDuc's book is by far the best seller, but even relative newcomers such as Middleton and Chamberlain's text have done well. The traditional or narrative texts clearly outnumber casebooks, but some mass communication programs have successfully used the Gillmor, et al. casebook even though it is geared principally to law students. Most of the publishers provide an annual update, although nearly all of them distribute copies only to the instructors, who then have the burden of arranging for photocopies to be available to the students. A few of the texts such as Middleton and Chamberlain's publish a convenient annual update sold with the book. Updates in some form are essential even though the instructor should continually compile stories and cases as they develop. Normally, the publisher grants copyright permission for the update to be reproduced if the book is adopted for the course, but permission should be sought in writing unless specifically granted in the update. Some of the updates are more accurate and comprehensive than others, but they all generally do a good job of covering major changes in the law, with the exception of changes in state law, which are the responsibility of the instructor. These changes should be compiled as a separate handout, with copyright permission requested as appropriate.

Consider the following points in choosing a textbook. Casebooks usually work well only with advanced students such as those who have taken a previous course in media law. Also, remember that none of the texts will be adequate unless supplemented by other materials. For example, students will gain little, if any, knowledge of the laws in their state, such as open meetings and open records laws, from reading only the textbook. Be sure to look closely at texts that have been recently revised or for which a revised edition will be available by the time the course begins. Having to update the text for several years rather than merely one year can be quite time-consuming for the instructor and confusing for students who have to constantly determine when a section of the book is out of date.

Unless extremely high, price should not be a major factor. Students will complain about any book's price, no matter how low, but they are better served by a well-written, comprehensive, and fairly expensive text than by a lower-priced one that may offer less extensive coverage or be woefully out of date. To lower costs, students can be encouraged to share textbooks or to read the copies on reserve in the library or college reading room. Always strongly discourage students, though, from ever photocopying portions of any text since such reproduction is nearly always a violation of copyright, a topic of discussion later in the term!

An enormous variety of supplementary materials is available for the mass media law course. Some of the materials are almost essential, while other resources will simply enrich the course. The American Bar

Association (ABA) [Public Education Division, 750 N. Lake Shore Drive, Chicago, IL 60611, (312) 988–5725] offers several excellent publications, including *Law and the Courts, A Journalist's Primer on Federal Criminal Procedure,* and *A Journalist's Primer on Locating Legal Documents.* The first, an eighty-page booklet of courtroom procedures and a glossary of legal terms, is relatively inexpensive and can be ordered for students through the campus bookstore. It is a very succinct review of the civil and judicial process and the state and federal court systems.

The primer on criminal procedure (fifty-two pages, including glossary) is the first of a series of pocket booklets published jointly by the ABA and the Society of Professional Journalists (SPJ). The two organizations have also produced an excellent videotape on the same topic, which can be purchased or rented from the ABA. Videotapes on other media law topics are planned. The primer is inexpensive when purchased in bulk, and the videotape is relatively inexpensive and can sometimes be rented free through the local bar association or the local chapter of SPJ. The ABA and SPJ are encouraging local and state bar associations to purchase the videotape for university and public libraries. Contact the state or local bar association president about the possibility of getting the tape for the school or college reading room.

Other valuable supplemental materials are state statutes on libel, invasion of privacy, contempt, open meetings, open records, obscenity, and protection of confidential sources (shield laws). The statutes, *without annotations,* can be reprinted and distributed to students without violating federal copyright statutes. In other words, the statutes themselves are in the public domain. However, annotations (which are usually citations of major court decisions and other comments at the end of a statute) are nearly always copyrighted by the publisher, such as West Publishing, listed at the beginning of the volume; thus, reproducing statutes with annotations could constitute copyright infringement. A good source for the noncopyrighted version of the statutes is the state attorney general's office. Permission should be obtained from the publisher before photocopying any annotated statutes.

Reprinting court decisions presents similar copyright problems. Unannotated versions (which are sometimes difficult to distinguish) are usually public domain, while annotated versions are nearly always copyrighted.

Three texts provide summaries of major U.S. Supreme Court decisions on media law:

Douglas A. Campbell, *The Supreme Court and the Mass Media* (New York: Praeger, 1990).

Kenneth S. Devol, *Mass Media and the Supreme Court*, 3rd ed. (New York: Hastings House, 1982).

Richard Hixson, *Mass Media and the Constitution* (New York: Garland Publishing, 1989).

Hixson's book is by far the most comprehensive but it is published in an expensive hardback that prevents it from being used as a supplemental text. Campbell's text provides an excellent overview of cases on selected topics and is affordable as a supplement since it is published in paperback. Although dated, the Devol book is a good source and is available in paperback.

A number of videotapes on media law and related topics have been produced. The Adult Learning Satellite Service of the Public Broadcasting Service (1320 Braddock Place, Alexandria, VA 22314–1698, 1–800–ALS–ALS8) delivers via satellite various programs, sometimes with media law-related themes, to colleges and universities across the country. Many schools are members of ALSS and can tape the programs as audio-visual resources either at no fee or at a reduced cost. PBS Video (same address as ALSS, 1–800–344–3337 or 1–800–424–7963) also makes available for sale or rent videotapes of various programs that have been broadcast on PBS such as Fred Friendly's excellent *The Constitution: That Delicate Balance*. (The book by the same title is an excellent resource as well.)

Media Law Reporter contains the full text of most major court decisions (state and federal) on media law and summaries of other developments. A subscription price includes a bound volume each year to replace the loose-leaf binder and the opportunity to purchase bound volumes of previous years relatively inexpensively. Many law libraries subscribe to this reporter, and college and university libraries are often willing to include a subscription in a program's annual library budget.

News Media and the Law appears quarterly and is available for a contribution to the Reporters Committee for Freedom of the Press (1735 Eye Street, NW, # 508, Washington, D.C., 20006) of at least $20.00. Back issues cost $5.00. The annual U.S. Supreme Court issue makes a useful supplemental text since it summarizes and analyzes all of the major Supreme Court decisions for the previous term. Copies for classes can be ordered through the college bookstore.

The *Student Press Law Center Report*, published three times each year by the same organization as *News Media and the Law*, provides a fairly comprehensive analysis and summary of "current controversies involving student press rights." Subscriptions are $10.00 annually. The reports are "researched, written, and produced entirely by journalism and law student interns."

Each year the SPJ produces an excellent report that is usually available in reasonable quantities for free distribution to media law and other students: *Ethics* (a report of controversies involving media ethics). Since the report is usually sent via fourth-class mail, contact SPJ several weeks before copies are needed to ensure that they arrive in time. An *F.O.I.* report, which was a separate publication by SPJ until 1990, now appears in a special edition of *Quill* magazine (typically in the November/December issue). This report focuses on freedom of information matters, including court decisions and regional reports.

Other resources that should be consulted regularly to keep current on media law matters are *Communication and the Law, Media Law Notes* (mentioned earlier; published by the AEJMC Media Law Division, which every media law instructor should join), *Communications Lawyer* (published by the ABA Forum on Communications Law at $15.00 annually for nonlawyers), *ABA Journal* ($48.00 for non-ABA members), and *Quill* (published by SPJ). While *ABA Journal* and *Quill* (except for the annual *F.O.I.* issue) are not geared specifically to media law, both feature occasional articles on the First Amendment and include summaries and analyses of recent court decisions. *ABA Journal* also features a "Supreme Court Preview" section that summarizes cases to be decided by the court.

CONCLUSION

The approaches to evaluating students in the mass communication law course are enormously varied. Some instructors swear by multiple-choice exams while others abhor them and cling religiously to essay tests. For particularly large classes (100 or more students), pure essay exams may be impractical, especially if the instructor has no teaching assistant and a heavy course load. Many instructors use a combination of objective and essay questions, with the objective items designed to test knowledge of basic concepts, while the narrative questions tap logical reasoning, including the ability to analyze a set of facts (usually in the form of hypotheticals) to arrive at defensible conclusions. Above all, exams should stress legal principles and concepts, not case names or dates, although the student should be conversant with the names of major cases such as *New York Times v.*

Sullivan and *Branzburg v. Hayes*. There is no ideal number of exams, but the amount of material is so overwhelming that a midterm and final exam only will probably not work well. Some instructors require a term paper or other final project, typically designed to demonstrate the ability to do competent legal research. Before the class embarks on such an adventure, have the students complete some routine, relatively brief exercises on legal research. Students will also appreciate a guided tour of the legal resources in the university library.

The typical format for the course is probably three or four one-to-two hour exams with a mixture of objective and essay questions. Some professors have students participate for credit in innovative projects such as mock trials or appeals. The more interesting and participatory the classes, the more likely the students are to enjoy learning. Guest speakers such as media lawyers, judges, and state attorney generals can heighten student interest, but such experts should be selected with care to ensure that they can relate well to the students. Local reporters who have experience in investigative reporting and searching public records, for example, can pique class interest. Finally, if there is a libel or invasion of privacy trial going on during the term, have the class observe the proceedings and write a news story or other report. Be sure to tell the court clerk in advance that the class will be attending.

Media law can be an exciting and yet challenging course. The course offers excellent opportunities for innovative and creative teaching and can serve as one of the most interesting and practical classes in the student's academic career.

NOTES

1. Association for Education in Journalism and Mass Communication, "Challenges and Opportunities in Journalism and Mass Communication Education," report of the Task Force on the Future of Journalism and Mass Communication Education, *Journalism Educator* 44 (Spring 1989): A–4.

2. Albert C. Skaggs, " 'Is This Libelous?' Simple Chart Helps Students Get the Answer," *Journalism Educator* 37 (Autumn 1982): 16.

3. Evan B. Smith, "Charting Complexities of Modern Libel Law," *Journalism Educator* 44 (Spring 1989): 20–26.

4. Ken Bush, "OK, Alex, I'll Take Libel for $200," *AEJMC Newspaper Division Newsletter* (June 1989): 7–8.

Chapter 13

MASS COMMUNICATION MANAGEMENT

John De Mott

One of today's most exciting challenges in social responsibility, for professors of journalism and mass communication, is the teaching of mass communication (masscomm) management—the economics and administration of private or public enterprises engaged in the creation and dissemination of public information (advertising, news reportage, and public relations communication). In response to continuing pressure from masscomm's professional organizations and industries, schools and departments of journalism and mass communication throughout the country are constantly striving to modernize and improve existing courses—and also to create additional courses of study with appropriate content and in appropriate mode.

As a part of that process for many years—I have now taught management at three universities, both graduate and undergraduate courses—I have discovered my own best results have followed, invariably, the use of a systems analysis approach I developed originally while teaching in Illinois.

BACKGROUND

Before considering the conduct of a masscomm management course using such an approach today, consider an analysis of the educational subsystem that appears to require instruction in masscomm management. In systems flow analysis, we need to focus—as sharply as possible—on three essentials: *input, process* (let's call it *throughput* for our purposes), and *output*. The prospective course of study we have under consideration, of course, is our *throughput*.

Determining output is not easy, although some educators make it appear so. Too often such courses are based on unrealistic aspirations or extravagant expectations. Consequently, such courses sometimes end up being over-specialized. Or because of other questionable decisions concerning the desirable output, such courses can be prejudiced toward management's point of view—or that of "labor." Or biased toward one particular management philosophy or "executive style," rather than taking an evenhanded position that is fair to those enrolled in such a course. Therefore, keen thought needs to be given the desired results of such study—the system's *output*.

Before the character and content of the course, or *throughput*, can be determined, we need to determine just how much knowledge of masscomm management theory and practice students need. Why? What do our students need to know about the management of masscomm enterprises? Not enough to actually administer or manage a professional masscomm enterprise, obviously, but enough to fit into such an organization reasonably well, at entry level, and function effectively with the organization's management.

That goal is supported by a survey among mass communication managers conducted in 1987. In the report of that research, published by the Media Management & Economics Resource Center (MMERC) of the University of Minnesota's School of Journalism and Mass Communication,[1] Daniel B. Wackman reported:

media executives hold the view that their future employees would benefit from exposure to some of the fundamentals of media management . . . helping them gain a basic knowledge of media industries as a whole, of the issues that managers and media companies face, and the perspectives and skills that managers utilize.

The first big decision to be made in implementing a faculty's decision concerning the extent and depth of knowledge needed is whether to use a single cross-media course to give all its majors their initial understanding of management, or—on the other hand—to provide separate media-based courses for majors in broadcasting, advertising, newspaper journalism, public relations, magazine editing, photojournalism, and so forth.

That decision is quite often dictated by a school's size—only a single offering is possible, in some cases—but I believe that a single integrated course for all majors is best, regardless of the school's size.

There is much to be learned about management in general from comparing management practices across the media, and extensive specialization can be quite dysfunctional on the undergraduate level—master's level, even.

During the mid–1970s, in an initial burst of enthusiasm for instruction in masscomm management, schools and departments frequently went overboard on specialization. That experience proved a sobering one for many. As a result, there has been a drift toward more generalized courses designed to meet the needs of students with diverse expectations and interests. In this regard, also, the educational situation appears to fit the need seen by executives themselves.

Because there is considerable staff crossover between media, also—and most journalism/masscomm students have little knowledge of organizational behavior, economics, and administration/management in general—the cross-media approach appears best in most cases.

Incidentally, let's reject out of hand the preposterous idea that the purpose of a masscomm management course is to provide specialized preparation or training for actual management in the professional field. Using such a premise constitutes incompetent decision making and planning in the educational context.

From our analysis of the output desired from our system of instruction in this course, we can create a statement of its general purpose and a set of appropriate objectives for it (in managerial terms, a mission statement and set of major goals).

ORGANIZATION

"The general purpose of this course," our syllabus states, "is to explore the ways in which mass communication organizations are managed today, in the United States, with special attention to the basic economic needs of masscomm enterprises, common problems encountered by all, current trends in the field, and management challenges created by attempts to anticipate future developments in the environment—economic, political, and other—of such enterprises." Specific objectives of our course are these:

1. Familiarity with the functions of the executive or management "team" in administration of a masscomm enterprise, and familiarity with the relevance of management science and its principles to the solution of problems in administration of complex organizations developed for operation of today's media of mass communication.

2. Knowledge of how various masscomm enterprises are structured over-all, as complex organizations, and substructured for particular functions like general administration, personnel recruitment and development, decision making, production, marketing, budgeting, distribution or dissemination of product, control of quality, financial accounting, research, and planning.
3. Understanding of how various masscomm organizations differ, in some administrative practices, and, on the other hand, how those organizations (television or radio broadcasting stations, advertising agencies or departments, newspapers or magazines, and public relations departments or firms) resemble one another in their efforts to solve common problems of administration.
4. Deeper appreciation for the role of masscomm in our democratic capitalistic society, and its impact upon the nation's industry, commerce, labor force, finance, trade, and overall economy.

Reexamining our desired output, before creating a throughput method and content for conduct of the course, we need to look at our input.

Given the preparation provided by lower level courses leading into masscomm management, what capabilities do our course's prospective participants possess? Have they taken any general course in management? Economics? Organizational behavior? Should some course of that kind be made prerequisite to enrollment in masscomm management? Is there any kind of selection process, or is the course to be required of all majors? What are the attitudes of prospective participants toward management? Is there adequate expertise in our faculty to conduct prospective participants on our assessed level of development to the level envisioned in our determination of the desired output for the course? in the time available? with the resources at hand? Is there sufficient instructional material available?

Depending on the answers to questions such as these, we may want to revise our analysis of output. Let's assume, however, for purposes of this discussion, that such reconsideration isn't necessary. Therefore, now consider our throughput—the course of study itself.

In introduction of the course to its participants, we need to point out that the course is designed to be of great benefit to those who never, ever, want to be masscomm managers, as well as any who may want to do so.

Whether a student of masscomm fancies himself or herself executive timber is beside the point, really. Every news reporter, advertising copywriter, public relations firm employee, photojournalist, will probably spend his or her entire career in formal organizations, being managed, if not managing, well or poorly. Moreover, most of every newsperson's daily job involves obtaining information from managers of complex organizations, public or private. Generally, one cannot conduct a journalistic investigation successfully without a sound knowledge of organizational structure and communication flow. Similarly, public relations and advertising professionals need to understand management theory and practice, regardless of their respective positions in their own organizations. Working successfully with other organizations and their personnel is generally a critical factor in success on the professional level.

Once that point is driven home in an orientation to the course, we can reasonably expect a high level of esprit de corps to prevail among participants.

In orienting participants, it's also helpful to point out that the basic concepts used in systems analysis have been developed from some questions familiar to journalism/masscomm students as well as anthropologists. Those questions are: WHO? WHAT? WHERE? WHEN? WHY? and HOW?

Each of those questions is related in a quite special way to one of these concepts used in systems analysis:

- Purpose of the enterprise—WHY?
- The environment—WHERE?
- Resources (with)—WHAT?
- Organization—WHO?
- Decision making—HOW and WHEN?

Having introduced the course participants to those concepts, we proceed to the implementation of our process, session to session.

The systems analysis and systems flow approach enables us to relate each individual participant's area of special interest to other kinds of enterprise, private or public, and make enterprising comparisons that best illustrate the basic principles and functions of management. The functions of management, common to all kinds of human enterprise, are:

- Decision making: the process by which a course of action is consciously chosen from available alternatives for the purpose of achieving a desired result;
- Organizing: the process by which the structure and allocation of jobs are determined;

- Staffing: the process by which managers select, train, promote, and retire subordinates;
- Planning: the process by which management anticipates the future and discovers alternative courses of action open to it;
- Controlling: the process by which management measures current performance and guides it toward the predetermined goal(s);
- Communicating: the process by which ideas are transmitted to others in the organization, for the purpose of effecting a desired result;
- Directing: the process by which actual performance of subordinates is guided toward common goals of those comprising the organization;

Each of those functions constitutes a unit in our course of study. Each unit includes these four activities:

1. Two assigned readings every week, one from the regular textbook and the other (related) from some research journal or professional "trade" periodical in the individual participant's area of special interest—advertising, news, public relations, and so forth.

2. Seminar discussion of assigned readings. Each individual participant reports on particular article read, and then the group discusses the assigned topic collectively, with discussion moderated by "course conductor." (I much prefer that identification. The term "teacher" is dysfunctional, a carry-over from elementary and high school. I find students much more receptive to the acceptance of personal learning responsibility when they have no "teacher.")

3. Seminar presentation, by a panel of professionals representing different types of masscomm organizations, followed by a question/answer session devoted to exploring similarities and differences in the ways different masscomm organizations carry out the same functions of management.

4. Special project, related to the function of management being studied in that unit of the course.

The special projects, which are particularly helpful in giving participants clearer insight into the related aspect of management, include these possibilities:

- Writing a detailed job description;
- Creating a "mission statement" for a selected medium of mass communication;
- Identifying objectives for a particular department's activity during the next year;

- Preparing a departmental budget using zero-sum method;
- Formulating an affirmative action policy;
- Creating a form for annual evaluation of achievement by an individual staff member;
- Writing a news release announcing an increase in price of some product or service;
- Analyzing cost of some operation by a particular department;
- Explaining an organization's economic "environment";
- Designing an organization chart;
- Writing directions for implementation of some revised policy;
- Preparing a proposed orientation manual's table of contents;
- Formulating a response to some consumer's letter alleging mistreatment by an employee of the organization;
- Analyzing a financial statement.

The following are two examples of instructions for special projects.

Organization Chart. For some enterprise of which you'd like to be a part, draw a chart explaining how you think the enterprise ought to be organized for best results—maximum effectiveness and efficiency. Show as clearly as possible to what part of the organization—division, department, section, office, or individual desk—each organizational unit reports, and then to what part of the organization that unit in turn reports. Examining your chart, an outsider should be able to figure out to what unit in your organization he or she would logically go in order to obtain the answer to any kind of question concerning your organization's services—and also to what unit he or she could appeal if dissatisfied with such service. Explain the reasons for your mode of organization and chain of command/responsibility.

Job Description. Write a description for a prospective job in some organization in your career field. Explain as precisely as possible exactly what the person occupying that position in the organization would be responsible for *doing*. (Do *not*, for example, describe the educational qualifications, skills, experience, etc., you logically would look for in assessing applicants for employment in the position. That's another function of management: recruitment.) Keep in mind that one use of a job description is to explain to the person employed in that position precisely what is expected of him or her. It should concentrate, obviously, upon the most important aspects of performance, leaving the employee and his or her supervisor as much freedom as practical to adapt the details of duty and performance to their unique experiences, abilities, and lifestyles. (Please don't spend any of your precious time telling *how well* the person in that position is expected to do his or her job. It's assumed, when writing job descriptions, that the best available person is to be recruited and that he or she is going to be motivated to do the best job possible, under the circumstances.) Describe the *job*—what is to be *done*, not how *well*.

The presentations by executives of local masscomm organizations are extremely valuable. One of the most common misconceptions harbored by advertising, news, and public relations students is that public relations firms, newspapers, magazines, ad agencies, or television and radio stations are somehow so different from other businesses that the same principles of management do not apply. Also, masscomm staffers tend to be afflicted deeply with a professional conceit, leading them to believe that standard administration practices are inapplicable to the media because masscomm folk are so much more creative, enterprising, self-motivating, resourceful, professional, and so forth, than men and women in other occupations. That's an interesting theory, but not much more than pleasant speculation at this stage in the evolution of management science.

Talking with professional managers representing the widest possible range of masscomm enterprise—advertising, public relations, and print and broadcast news—students see readily that masscomm enterprises share (with other kinds of businesses, as well as among themselves) common problems of organization, efficiency, decision making, planning, formulation of policy, resource allocation, recruitment of staff, financing, in-service training, budgeting, performance evaluation, cost accounting, consumer relations, and quality control.

For those reasons, it's important that each panel of resource persons represent as nearly as practical the full spectrum of masscomm enterprise, and also that each panel devote itself to the exploration of the particular function of management being studied in that particular unit of the course. For example, one unit's panel—an ad agency vice president, a newspaper editor, a public relations firm's chief executive officer, and the assistant general manager of a television station—can be asked to explain and compare their respective methods of budgeting—Management By Objectives (MBO), zero-base, line-item, etc.—as a subfunction of the budgeting process. The members of another panel can be asked to explain how their organizations go about the recruiting and training of staff. Or the planning of their production operations. Controlling of quality. Monitoring the implementation of delegated authority. Conducting internal communication, and so forth.

For schools situated in large metropolitan areas, such presentations can be arranged easily, with adequate lead time for planning. In smaller cities, of course, such presentations will require more effort. Usually, however, the necessary arrangements can be made. It has been my experience (and that of others teaching management) that masscomm professionals are generally willing—eager, even—to assist. They have a vested interest, obviously, in cultivating greater understanding of management and its functions. Such an interest is recognized by virtually all professional associations in masscomm, and most of them tend to be helpful in providing panelists. For schools situated in small traditional university towns, a telephone call to the nearest metropolitan area, if sufficient lead time is provided, can produce the needed resource people (also some helpful public relations for the university).

Bringing individual managers in one at a time to talk about their particular enterprises—once a common practice in teaching masscomm management—can reinforce, unfortunately, the idea that such enterprises are quite peculiar and therefore have little in common. Furthermore, a manager given lots of time to talk about his or her business frequently will drift into "war-story-land" or go into a recital of nitty-gritty kinds of detail that add little to the seminar participants' grasp of management's essentials. The presentation of a panel generally avoids such things, however, because its members tend to keep one another on target.

Another note of caution here. Special attention needs to be given during question/answer periods following the panel presentations to preventing such sessions from degenerating into discussions of employment opportunities in a particular field or the local market area, entry-level salaries, writing of resumes and applying for employment, and similar activities more appropriate to the meetings of student organizations in masscomm. Seminars in masscomm management are not the place for establishment of job contacts, networking, arranging internships, or cultivating relationships with prospective employers that can be exploited upon graduation.

Following each panel presentation, an attractive "Certificate of Appreciation"—signed, ideally, by the department's chairperson, dean of the school or college, or director—should be sent to each panelist. That practice is most effective, I've found, in ensuring repeat performances.

TEXTS

Whatever the degree of a professor's own expertise, and the number of outside reading assignments, handouts, and so on, the average group of students still needs the "security blanket" provided by a common textbook. The best available now is John M. Lavine and Daniel B. Wackman, *Managing Media Organizations* (New York, NY: Longman, 1988). It contains an abundance of insights, knowledge, and perspectives on management of masscomm.

Several articles that provide additional perspectives on the teaching of masscomm management have appeared in *Journalism Educator* and related periodicals, and papers presenting different ideas have been read at meetings of journalism/masscomm educators. To keep up to date, one needs to monitor the media management articles in *Journalism Quarterly*.

However, I don't let the text or readings dictate my own course schedule. Rather, I proceed in the following manner, which emphasizes a systems flow and analysis approach.

1. Mass communication system input:
   - The economic condition of U.S. society today, and the resources for masscomm enterprise inherent in that environment;
   - Financial support available to private enterprise (ownership patterns, the trend toward greater concentration of ownership, competition for consumer money and time, etc.);
   - Today's labor force (education, research, and knowledge levels);
   - Modern technology and its application potential;
   - Materials needed (newsprint, etc.);
   - Latitude available under relationship to government, law, etc.
2. Throughput (Process):
   - Management theory;
   - Functions of management (discussed previously);
   - Production method(s);
   - Maintenance of quality.
3. Output:
   - Distribution, dissemination, etc.;
   - Research on market reaction (acceptance of product, etc.).

Problems of law and ethics—like many other educators conducting courses in management, I also teach law and ethics—are discussed as they arise in connection with functions of management and case studies.

From time to time, group analysis and discussion of particular cases in masscomm management is incorporated into the sessions.

Other techniques like computer simulation can be used, and masscomm management adapts itself beautifully to the use of graphic presentations of organization patterns, diagrams explaining systems design, financial accounting/analysis, and so on. Nevertheless, I find that tying the entire course to a method-like case study or to computer simulation of a particular organization's operation is too narrow and restrictive an approach. The tail begins, too often, to wag the dog.

While following my own schedule for discussion sessions throughout the course of study, rather than following the textbook's organization and table of contents, I assign related readings in the textbook, and the text is read in its entirety. Knowledge gleaned from reading the text, as well as that gained from my own presentations and assignments of outside reading, is included on two midterm examinations and the final exam. There are also ten-minute quizzes given from time to time.

The evaluation of each participant's achievement is based on this formula:

Final exam	25%
Hour exam I	15%
Hour exam II	15%
Special projects	25%
Quizzes	10%
Contribution to discussion	10%

For enrichment of the discussion sessions, each participant in the course is urged to acquire a supplementary text related to his or her special area of interest in masscomm management. Quite good books are available on the management of newspapers, magazines, broadcasting stations, public relations, and advertising. They are listed, with many additional sources of such information, in the Lavine/Wackman book. Moreover, a bibliography with about 500 entries is available from the Media Management & Economics Resource Center (MMERC). The center also publishes a newsletter which contains items about masscomm management generally as well as tips on teaching.

Up-to-date news about management practices and problems in the respective media and/or areas of masscomm can be obtained from trade publications like *Editor & Publisher, Broadcasting, Public Relations News, Advertising Age, Folio* (magazine management), *Publisher's Weekly, Electronic Media, Presstime* (a publication of the American

Newspaper Publishers Association), and many other similar periodicals. There are news media in every area of mass communication.

CONCLUSION

Numerous opportunities exist today for one's own continuing education in management. For several years, the Poynter Institute for Media Studies at St. Petersburg, Florida, has awarded special "teaching fellowships" to selected professors of journalism and mass communication, and educators are eligible for management programs conducted by the American Press Institute, Southern Newspaper Publishers Association, and other professional organizations. National, regional, and state meetings of professional associations frequently include sessions on management.

Furthermore, the employee or internal publications ("house organs") of individual companies, like the *Gannetteer* and *Scripps Howard News*, offer helpful perspectives on functions of management. I examine for statistical data and trend perspectives the "Communications Industry Report" published by Veronis, Suhler & Associates. Moreover, every association in the professional field has some kind of newsletter or journal. Most provide free subscriptions to schools and departments of journalism and mass communication. To summarize, there is instructional material galore, and has been for many years, for every area of masscomm management. Pulling it together takes some effort, and precious time, of course.

NOTE

1. The MMERC is now at Northwestern University's Medill School of Journalism.

Chapter 14

MASS COMMUNICATION HISTORY

Maurine H. Beasley

To teach mass communication history successfully, one must be committed to its worth as an integral part of the academic program. During the last three decades, some critics have, unfortunately, attacked journalism history, long the foundation of mass communication history, by contending that it had lost relevance to the main body of knowledge presented in colleges of journalism and communication.[1]

Since these challenges, significant developments have occurred to uplift the entire field. New reference books and textbooks have appeared, scholars have broken away from traditional approaches, a substantial number of monographs and books have been published in journalism history, and efforts have been made to uncover the history of women and minorities in journalism. Organization of a scholarly group devoted solely to the study of journalism history took place in 1981 with the founding of the American Journalism Historians Association. Along with the History Division of the Association for Education in Journalism and Mass Communication (AEJMC), the new organization has encouraged scholars to bring fresh perspectives to the study of journalism history.

Two journals present fresh ideas that can be used to enliven classroom lectures. They are *Journalism History*, published at California State University–Northridge, and *American Journalism*, published by the American Journalism Historians Association. Although *Journalism History*, which published James Carey's attack[2] in its first issue in 1974, is not officially connected with the History Division of AEJMC, it receives a subsidy from that group. While neither group is large, with the History Division having about 450 members and the American

Journalism Historians Association about 300, the fact that the field is able to sustain two separate organizations and publications testifies to its vitality.

Carey, once the preeminent critic, no longer thinks the field is in a desperate situation. In 1985 he wrote: "Today there is no longer any one point of view or fixed school of historiography or single center of training that dominates journalism history."[3] He attributed the change to social movements that have broken down old ideas of history and substituted new ones such as black/white and male/female relations.[4]

BACKGROUND

No current statistics exist on the number of students enrolled in journalism or mass communication history courses. Similarly, there is no information on numbers enrolled in courses that relate to historical study—such as philosophy and ethics. The last surveys of journalism history courses, done a decade ago, offered assurances of the viability of the field. Ted Curtis Smythe of California State University–Fullerton reported in 1981 that journalism history courses were "alive and doing well," according to a survey of schools affiliated with the American Society of Journalism School Administrators, which represented nonaccredited programs.[5] Reg Westmoreland of North Texas State University found in another study published the same year that "journalism history continues to be a popular offering in the curricula of accredited schools and departments."[6]

Both Smythe and Westmoreland determined that relatively few schools required all journalism students to take courses in history within their professional programs. Smythe's data showed that twenty-four schools did not offer separate journalism history courses, covering the subject, if at all, in survey courses or other classes, while of the seventy-three that did offer history, only forty-three required it for some or all sequences. Of the sixty-one accredited programs responding to Westmoreland's survey, sixteen required all majors to take a journalism history course, thirty-five required it in at least one sequence, and five offered it as an elective.

Smythe noted a disturbing trend: The percentage of schools reporting that journalism history was required had dropped dramatically over a ten-year period, from 76 percent of the institutions responding, to 59 percent. This was linked to the growth of sequences in journalism programs that did not require history—sequences in advertising, public relations, broadcasting, and other areas. History traditionally has been required by the news-editorial sequence. It still continues to be in some schools.

The sale of textbooks alone indicates that several thousand students each semester are studying journalism or mass communication history. What is the content of these courses? Should they be required? What textbooks are available? What approaches to the material are taken by successful teachers? Each of these topics will be examined in turn.

ORGANIZATION

To determine what should be taught in a journalism or mass communication history class, one must begin by thinking through the rationale of the course. Traditionally, journalism history traced the growth of the American newspaper from colonial to contemporary times, with a heavy emphasis on the development of professional standards. When journalism schools broadened their focus to include the study of diverse forms of mass communication, journalism history courses often were renamed mass communication courses.

But in many cases the content did not change substantially. Although some attention was given to the rise of electronic journalism, the evolution of mainstream newspapers and, to a much lesser extent, of magazines continued to dominate the subject matter. Very little attention centered on the history of advertising or public relations, in part because almost no research has been done in those areas. Consequently, for many years, instructors had practically no materials on which to draw.

Since newspapers traditionally have been a male-dominated medium (and still are), journalism/mass communication history courses have tended to concentrate on biographical studies of prominent white male editors. These are figures such as Benjamin Franklin, James Gordon Bennett, Horace Greeley, Adolph Ochs, Joseph Pulitzer, William Randolph Hearst. Women and minorities have been virtually excluded, although in recent years many instructors have added a lecture or so on the history of women and minorities. The alternative press has received little attention.

This is not to say that the traditional history/mass communication course has not served a worthwhile purpose. Such courses generally have emphasized the role of the free press in criticizing the government and in serving as a watchdog on behalf of the citizenry. If the purpose of a history/mass communication course is to acquaint students with the origins of contemporary practice and to explain why things are-as-they-are, as well as to introduce students to famous figures within the field, the traditional approach is appropriate, although Carey's criticism should be kept in mind. It also needs to be understood that a cultural history is in the process of being created but still does not exist in a form that can be easily translated to undergraduate classes.

Let us look at the content of a traditional course. Here is a sample syllabus, which represents a compilation of material often covered. The syllabus is divided into nine sections. Under each section key ideas are explained and main points are identified.

History of Mass Communication in the United States
  I.   Historic Roots
       A.   Key Ideas: Origins of a responsible journalism for a
            democratic society; the relationship of journalism to
            government; journalism as a reflection of events.
       B.   Main Points
            1.   News existed before newspapers (e.g., *acta diurna* of
                 ancient Rome and the *gazetta* of Venice)
            2.   First actual newspapers printed in Germany in the 1600s
            3.   Arguments developed in England over press control
                 (e.g., Milton's *Areopagitica*)
            4.   *Oxford Gazette*—first English newspaper appeared
                 (1665)
            5.   Libertarian theory of press evolved in England in the late
                 1600s (this theory parent to social responsibility theory
                 born in the U.S.)
  II. Colonial Period
       A.   Key Ideas: Struggle laid down which still continues—efforts
            of the Establishment to control the news versus attempts of
            private individuals to disclose it without restriction.
       B.   Main Points
            1.   *Publick Occurrences* (1690) published in America by
                 Benjamin Harris
            2.   *Boston News-Letter*, first continuously published
                 American newspaper, appeared (1704); published by John
                 Campbell under the designation "by authority"
            3.   James Franklin unshackled the American press through
                 publication of the *New England Courant* (1721), first
                 continuous unlicensed newspaper

4. "Cato Letters," written by John Trenchard and Thomas Gordon, were published in the *London Journal* (1720–23), widely reprinted and read in the colonies

5. Ben Franklin took over as publisher of the *Pennsylvania Gazette* (1729)

6. Trial of John Peter Zenger (1734–5)—Andrew Hamilton makes case that jury should judge a point of law as well as of fact

III. The Revolutionary Period

A. Key Ideas: The press helped sow the seeds of revolt against the British Crown, and news was subordinated to political ideology particularly spread by pamphlet (e.g., Tom Paine's work).

B. Main Points

1. Colonial newspapers revolted against the extension of the Stamp Act to the colonies (1765)

2. Three political ideas denoted the Revolutionary press—Tory, Whig, and Patriot—or radical

3. Isaiah Thomas, editor of the *Massachusetts Spy*, wrote the most famous news story of the Revolution (on the Battle of Lexington and Concord)

4. Women printers and publishers, particularly Mary Katherine Goddard of the *Maryland Journal*, contributed to journalism

IV. The Party Press Period

A. Key Ideas: Following the Revolution, the press was dominated by political interests eager to influence public opinion even though the electorate was limited.

B. Main Points

1. Hamilton and Jefferson struggled for control of the new government via their respective newspapers; discord, which continues today, began between presidents and the press

   a. Federalists controlled the *Gazette of the United States* (1789), edited by John Fenno, and *Porcupine's Gazette* (1798), edited by William Cobbett

   b. Jeffersonian Republicans (who became the Democratic party) founded the *National Gazette*, edited by Phillip Freneau, and the *Aurora*, edited by Benjamin Franklin Bache

2.   The Alien and Sedition Acts were passed (1798) to control the Anti-Federalist press, but they also recognized truth as a defense in libel

3.   Jefferson, although a firm believer in press freedom, allowed prosecution of the seditious libel case (1804)

4.   Benjamin Towne established the first daily newspaper in America (1783), the *Pennsylvania Evening Post*

5.   Frontier migration created westward expansion of the press

6.   A mob attack on the *Federal Republican* of Baltimore during the War of 1812 raised the still-debated question —when does treason become the outgrowth of honest criticism?

7.   The *Washington Globe*, edited by Francis P. Blair and influenced by Amos Kendall

V.   Newspapers for the Masses

A.   Key Ideas: The period from 1833 to 1883 saw the press turn increasingly to entertainment and news rather than political views as technological advances brought the advent of "the penny press" and the Civil War led to major changes in reporting practices; editors made this the "era of personal journalism"; blacks and women entered journalism.

B.   Main Points

1.   Improvements in printing and paper-making during the early 1830s permitted establishment of the first successful penny paper, the *New York Sun* (1833), edited by Benjamin L. Day

2.   Editors built great publications

a.   James Gordon Bennett—*New York Herald* (1835), known for its newsgathering and sensationalism

b.   Horace Greeley—*New York Tribune* (1841), known for its able staff including Margaret Fuller, first woman foreign correspondent

c.   Henry J. Raymond—*New York Times* (1851), known for balanced and accurate news

d.   Regional editors, as represented by Samuel Bowles III, editor of the *Springfield* (Mass.) *Republican*, built influential publications

3.   Samuel B. Morse invented the telegraph (1844), which increased the speed of news transmission

4. Development of railroads aided in speeding the collection and distribution of news (e.g., Mexican War news)

5. New voices emerged

   a. *Freedom's Journal* (1827), the first black newspaper, edited by the Rev. Samuel Cornish and John Russworm, fought against slavery

   b. Black and white abolitionist editors served to polarize public opinion on slavery (e.g., Frederick Douglass and his *North Star*, black, and William Lloyd Garrison and his *Liberator*, white)

   c. Women defied convention to enter political journalism (e.g., Anne Royall, Jane G. Swisshelm, "Grace Greenwood," and Mary Clemmer Ames)

6. The Civil War dramatically created the "reporter"— an individual who "looks" for news—and spurred the press to take advantage of new technology such as stereotyping (developed about 1861) and the web-perfecting press (which printed on both sides of a continuous roll)

   a. Relations between the government and the press were formalized as battles over censorship occurred

   b. Summary leads and forerunners of headlines appeared as did the forerunners of photojournalism (e.g., *Harper's* and Frank Leslie's *Illustrated Newspaper* and the work of Mathew Brady)

7. After the Civil War, the press revealed the scandals of Grant's administration; the *New York Sun*, rejuvenated by Charles A. Dana, exposed corruption in Congress; and the *New York Times* fought Boss Tweed in New York City

8. Magazines assumed more importance with the *Nation* (1865), founded by E. L. Godkin, reaching an influential audience

9. The Trans-Atlantic cable (1866) connected the United States with Europe, and another cable stretched to the Orient

VI. "New Journalism" Period (1883–World War I)

A. Key Ideas: A wave of sensationalism carried the American press to unprecedented circulations as the daily newspaper became a complex corporate institution; editors like Joseph Pulitzer (*St. Louis Post-Dispatch* and the *New York World*) and William Randolph Hearst (*San Francisco Examiner* and *New*

York Evening Journal) battled for supremacy, while E. W. Scripps (*Cleveland Press* and other newspapers) viewed newspapers as schools for the "working man" and symbols of civic spirit.

B.   Main Points

1.   "Yellow Journalism" (1890–1905) depended on technology (fast presses, halftone photographs, colored ink, typewriters, automatic typesetting machines) to win more and more readers through sensationalized, entertainment-type content (e.g., Richard Outcault's "Yellow Kid," a comic-strip figure)

2.   Wire services (Associated Press reorganized in 1900) and United Press (founded 1907) gathered news from all over the world, fitting it into a formula acceptable to publications of different political views; the advent of the telephone in the 1870s aided newsgathering enormously

3.   Women "stunt girls" and "sob sisters" (e.g., "Nellie Bly") were exploited to concoct news

4.   Hearst and Pulitzer whipped up public support for the Spanish-American War

5.   Crusading in the public interest led to "muckraking," a series of reform crusades conducted by investigative journalists (e.g., Ida Tarbell, Lincoln Steffins, and Ray Stannard Baker of *McClure's* magazine)

VII.   World War I and "Jazz Journalism" Period (1914–1930)

A.   Key Ideas: Mass communication was used to mobilize the public for war; disillusionment after the war helped produce climate for tabloid "gutter sheets" of the Roaring '20s; revolutionary developments in photojournalism attuned the public to visual images; newsmagazines were started to "organize" the news.

B.   Main Points

1.   The Committee on Public Information, headed by George Creel, established a record for accuracy as the government's World War I propaganda arm

2.   Adolph S. Ochs made the *New York Times* the premier paper of record during World War I, but the *Times* failed to support civil liberties during the "Red Scare"

3.   Joseph Medill Patterson founded the *New York Daily News* (1919), capitalizing on the new technology of photography to draw millions of new readers to tabloid journalism

4. *Time* magazine (1923) was started by Henry R. Luce and Briton Hadden to compartmentalize the news for "the busy man"; Luce also started *Life* (1936)

VIII. The Press After 1930

A. Key Ideas: The newspaper declined as the prime medium for spot news; the Depression of the 1930s, which led to massive intervention in the economy by Roosevelt's "New Deal," created a need for explanatory or interpretative journalism; the press complied with restrictions during World War II and the Korean conflict but became increasingly critical of government action in the Vietnam period, culminating in the Pentagon papers case and the Watergate revelations; public debate arose over journalistic performance.

B. Main Points

1. Concentration of ownership and newspaper monopolies in most cities marked the newspaper field

2. Newspaper personnel organized to improve conditions (American Newspaper Guild founded in 1933)

3. Interpretative journalism gave rise to influential columnists (e.g., Walter Lippmann) and to attempts by Roosevelt and other presidents to "manage" relationships with journalists

4. The government instituted control of the media during World War II through the Office of Censorship and the Office of War Information

5. The mainstream media, in sympathy with the aims of World War II, made no objection to government actions, which included surveillance of the black press

6. Eleanor Roosevelt's White House press conferences for women only helped women gain recognition in journalism, but women were forced out of newspaper jobs after World War II ended

7. Journalists, trained to be accepting of authority, found themselves manipulated by the red-baiting Senator Joseph McCarthy during the Cold War

8. The civil rights struggle and the Vietnam era brought the press into conflict with established government authority; this climaxed in the *New York Times*'s decision to publish the Pentagon papers and the *Washington Post*'s investigation of Watergate

9. Protest journalism arose in the 1960s (underground newspapers and a new "New Journalism," which involved use of literary techniques)

10. Movement for public accountability resulted in external and internal examination of journalism (e.g., journalism reviews)

IX. Age of Electronic Journalism

A. Key Ideas: Radio and then television created a new technology which refused to translate into print, challenged the newspaper for advertising and audience, and changed the way in which news was presented; unlike the print media, broadcasting outlets were licensed by the government.

B. Main Points

1. Italian physicist Guglielmo Marconi applied for the first British patent for wireless telegraphy (1896) and Dr. Lee DeForest improved the vacuum tube (1906), making possible the transmission of voice broadcasting

2. Commercial radio began as a way of promoting newspapers and other companies (e.g., *WWJ* and the *Detroit News*)

3. Motion picture newsreels, often showing faked events, reached a large segment of the public during the first half of the 20th century

4. Radio networks were extended coast to coast (1927), and Congress established the Federal Radio Commission

5. Radio news proved itself during World War II (e.g., Edward R. Murrow's broadcasts from Europe)

6. Commercial telecasting began (1941) but was slowed by World War II; by 1949 there were 108 television stations, and television soon blanketed the nation

7. Murrow's "See It Now" programs represented the golden age of television news (1950s)

8. Telstar was launched in 1962, making possible instantaneous inter-continental transmission of news and pictures

9. Television news changed news coverage in print (1960s and 1970s), leading to more soft news and entertainment; television coverage of Vietnam brought war home as never before to Americans; television led to death of picture magazines and to new forms of newspapers (e.g., *USA Today*, 1982)

As the sample syllabus makes plain, there is no lack of material to cover in a mass communication history course. Numerous questions arise: Is the context too narrow? Should methods of historical research themselves be considered? Should broad topics like literacy itself and technology be covered in more depth? Does a course of this sort truly address the needs of advertising and public relations students? Is a student likely to get bogged down in detail? Should the roles of women, radicals, blacks, and other minority groups be given far more attention? All of these points need to be addressed in a discussion of whether a mass communication history course should be required.

In a national survey of philosophies, practices, and problems related to journalism history courses, Fred Endres found two chief rationales given for offering these classes.[7] One was "internal," to pass on the traditions of journalism, while the other was external, to offer an "interdisciplinary perspective," linking the development of journalism to American economic, political, and cultural history.[8] Either reason might be seen as a rationale for requiring the course, but in each instance questions immediately arise as to the wisdom of doing so.

Today journalism education is flooded with students interested in areas allied to, but still quite different from, traditional newspapers. Accredited schools require students to take at least ninety hours of work outside journalism. That leaves only thirty hours of professional coursework in journalism. With the majority of students seeking careers in advertising, public relations, broadcasting, or other communications fields, is it justifiable to compel students to take a course that deals mainly with newspaper traditions? It may well be, but if student interest is to be maintained, instructors need to develop materials that pertain to the history of advertising and public relations as well as to the history of communication theory.

If, on the other hand, the rationale is to link the story of journalism to broad trends in American history, then instructors still are confronted with an enormous challenge. How does one cover an infinite amount of material in one semester? Why teach a history course that is outside of the history department? How does one overcome student resistance to history in general, particularly if the class is so large that instructors tend to rely on objective tests of the "names and dates" variety?

One of the best reasons for not requiring a mass communication history course is class size. If the course is required, financial and scheduling considerations may force the course to be taught to hundreds of students in a large lecture setting. Although the occasional instructor may be able to teach effectively in such a situation, most find it almost impossible. Some devise techniques to deal with large groups that involve dramatizations, audio-visual materials, and even comedy routines. While these may represent good teaching, depending on the personality and skill of the instructor as well as the worth of the materials presented, they frequently substitute entertainment for education.

In short, if mass communication history courses are required, they should not be seen simply as tradition-laden classes that ought to be administered to students like bad-tasting medicine because they are "good for them." Instead, history classes must be updated to current realities of the curriculum. They also need to be viewed as valid history courses that interpret history from a communications perspective. Although many scholars are working toward that end, perhaps it is not an unfair statement to say that the ideal course remains to be developed.

TEXTS

Textbooks represent key elements in the teaching of mass communication history courses, although some instructors prefer separate readings supplemented by works on American history. Of course, not all instructors do, or should, use texts the same way. Nevertheless, for many instructors, textbooks are crucial elements in structuring courses.

Currently the field of mass communication history offers three main texts.[9]

Edwin and Michael Emery, *The Press in America: An Interpretive History of the Mass Media* (Englewood Cliffs, NJ: Prentice-Hall, 1990). Now in its sixth edition, this book offers detailed information touching on all forms of media.

Jean Folkerts and Dwight L. Teeter, *Voices of a Nation: A History of the Media in the United States* (New York: Macmillan, 1989). Divided into four chronological parts, with brief introductory essays for each part, aimed at giving thematic overviews. Easier to read than the Emery book, but unlike Emery and Emery, it contains little material on the last two decades.

William David Sloan, James G. Stovall, and James D. Startt, eds., *The Media in America* (Worthington, OH: Publishing Horizons, 1989). Eighteen scholars contributed.

Instructors using these books or separate readings still have the challenging task of making the mass communication history course come alive for students. One way is to use a "show-and-tell" approach, sending students to libraries to look at actual publications of various periods and to report on them to the class. Another is to have students pick mass communication professionals from history who can be their own "role models" for professional excellence. A third way is to introduce students to primary source material by having them explore university archives, community newspaper offices, and local libraries for unpublished material pertaining to the history of the media around them. A fourth way is to have them do oral history interviews with veteran professionals.

The list of ways in which inventive teachers can breathe life into mass communication history courses is almost endless. A good source of new ideas is *CLIO*, the quarterly newsletter of the History Division of the Association for Education in Journalism and Mass Communication. Often successful approaches are presented at meetings of both the History Division and the American Journalism Historians Association.

CONCLUSION

Today mass communication history is still very much a challenge. The instructor needs to think carefully about the course rationale and devise an appropriate approach, always attempting to communicate to students the inherent fascination of the field of history itself.

NOTES

1. James W. Carey, "The Problem of Journalism History," *Journalism History* 1 (Spring 1974): 3. Carey listed reasons given for the low status of the field.

2. Carey's criticism of journalism history was that it was a myriad of great or significant person biographies that was outmoded; see Carey, "The Problem of Journalism History."

3. "'Putting the World at Peril,' " A conversation with James W. Carey, *Journalism History* 12 (Summer 1985): 38.

4. Ibid., 40.

5. Ted Curtis Smythe, "Journalism History Enrollment Trends," *CLIO* (Newsletter of the AEJMC History Division) (Summer 1981): 1.

6. Reg Westmoreland, "J-History Course Very Much Alive in AASDJ Schools," *Journalism Educator* 35 (January 1981): 12.

7. Fred F. Endres, "Philosophies, Practices and Problems in Teaching Journalism History," *Journalism History* 5 (Spring 1978): 1.

8. Ibid., 30.

9. For a composite review of media history texts, see Karen List, "Journalism History Textbooks and Their Uses," *American Journalism* (Spring 1990): 114–18.

Chapter 15

MASS MEDIA AND POLITICS

Dan Nimmo

Course work in the area of mass media and politics comprises one dimension of not only the field of *mass communication*, which has been a field of communication studies for decades, but also of the newer and expanding cognate field of teaching and research designated as *political communication*. This has not always been the case. As short a time as a quarter of a century ago, the course in mass media and politics at most institutions of higher education—if such a course existed at all—constituted the whole of the content of the merging field of political communication. Today political communication offerings are far more numerous and diverse in content. Included are separate courses in political language/linguistics, political rhetoric, public opinion, public relations and politics, political advertising, communication and political decision making, and others—along with such staples as communication in election campaigns and government-press relations. Moreover, such courses are located in a variety of academic departments including mass communication, journalism, public relations, broadcasting, political science, sociology, linguistics, and elsewhere.

Given the pluralist, perhaps even fragmented, development of the field of political communication, it is necessary when discussing a single course, in this case one titled Mass Media and Politics, to distinguish it at the outset from at least two other course offerings with which it frequently overlaps. First, although mass media and politics, as noted above, once served as the core survey course in political communication—and still does in institutions with limited curricula in political communication—the rich diversity of the generic field is currently such that it is too much to expect that a single course in mass media and politics can bear that burden. Today a survey course must treat in detail several key areas: political symbolism, political communicators, language and politics, campaigns and elections, political media (interpersonal, organizational, and mass), institutional communication, policy making, international communication, and many more. By contrast, a course in mass media and politics is a specialized offering within that overall context and must be so designed and taught.

Second, the mass media and politics course should be distinguished from another specialized offering with which it is often confused, the skills course in political campaigning. The typical fare of such skills courses includes hands-on instruction in organizing campaigns, conducting polls, speech writing, preparing press releases, designing ad copy, scripting and shooting television commercials, and other techniques used to win political office. Frequently instruction in campaign skills takes place within the context of a simulated election campaign involving members of the class. Such courses are valuable instructional experiences for both the teacher and student. However, their foci of necessity are more narrow and, frequently, more a-theoretical than a general course in mass media and politics.

Within the context described, that is, of the more encompassing fields of mass communication and political communication, this essay describes the general contours of the specialized course in mass media and politics. It considers generic topics included in the course content, possible exercises and resources, available texts, and additional relevant materials. It omits many of the topics that would be included in a political communication survey course as well as efforts to instruct students in campaign skills. The purpose of the course in mass media and politics described here is to provide students with an understanding of how and why, in the contemporary world, mass media and politics are conjoint activities comprising a single, seamless process. To say "politics" in the contemporary era is, in large measure, to say "mass media" and vice versa.

Before describing the course content, organizational possibilities, resource materials, textbooks, and supplementary materials, a word is in order regarding evaluation procedures for students. The course assumes two or three examinations during the semester along with a comprehensive final. In addition there is a minimum of one written assignment based upon student research and a minimum of one oral presentation. Overall grades reflect a weighting of the various examinations, written materials, and oral presentations, a weighting that varies from one semester to another depending upon the varying content emphases of the course.

BACKGROUND

Depending on a host of factors, individual instructors will prepare course outlines and syllabi that differ markedly in organization, scheduling, assignments, and so on. What follows is a discussion of the minimum set of topics that would be included in a typical course and a rationale for them and their content. At the close of each segment of the essay describing a course section, there is an outline of suggested topics summarizing the discussion. Those outlines assume a one-semester course, normally enrolling advanced undergraduates; it would be necessary to tailor the course outline for other instructional situations.

One of the key problems in approaching a course in mass media and politics is that students typically take for granted, without reflection, that they "know" what politics and the mass media "are." Politics "is" what an abstract set of persons called "politicians" do—usually a self-serving enterprise, limited (depending upon the sophistication of the student) to relatively small numbers in the nation's capital. The mass media "is" TV. (Obviously, if introductory courses in government/political science and mass communication are prerequisites for a course in mass media and politics, students can be expected to have broadened understandings. However, such prerequisites are not always the case; even when they are, the instructor's expectations are often not realized.) An initial task, then, is to deal in concrete ways with three very broad concepts—*power*, *politics*, and *mass media*.

Whether providing information, entertainment, babysitting, background diversion, or whatever, the media act as *political* institutions. As David Altheide so deftly argues, to speak of media is to speak of "media power."[1] A useful place to begin a course in mass media and politics is with consideration of the nature of power in the everyday lives of students themselves, then extend the discussion to less directly experienced arenas of power. There are several ways of doing this. One is straightforward, that is, to provoke discussion of power relations among the students as they are acting within the here-and-now of the classroom setting: who speaks, who doesn't; who argues, who acquiesces; who pays attention, who escapes—these are all matters involving power, authority, and participation. By extension, discussion can move to power in other settings: family, courtship, getting an auto repaired, shopping, having hair styled, trying to find employ-ment, and all manner of other everyday occurrences. Once students grasp that their daily lives are replete with power situations, they have no difficulty in adding their own "for instances" and "it's like" (to use their vernacular). It is then possible to move to the more remote dimensions of political power to provide students an essential theoretical grounding—that is, power as normally associated with "politicians."

Gaming exercises provide another entree to the power discussion. A useful resource here is Michael Laver's *Playing Politics*.[2] Laver provides a series of nine classroom games; two of those offer ex-perience in basic power relations, "Primitive Politics" and "Entrepreneur." Each pits students against one another in competi-tion to allocate and coordinate power resources and values. (Laver's games are suggestions; instructors will have little difficulty originat-ing equally provocative exercises.)

ORGANIZATION

Whatever the approach, the intent is to present the relationship of power and politics so as to impress students with a sense that politics is not an activity removed from their lives but one at the core of much they do. With that in mind, politics is no longer "them" but "us." Also "us" is the mass media. There are several resource materials, from which appropriate selections can be assigned as readings, to which instructors can turn in fashioning lecture and/or discussion topics exploring the political status of the mass media as diversified power complexes.[3] It is particularly helpful to the student to tie what media power complexes do (inform, entertain, advertise, etc.) to everyday living. As is the case with everyday politics, media influence is not abstract and remote, for there is an everyday mediation of students' lives via mass media.

A summary outline of this opening section of the course is as follows:

I.   Introduction: Power, Politics, and the Mass Media
   A.   Power Relations for Us and Them
      1.   Power in everyday discourse and life
      2.   Power at large: a general definition of power
   B.   Coping with Power's Tensions: The Art of Politics

      1.   Politics in everyday life

      2.   What politicians do: a definition of politics

  C. Enter the Mass Media

      1.   Using the mass media in practicing daily power

      2.   The mass media as political power complexes

This portion of the course has two aspects. The first deals with areas involving overt political activities, relationships, and content of the mass media; the second involves consideration of the latent, less clearly visible political content in media messages.

Central to any course in mass media and politics are selected topics: (1) the mass media and public opinion; (2) mass media and electoral politics; (3) government-press relations; (4) mass media in policy making; (5) the mass media role in international politics; and (6) crisis politics and the mass media. A must resource that provides an overall assessment of key ideas in many of these areas is Walter Lippmann's classic 1922 treatise, *Public Opinion*.[4] Granted, the work is almost seven decades old, it is primarily remembered for Lippmann's discussion of stereotypes, and he made no allowances for the electronic media yet to dominate the scene. Yet, Lippmann's accounts of the nature of news and the news media, public opinion, governmental institutions, and problems of enlightened self-government hold insight for those attempting to describe and analyze the political role of the mass media today.

Among the matters for class consideration in each of the six areas listed above a partial listing would be as follows.

Mass Media and Public Opinion. In discussion, it is essential to ponder the nature of the public, the mass, and public opinion as well as whether public opinion exists and, if so, how we know it. This introduces such topics as the political roles of groups, organizations, mass movements, crowds, and other social aggregates. Here students can be invited to prepare arguments regarding the role of the mass media in covering politics versus promoting selected social interests in competition with one another. Murray Edelman's analyses are excellent background resources for these topics.[5]

In addition, the topic of what people learn about politics, that is, political socialization, is appropriate for consideration at this point. An excellent student exercise is to assign each class member the task of preparing a brief "political media autobiography" comparing the earliest political events students can recall learning about through media coverage (and what they remember about them) to more recent recollections. The exercise serves two purposes. First, it reveals to students how much of the politics outside their daily lives (i.e., directly experienced politics) consists of the secondhand realities provided by the mass media. Second, the exercise serves as a jolting reminder to instructors of how short a political life span their students have experienced (only dimly recalling, for example, having seen an incumbent Democratic U.S. president on TV!).

Mass Media and Electoral Politics. There is no dearth of materials concerning the contemporary role of this topic. Definitely to be included are lectures and discussions on news coverage of presidential primaries; news coverage of general election campaigns; broadcast debates between candidates; print and televised political advertising; the role of professional political consultants in shaping mass media responses to campaigns and candidates; horserace and/or issue coverage of election contests; and election night coverage and analysis.

Of the above lecture/discussion items, students have considerable exposure to televised political advertising, particularly during election years. Given the existence of various archives of such commercials and the relative ease of taping televised ads, it is useful to compile tapes and to devise class exercises for critiquing ads. (For example, instructors can obtain compilation tapes tailored to their particular students' backgrounds and interests from the Political Commercial Archive, University of Oklahoma). Of particular value to instructors and students in suggesting guidelines for such analysis is Hugh Rank's *The Pitch*.[6] Rank's "30-second Spot Quiz" for the analysis of both product and political ads is a four-step procedure that students can readily grasp and apply.

For those teachers having access to computer instructional facilities, two computer simulations emphasizing the relationship of the mass media to electoral politics are available. One is provided under the auspices of the American Political Science Association program of "APSA Setups" (Supplementary Empirical Teaching Units in Political Science). It is entitled *Elections and the Mass Media*. The other is provided via the publication, *Campaigns & Elections*. Under the authorship of Murray Fishel, David Gopoian, and J. Michael Stacey, *On the Campaign Trail: The Ultimate Campaign Computer Simulation* offers a brief textbook, workbook, personal computer diskette, and instructor's guide.

Government-Press Relations. A key aspect in introducing students to this general topic is to specify similarities and contrasts in those relations deriving from differing institutional complexes (executive, bureaucratic, legislative, and judicial) of government and of mass media (newspapers, newsmagazines, opinion media, radio, over-the-air and cable TV, etc.). In addition to lectures based upon general resource materials, it is useful to provide illustrations of such similarities and contrasts by examining coverage in differing media of events/issues involving various governing bodies. For example, the confirmation hearings and later rejection in 1987 of Robert Bork as appointee to the Supreme Court involved executive nomination, Federal Bureau of Investigation and other bureaucratic processing, legislative testimony and voting, and controversy over the judicial office at stake—all covered extensively in all news media. Samples of print and video treatment of the story from various media perspectives, along with excerpts of the Cable Satellite Public Affairs Network's (C-SPAN) coverage of the Congressional hearings, are readily available for compilation and examination.

Mass Media in Policy Making. This topic is a sparsely researched area. Consequently, course instruction is limited in part by a lack of materials. However, the general rubric under which the topic can be approached most fruitfully is agenda setting—more specifically, exploring how the issue agendas of citizens are set by the relative emphases given various social problems by the news media, and how policy agendas are set by the joint influences of media emphases and political pressures. To follow this line of thinking, instructors may find it helpful to link two largely separate bodies of literature dealing with agenda setting. One consists of theory and research conducted by scholars in mass communication,[7] the other by political scientists.[8] Both lines of thinking suggest a variety of subtopics and case studies that can be readily adapted to classroom use.

Mass Media Role in International Politics. The impact of mass media in this area is a major one. From William Randolph Hearst's widely debated provocation of the Spanish-American War, through former CBS News anchor Walter Cronkite's joint interview of Egyptian President Anwar Sadat and Israeli Prime Minister Menachem Begin, to television's coverage of and role in movements for reform in the Philippines and China, there are numerous examples of the controversies spawned by the impact of news coverage on international relations. Fortunately, there are several convenient resource materials available. Moreover, with the advent of the VCR, it is convenient to compile tapes of such materials as ABC's "Nightline" and PBS's "Frontline," both of which are replete with examples of mass media participation in, as well as coverage of, international events.

Crisis Politics and the Mass Media. Mass media's coverage of political crises—such as terrorist acts, seizures of hostages, political protests, armed confrontation, and so on—merits consideration in any course on mass media and politics. A key question for class consideration is whether news coverage of such crises, thereby providing publicity for terrorists, kidnappers, protestors, and so on, is itself a major cause of the crises. Useful source materials for exploring the nature of crisis, along with suggestions for the use of case materials, including videotapes of crisis coverage, can be derived from *Nightly Horrors* by Dan Nimmo and James E. Combs.[9]

Not all of the political fare in the mass media consists of news, interpretation, editorials, commentary, and discussion. Much of popular programming on television, the diverting content of newspapers ("Dear Abby" or cartoon strips), play content in magazines, and entertainment in popular movies carry implicit political messages—about power structures and relationships; the political and social status and standing of racial, gender, and ethnic groups; the nature of political enterprises such as space exploration, war, conquest, and combat against drug abuse, diseases, or crime. (To take popular movies as an example, an excellent guide to their political content, explicit and implicit, is Terry Christensen's 1987 book *Reel Politics.*[10])

The purpose of this section of the course is to assist students in developing a critical attitude toward such latent political messages in mass media "texts." Numerous source materials are available to instructors providing examples of textual readings. An insightful series of essays aimed specifically at political texts, which introduces instructors to analytical frameworks derived from contemporary modes of political language analysis, is Michael Shapiro's *Language and Politics.*[11] More readily comprehended and applied by students in class exercises is the scheme developed by Hugh Rank in *The Pep Talk: How to Analyze Political Language.*[12] Also helpful are selected articles appearing in the professional journal, *Critical Studies in Mass Communication.* Each issue of the journal contains critical analyses of political content in horror films, TV shows, cartoons, rock music, and other forms of popular culture. One of many possible class projects that can be used in addressing this topic is to ask each student to select a single prime time televised series—say "The Cosby Show," "Golden Girls," "Murder, She Wrote"—and, having provided instruction in textual analysis, require a written or oral critique of the latent political content encountered.

Again, to summarize, a syllabus outline for this second major portion of the course would be as follows:

II. Politics in the Mass Media
   A. Conventional News and Public Affairs Topics
      1. Mass media and public opinion
      2. Mass media and electoral politics
      3. Government-press relations: news management and newsgathering
      4. Mass media in policy making
      5. Mass media and international politics
      6. Mass media and political crises
   B. Unconventional Politics

Certainly one of the principal topics of concern for scholars of mass communication with respect to political matters has been the effects that the mass media have upon the political attitudes, values, and behavior of audience members. There has been considerable speculation, research, and theorizing about those effects. This section of the course endeavors to summarize and explain posited effects. There are several approaches to the discussion and classification of effects. One convenient approach is to distinguish for the student media-centered, source-centered, message-centered, and audience-centered effects. Whatever the mode selected, however, there are numerous mass media textbooks that discuss effects, thus providing instructors with guidelines appropriate to the level of the course and student backgrounds encountered.

One of the earliest, and still argued in some circles, theories of media effects is that of the "all powerful media" school. Variously labeled the "hypodermic" or "bullet" theory, the view held sway for several decades. A discussion of it—its origins, impact on how people began to think of the mass media, policy implications, and limits—is a convenient starting point. In incremental steps the instructor can then move to other theories of effects in the media-centered tradition, but which move away from direct to marginal media effects: agenda setting, cultivation theory, the knowledge gap hypothesis, social versus perceptual effects as contrasted in the views of Harold Adams Innis and Marshall McLuhan, and a return to preliterate politics as a function of the growth of the electronic media.[13]

The sources of political messages in the mass media are individuals, that is, political leaders (office-holders, interest spokespersons, and candidates), political journalists, political analysts and private citizens, and political organizations and institutions ("Congress," "ABC News," etc.). There is a body of research that probes the relationship between characteristics of personal sources—particularly the credibility of individual sources—and the persuasive effects of messages. Another body of research explores the relationship between the confidence that citizens have in social, political, religious, and economic institutions, and persuasive effects. Standard texts in mass media and politics (see below) provide guides to both bodies of research.

Several scholarly traditions focus attention on the relationship of message content to effects: rhetorical theory, experimental studies probing message structure and organization, argumentation theory, forms of textual analysis alluded to earlier, content analysis of themes in political messages, language analysis, and so on. The works of political scientists Doris Graber and Paul Corcoran provide succinct guides to such traditions.[14]

A prime consequence of the scholarly debunking of the "all powerful media" view was to locate media effects in audience perceptions—a move away from the concept of a passive, mindless, reactive audience to that of an active-minded, responsive audience constructing meaning out of media messages. The shift was summed up in the phrase that became fashionable, that is, what is key is not what the media do to audiences but what audiences do with the media. Numerous research efforts produced theories of audience-centered effects: uses and gratifications theory, play theory, spiral of silence theory, parasocial theory, diffusion analysis, accommodation theory—to name but a few. The problem of instruction posed by the abundance of such audience-centered theories of effects is to avoid leaving the impression that research produces nothing more than an ever-lengthening laundry list. One safeguard against that tendency is continuously to return (not only in this section but in all sections of the course) to the framework sketched at the beginning, that is, asking students to relate "effects" to the principal concern of the course—the joint relationships of media, power, and politics. Students will recognize that some posited media-, source-, message-, and audience-centered effects are political by their very nature; others are less so; others are not.

A topical summary for the course section on mass media effects is as follows:

III.   Political Effects of the Mass Media
    A.   Media-Centered Effects
        1.   The all powerful media view
        2.   Agenda setting

3. Cultivation theory
4. The posited knowledge gap
5. Social vs. perceptual determinism
6. Return to preliteracy

B. Source-Centered Effects
1. Credibility views
2. Confidence in institutions

C. Message-Centered Effects

D. Audience-Centered Effects
1. Uses and gratifications
2. Play theory
3. Spiral of silence theory
4. Parasocial theory
5. Diffusion theories
6. Accommodation theory

The closing section of the course highlights disputes and controversies. Some of these issues touch upon interpretations of research purporting to explain the media, power, politics mix. Others involve matters of doctrinal preference. And others deal with philosophical differences. In any event, selected issues provide the instructor with an opportunity to provoke class discussion and to ask students to draw upon what has transpired earlier. Exercises can include debates, preparation of position papers, or various forms of simulation, depending upon the time and resources available.

One set of issues that flows from the course section on effects is that of direct versus minimal effects of the mass media on political behavior. Enough has been introduced on that topic to promote class discussion. It is useful at this point to move from the consideration of *effects* on individuals to the political *impact* of mass media on the policy as a whole. Here the issue of media hegemony, that is, whether the mass media shape a dominant pattern of political life and thought, can be introduced. Juxtaposed to the hegemonic viewpoint are those arguing that the mass media supplant political logic with media logic, the view that the mass media are the prime institutions in negotiating social order (even if not all powerful), and the argument that people live in a world of mediated politics rather than directly experienced politics.

A second set of key issues derives less from research into media effects and impact—and the interpretation of findings—than from philosophical controversies. For example, a course in mass media and politics should debate the issue of the freedom of mass media. Several topics are relevant: government control over and manipulation of information and the mass media (censorship, security classifications, orchestration of political events); slander and libel laws; and doctrines of fairness, equal time, and popular access to the media. Ethical issues are also numerous: the accountability of the news media; dimensions of confrontational journalism; media staging of events; fabrication of news sources; journalistic probing of the private lives of public figures; friendships between journalists and official news sources; conflicts of interest of journalists; and a code of ethics for journalists. Economic disputes include the influence of audience ratings on news programming; sponsorship and advertising censorship of public affairs content of the media; the role of economic conglomerates in the news industry; the decline in the number of cities with competitive newspapers; the homogeneity of newsmagazines competing for the same market share; the impact of celebrity journalists in politics. Finally, there is an overarching political issue, that is, to what degree has representative democracy, which involves governance by accountable intermediary elective and appointive officials, been supplanted by a mass democracy through mediating (media) institutions?

A summary topical outline for the closing section of the course highlighting these issues:

IV.   Issues in the Mass Media-Politics Relationship
    A.   Issues in Political Effects and Impact
    B.   Continuing Controversies
        1.   Media freedom and accountability
        2.   Ethical considerations
        3.   Economic questions
        4.   Media/political power

TEXTS

Throughout this essay pertinent sources have been cited providing instructors with background material for various topics. For the most part those sources are specialized as to subject matter. With respect to the overall course in mass media and politics, and to materials that students might read to obtain an overall view, there are relatively few textbooks currently on the market. What is more common are texts for more generic courses surveying the whole of political communication, or texts in specialized topic areas such as communication in election campaigns, political persuasion, or political news coverage. Here we consider texts primarily focusing upon mass media and politics that cover the range of topics described in this essay.

> Lance Bennett, *News: The Politics of Illusion* (New York: Longman, 1988). Develops a framework for thinking about mass media and politics. In its revised edition, focuses upon the relationship of reporters and officials.

> Doris Graber, *Mass Media and American Politics* (Washington, DC: Congressional Quarterly Press, 1988). Graber is meticulous in relating the results of empirical research to each topic considered.

> David L. Paletz and Robert M. Entman, *Media Power Politics* (New York: The Free Press, 1981). Another text with a point of view, it explores the effects of television, newspapers, and newsmagazines on the distribution of power in America. Now dated, it is useful as a supplement.

> Charles Press and Kenneth Verburg, *American Politicians and Journalists* (Glenview, Ill.: Scott, Foresman and Company, 1988). Places the "star-crossed romance" of politicians and journalists within a broader institutional setting.

Also, avowedly intended as supplementary is *Mediated Political Realities* by Dan Nimmo and James E. Combs (New York: Longman, 2nd rev. ed., 1989). The text argues that citizens seldom experience the multiple, complex, and contradictory realities of politics directly; instead mass and group media fashion simplified, single pictures of politics presented in the form of dramatic fantasies. The mass media covered in this text include not only the news media but popular magazines, movies, sports, religion, and movements.

CONCLUSION

It should be clear from this brief survey that no single text will suffice for a course in mass media and politics. As new textbooks appear on the market, this may change, although the likelihood of any one text filling all of the instructor's needs is small. Depending upon the mix of topics selected by the instructor, it will be necessary to adopt a combination of texts and/or separate readings.

NOTES

1. David L. Altheide, *Media Power* (Beverly Hills, CA: Sage, 1985).

2. Michael Laver, *Playing Politics* (New York: Penguin, 1979).

3. See particularly Altheide, *Media Power*, op. cit., and Andrew King, *Power & Communication* (Prospect Heights, IL: Waveland Press, 1987).

4. Walter Lippmann, *Public Opinion* (New York: Macmillan, 1922).

5. Murray Edelman, *Political Language* (New York: Academic Press, 1977).

6. Hugh Rank, *The Pitch* (Park Forest, IL: The Counter-Propaganda Press, 1984).

7. Donald L. Shaw and Maxwell E. McCombs, *The Emergence of Political Issues* (St. Paul, MN: West, 1977).

8. Roger W. Cobb and Charles D. Elder, *Participation in American Politics: The Dynamics of Agenda Setting* (Baltimore, MD: The Johns Hopkins University Press, 1975).

9. Dan Nimmo and James E. Combs, *Nightly Horrors* (Knoxville, TN: University of Tennessee Press, 1985).

10. Terry Christensen, *Reel Politics* (New York: Basil Blackwell, 1987).

11. Michael Shapiro, ed., *Language and Politics* (New York: New York University Press, 1984).

12. Hugh Rank, *The Pep Talk* (Prospect Heights, IL: The Counter-Propaganda Press, 1984).

13. Consult James W. Carey, "Harold Adams Innis and Marshall McLuhan," *Antioch Review* (Spring 1968): 5–39; and Paul Corcoran, *Political Language and Rhetoric* (Austin: University of Texas Press, 1979).

14. See Doris Graber, "Political Languages," in Dan Nimmo and Keith Sanders, eds., *Handbook of Political Communication* (Beverly Hills, CA: Sage, 1981), 195–223; and Paul Corcoran, "Political Language," in David Swanson and Dan Nimmo, eds., *New Directions in Political Communication: A Resource Book* (Newbury Park, CA: Sage, 1990).

Chapter 16

MEDIA CRITICISM

Michael A. Russo

For the twenty or so students usually enrolled in an upper division course in media criticism at Saint Mary's College, a small liberal arts college near San Francisco, the goal is to get behind the illusory world of film and television for the purpose of introducing criteria, strategies, and sensibilities essential to criticism. As described in this essay, among its chief features is a four-day tour of the "Entertainment Capital of the World," Hollywood, California. One further introductory note: our institution maintains a four-one-four schedule, which includes a January term, thus providing an opportunity for students to concentrate on a single course and allow for a travel component.

In the opinion of students, the course meets with a measure of success in both expected and unexpected ways. For example, following a first venture into Hollywood—complete with lectures, seminars, screenings, and a "behind-the-scenes" look at the studios—we returned to the everyday "less glamorous" life of the classroom. The session opened with a roundtable discussion of what we had experienced the previous week, and I heard comments that the course had shattered illusions and dreams about the "world of Hollywood." I explained to the students that, indeed, one aspect of this course may be a shattering of illusion, dreams, and myths, since all of film and television deals with illusions.

Thus, the purpose of the course is to get behind the mystique and fantasy in order to render an understanding of the layers of meaning that surround film and video narratives—an understanding that must include the economic and commercial environment of an industry that creates visual and written texts. This has become an essential goal, namely, to develop a sensibility about film and television, and also to express in conversation and written form those associations, ideas, comments, and appreciations.

BACKGROUND

We live at a time when everyone is a media critic. And, perhaps, that's a clue to the importance our culture attributes to film and television generally.[1] Two experiences drawn from my own education may help illustrate the design of the media criticism course.

When I was a student at Seton Hall Preparatory School in New Jersey, our high school shared the South Orange campus with a growing university. With classroom space being scarce, occasionally high school and college students took courses in close proximity. Moreover, several of the faculty taught on both the high school and college level. The instructor who taught us religion also had a part-time appointment in the college psychology department. He had an avid interest in two professionally related subjects, namely sex and the movies.

One day two professors from the college English department stopped by our class and attempted to sign us up for the newly created "Film Society." We were informed that we would get "extra credit" for attending film showings since "these movies would teach us about life," something we had not previously experienced according to the instructor. Among the first viewings was Fellini's *La Dolce Vita*. My initial impressions of Anita Ekberg awash in a Roman fountain made me concur with my teacher. Now I eagerly wanted to know more about life. During these months we watched an amazing list of wonderful movies: *Seven Samurai; Jules and Jim*; Lawrence Olivier's *Henry V; On the Waterfront; Wild Strawberries*.

Into this picture came a member of the college English department, Father William Keller, who was on hand to act as our interpreter, guide, and discussion leader. It was here that I came to appreciate the difference between high school and college learning. Keller did not fear any comment, idea, laughter, or criticism. Since most narrative films have a degree of accessibility, all the students had opinions and the teacher welcomed their ideas wherever the exploration took us. These were the days of the draconian Legion of Decency, and for Catholics most of these films were considered "forbidden fruit." I often think back to this film club and ponder how all this was possible in those days.

A decade later, in graduate school at New York University, I had the opportunity to take a film course with Joy Gould Boyum, the former film critic of the *Wall Street Journal* and writer of several important books on how to translate the literary text into film. She, too, was an extraordinary teacher. In the vernacular, she "took no hostages." Everything one wrote or said counted, and was to be lean, concise prose reflective of deep association with the film moment.

Among primary concerns were the criteria for judging film as art: What does the film mean? How does it reflect society? What techniques are employed to create the film's illusion? Is this film art? Is this a "good" film?[2] From this instructor, one learned to develop a taste, a sensibility as well as the academic grounding in the literature of film criticism. All of these are important aspects when one is confronted with the task of writing about film and television narratives.

In two distinct yet complementary approaches, Keller and Boyum made the classroom an effective critical environment for examination of the public arts. Indeed, the acknowledgement and recognition that there is something of significance about film and television art requiring conversation and consideration within the college academic setting is all important. Along with many more avenues and sources of experience and thought, I had for the first time the opportunity to trust my own judgments. And it is here where my approach to criticism begins, namely, allowing students to consider a range of film and television fare for the purpose of increasing the possibilities of meaning available. Consequently, the design for such a course comes out of an experience where the media of film and television are understood, appreciated, and respected.

TEXTS

What then is "film art"? And, by extension, are there forms of "television and video art"? At the very outset of an undergraduate course, it is important to establish helpful linkages to the visual arts and the understanding of "art-form." Important concepts such as "visual thinking" borrowed from art criticism can be useful when considering Walter Benjamin's notion of film "aura" and the art of mechanical reproduction.[3] The linkage to the arts provides an important stance from which to judge film and forward an appreciation for the overall artistic process. At the same time this should provide openings for establishment and vernacular expressions and interpretations. In other words, one should leave open the boundaries and appreciations for popular, mass, folk, and elite representations or forms of expression.

This is especially useful when considering television drama and situation comedy. Borrowing an idea from critic John Leonard, it is important to consider those television programs which are crossovers from film models. For example, according to Leonard, particular episodes of CBS's "Murphy Brown" are an improvement over *Broadcast News*. Or, careful study proves that "China Beach" and "Tour of Duty" have dramatic importance and make significant statements about the Vietnam War. I tend to agree with Leonard on this. To sort out mixed impressions about television drama and comedy, the following books are useful:

Todd Gitlin, ed., *Watching Television* (New York: Pantheon, 1986).

David Marc, *Comic Visions: TV Comedy and American Culture* (Boston: Unwin Hyman, 1989).

Horace Newcomb, ed., *Television: The Critical View*, 4th ed. (New York: Oxford University Press, 1987).

Among the many resources available to instructors are two books which are especially helpful during the writing phase of the course:

Tim Bywater and Thomas Sobchack, *Introduction to Film Criticism* (New York: Longman, 1989).

Brian G. Rose, ed., *TV Genres* (Westport, CT: Greenwood Press, 1985).

Another helpful possibility is a slide series that suggests boundaries of artistic representation: folk art, abstract expressionism, and the conventional "masters" of painting and sculpture. This is meant to be a helpful test of one's sensibilities about art-forms. Since it sparks controversy, an untitled work from the 1960s by Robert Morris is a favorite of mine. The sculpture is from the Whitney Museum in New York City. Looking like dark-grayish clutter, this piece is essentially strips of felt attached to the wall and floor. Most observers have a hard time seeing this as an art-form; yet the artist is prompting questions: What are the limits of sculpture? Is this the time for an art that comes on like something else? It may be helpful to identify important new movements in the arts such as the introduction of "video art" by artists Nam June Paik, Richard Serra, and Peter Campus.

From this and other examples, I make the case that forms of expression become works of art in their capacity for complexity, density, and intensity. This works easily when considering the conventional media of expression; however, film and television, like Morris's sculpture, have other problems related to authorship. Early critics such as Vachel Lindsey in the *Art of the Moving Picture* (New York: Liveright, 1916) took note of the collaborative nature of the film medium. To make judgments about film-art or television-art requires an understanding of the responsibilities for the work from the perspectives of the writer (complexity of the text), the director (density of the medium), and the actor (intensity of emotion). Our conversations in class, and later while on tour in Hollywood, are assessments of what individuals bring to the collaborative art-form. Thus our meetings with members of the film and television industry take on genuine importance.

ORGANIZATION

The late A. Bartlett Giamatti, former commissioner of baseball and president of Yale, once remarked that the primary task of the teacher is that of choice.[4] To be effective in the classroom requires selection of one text over another for the purpose of setting an agenda for learning and making connections between and among ideas. In developing a course in media criticism, choice is especially crucial since there are innumerable possible texts and almost as many critical theories worthy of consideration. Consequently, instructors have the task of organizing resources to advance the goal of the course.

First, I am describing here an undergraduate course for upper division students who have an expressed interest in film and television. At the outset, the goals of the course should clearly state that high levels of analysis both in conversation and written form are expected. While students need not be film or communications majors, it is imperative that students have an adequate background, especially in film and television history and theory. Courses which expose students to a canon of film and television texts are especially helpful since the instructor must call upon key films, directors, actors, and film and television genres.[5]

Second, the instructor should be demanding. A critical mind and conversation as well as class attendance should stimulate and inform discussion inside and outside the class. Every school has its core courses. At our college, all undergraduates participate in a four-course Collegiate Seminar that traces the Great Books of Western Civilization. Drawing on this model, I have developed a course reader that contains an appropriate level of critical approaches to film and television. It is intended to spark class discussion and inquiry into the theoretical foundations of criticism. Included are selections from both film/television reviews as well as critical essays by Gilbert Seldes, Pauline Kael, Walter Benjamin, David Marc, and others. The intent is an exposure to a range of opinion as well as models of written criticism, which may inspire strategies for student writing.

Third, the media criticism course fits neatly into a January term of four weeks. This is not essential, but for efficiency, focus, and travel, the January term works well. The class meets Monday through Thursday for a minimum of two-and-a-half hours. Week one deals with film. Week two considers television. Week three takes place in Los Angeles. And finally, week four is given over to class discussions of student essays.

Each class session contains a one-hour presentation or lecture concerning a reading or an aspect of critical film or television theory. Another hour is for student discussion and criticism of the previous day's screening. Students are expected to take notes and provide impressions concerning movies and television programs assigned. Each day one student is asked to research what critics have said or written about a particular work. Lastly, after an appropriate break, the class watches a full length feature, which will be the subject of the next day's session. Often, the class time goes well beyond the stated two-and-a-half hours.

My choice of films and television programming is always based on my knowledge of the students. The purpose is to broaden their range and stretch their interests in visual media. Nonetheless, sometimes my expectations of student likes and dislikes fail. For example, one class simply raved about Kurosawa's *Ran*, despite its length. On the other hand, thinking that the recent success of *A Fish Called Wanda* might serve as bait, I showed its model, *The Lavender Hill Mob*. It did not work. I was the only one in the class laughing at Alec Guinness.

At the beginning of the course, after the students have seen a film, I assign brief "reaction papers" in order to get them thinking about how to write about the visual media. In the early stages of the course it is important for the teacher to watch student reaction to particular films or television programs. I will often accompany students assigned to view particular films at theaters. This is an especially interesting experience since undergraduates seeing an important film for the first time provide the instructor with fresh perspectives. When my classes saw the newly reedited version of David Lean's *Lawrence of Arabia*, it was an opportunity to witness student response to this example of filmic art.

Another consideration is resources. Back in the pre-videotape era, Ted Perry, among others, wrote about the difficulties in establishing film programs, due to the expense of film rental and inadequate facilities on college campuses. For the most part, this has all changed. Our college library contains a media resource center, complete with VHS versions of most of the classic titles. It is helpful to the course when the library has the published text of the films. It can assist analysis and save time, and often the printed texts contain important notes for discussion.

Finally, among the primary goals of the course is for each student to write an original piece of film or television criticism. Students propose individual topics based on an analysis and/or interpretation of a film and/or television program. Sufficient time must be given to assist in the selection of the appropriate film or television narrative. In addition, students must develop a series of questions which frame the scope of the essay and act as criteria for the analysis. The student essays should undergo a series of revisions before the final presentation. When possible, I ask students to show specific scenes from the film or television program to the class. This helps to focus attention on the film or television text, and at the same time informs those in the class who may not be familiar with the work. For the January term course, there is no final examination. Grading is based on active participation and the completion of the essay. Should the course be taught in the normal fall or spring terms, I would recommend that midterm and final examinations include student analyses of class lectures and readings.

Charles Champlin was the keynote speaker for the 1989 tour of Hollywood. As the arts editor and film critic for the *Los Angeles Times*, he has a very difficult vantage point from which to write. According to Champlin, the primary problem for the critic is the very task of writing itself: finding a voice, weighing all the collaborative inputs, balancing off the positive and negative in a way that demonstrates a love of the medium and extends the boundaries of the art-form, while pursuing excellence. "Ultimately, the critic," Champlin concludes, "would rather say yes!"

These words act as a summary of our four-day exploration in Los Angeles. Here I bring twenty students to an active experience for the purpose of finding a voice and developing criteria from which to examine and, finally, judge film and television.

Our primary goal is the meaningful response to film and television art. Naturally, at the same time, undergraduates have a way of creating their own secondary goals; chief among them is the consideration of possible careers within the industry. Luckily, our college has several alumni who have been generous in helping to set up the tour as well as provide professionals to speak to the group. A few of our more recent alumni have provided the most realistic insights and advice about job prospects after college. As one might expect, this becomes an important and worthwhile subtext for many of our discussions and conversations during the week.

Our time in Hollywood is divided into morning presentations and panels at the hotel, afternoon tours of the studios, and evenings at studio tapings or filmings. After my first experience at this, I came to the awareness that Los Angeles is immense.[6] Naturally, freeways and proper directions are key. I recall on my first venture to Hollywood making a mad dash from Paramount Studios to the set of "L.A. Law" at Fox Studies in Century City. Attempting such a trek on a Friday afternoon is virtually impossible! Consequently, the primary improvement to the second tour was our hotel location in the most central place, Burbank, and having our guests come to us. Thus, careful planning and logistics are important to the number and quality of opportunities available.

The morning panels probably required the most careful planning and attention. Each was composed of two to six members who addressed a particular area of interest or concern. Topics ranged from the business of Hollywood, scriptwriting for film and television, and social responsibility and the media. Here contacts and networking eventually produce panelists. While my years of television producing come in to play, there is an articulate and active creative Hollywood community eager to tell its story. We had more panelists and contributors to the tour than we had time in our very tight schedule. The American Film Institute, the University of Southern California, and the University of California–Los Angeles are helpful resources for contacts and assistance when setting up panels.[7]

The scriptwriter panels are often the most helpful for the critic.[8] To learn about the internal design of a production is to peer into the complex nature of any film. It is useful to the student to understand the process of writing, rewriting, production, and editing. We were fortunate to have two panels address this aspect of film and television making.

Scriptwriter Victoria Trostle and two film editors from Lucasfilm, Ltd., showed the class two edited versions of a Hallmark Hall of Fame production, "The Resting Place." It is the story of a soldier's burial and a town coming to terms with its past. Actor John Lithgow plays an officer who confronts the local townsfolk and their racism. The class had the chance to read the script in its various stages. After viewing the final version of the made-for-TV movie, we discussed the nature of the changes in the script, the actors' needs, the director's selections, and the final editing process. Essentially, this was a conversation about postproduction from the viewpoint of key artistic collaborators.

A second panel was comprised of writers from NBC's "Night Court" who addressed the problems of a production in progress. Gary Murphy, the chief writer, described that week's program: what was and was not working in the particular script. He insisted that writing under the pressure of a weekly sitcom requires special "energies of the mind" and, most of all, a broad education.

The next evening, the class was at the Burbank Studios for the weekly taping of "Night Court." As critics-in-the-making, we saw the production process and the problems that arise. Among its more difficult aspects was a storyline that brought several dozens of extras into the limited space of the courtroom set, requiring fast movements on and off stage. The timing of the cast and the orchestration of action with the cameras did not work.

Between takes, a young comedian who acted as host for the production had the added task of entertaining the audience. That night he was fast running out of jokes and gags. During the long hours the actors, producers, and writers were on the set, I could see the emotions range from boredom to panic until they got to the carefully executed final scene. The taping was completed around 11:30 PM, and the class had an opportunity to say goodbye to Gary Murphy and actor John Laroquette. Both admitted it was a tough night at "Night Court." The following morning my students and I left Hollywood for the Bay Area and our college.

CONCLUSION

For many of us, this detour into the backstage life of actors, producers, writers, and technicians increased our knowledge and sparked ideas and ways to see film and watch television. We were especially interested in the ability of film and television to tell a good story. To this end, the course helped define the parameters of film and television art and assisted us in our conversations and writing. Ultimately, we saw moments of illumination and entertainment, and knew the difference.

NOTES

1. Neil Postman, *Amusing Ourselves to Death—Public Discourse in the Age of Show Business* (New York: Viking, 1985).

2. Joy Gould Boyum and Adrienne Scott, *Film as Film: Critical Responses to Film Art* (Boston: Allyn & Bacon, 1971).

3. Walter Benjamin, "Work of Art in the Age of Mechanical Reproduction," in *Video Culture: A Critical Investigation*, John G. Hanhardt, ed. (Rochester, NY: Visual Studies Workshop Press, 1987).

4. A. Bartlett Giamatti, *A Free and Ordered Space: The Real World of the University* (New York: Norton, 1989).

5. The British Film Institute has published a resource guide that may be helpful to those requiring background on the history of film and film study: Pam Cook, ed., *The Cinema Book* (New York: Pantheon, 1985).

6. The two best guidebooks for our purposes are Richard Alleman, *The Movie Lover's Guide to Hollywood* (New York: Harper & Row, 1985); and Richard Saul Wurman, *Los Angeles Access* (New York: Access Press, 1987).

7. Two additional books that may be helpful in suggesting topics and framing the discussion for the panels are Horace Newcomb and Robert S. Alley, *The Producer's Medium: Conversations with Creators of American TV* (New York: Oxford University Press, 1983); and Jason E. Squire, ed., *The Movie Business Book* (New York: Simon & Schuster, 1983).

8. Another resource that has proven helpful to students is a PBS series entitled "Word into Image: Writers on Screenwriting" (American Film Foundation, 1981), produced by Terry Sanders and Freida Lee Mock. This series of six half-hour documentaries considers writing for film by examining the works of William Goldman, Paul Mazursky, Neil Simon, Eleanor Perry, Carl Forman, and Robert Towne.

Chapter 17

MEDIA ETHICS

Jay Black

Let's begin with a deceptively simple question: What are our objectives in teaching and studying mass media ethics? It is easy to become confused in attempting to answer this question, because the teaching of ethics somehow seems to be a different enterprise than the teaching of law or history or any of the other subjects discussed in this book. The confusion arises because the subject matter seems to lend itself on the one hand to investigation into a body of knowledge or academic concepts and, on the other, to the teaching of values, moral character, and "good" behaviors. In professional programs such as those at journalism or mass communication schools and colleges, the focus of ethics instruction may vary from purely academic to highly applied, from broadly interdisciplinary to narrowly professional. Some faculty and media critics would have us prepare students for examined professional lives, while others suggest that we should impose "right" attitudes and inculcate "good" behaviors—whatever they mean by such terms. Unless we are careful, some questionable underlying assumptions may end up driving the enterprise.

BACKGROUND

Before going any further, we should make one observation very clear: There is a major difference between helping students learn how to become autonomous moral agents and imposing our value systems on them. It is the difference between moral philosophy and moralizing, and there is little room in the university setting for the latter.

Ethics is a branch of moral philosophy, or philosophical thinking about morality, moral problems, and moral judgments. At the outset of any discussion of ethics, we should recognize that moral philosophy differs in critically important ways from moralizing. Whereas moral philosophy consists of "thinking about ethics," moralizing is "giving advice." That difference is one of the distinctions between blind adherence to standard operating procedures or traditions of the craft and the pluralistic decision making so essential to the functioning of a participatory republic.

In thinking about ethics, we are dealing with general advice, advice that is consistent—over time, from case to case, from rule to rule, from person to person. This process demands consistency between what we say and what we do. Moral philosophy also involves dialectical, analytical, and cathartic thinking, talking, and enacting of ethical principles. On the other hand, when we moralize we merely give advice—specific, particular advice that lacks consistency over time, from case to case—and advice that may well be inconsistent with what we do. Whereas moral philosophy is dialectical, analytical, and cathartic, moralizing tends to be dogmatic, pragmatic, and advisory. That is, moral philosophy fosters openness, searching, and intellectual "cleansing," whereas moralizing is reflective of closed-mindedness and narrowness.

The distinctions between moral philosophers and moralizers are mentioned for two reasons. First, the moral development of mass media practitioners demands that individuals act with consciousness of moral philosophy rather than responding with the narrow, thoughtless precepts of moralizers. Second, there is a danger that enforceable ethics, whether by professional groups or by government or by public interest groups, will be more concerned with institutional image and accountability than with moral development. Those ethics imposed upon the media personnel may emerge from and pander to moralistic thinking patterns rather than intellectually mature moral philosophy.

Moral philosophy, with a consequent mature social development, appears when, like Socrates, we pass beyond the stage in which these rules are so internalized that we are under the illusion we are inner-directed, to the stage in which we think for ourselves in critical and general terms—and achieve a kind of autonomy as moral agents.[1] This is the autonomy anticipated by the First Amendment; it is built into the "civic" of the educated, examined professional communicator's life. That is, if vital information is to be generated and distributed for the public good, individuals should not be required to be bound by the "moralizing" of others.

We assume that most teachers of mass media ethics believe that the development of the individual moral agent is necessary for the mass media to fully assume their important and constitutionally protected roles in American society. Mass media products that reflect the collective judgment of "moral agents" are far preferable to media content determined by unquestioned adherence to tradition and myth, or to codes of ethics drafted by management and applicable only to staffers, or to the judgment of government imposed upon individual practitioners. The constant struggles between or among these forces for autonomy and conformity make a course in mass media ethics one of the most interesting and challenging courses in the professional curricula. One valuable result of these academic tussles is the students' increased awareness of how traditional philosophic principles interface with the daily lives of professional media practitioners. In short, there is a premium placed on understanding and applying normative ethics to the world of mass media.

OBJECTIVES

One of the most influential agencies in helping academics frame their courses in ethics has been at the Hastings Center, Institute of Society, Ethics, and Life Sciences. This think tank suggests that five instructional goals appropriate for any ethics course are to help students (1) recognize moral issues; (2) develop analytical skills; (3) tolerate—and resist—disagreement and ambiguity; (4) stimulate the moral imagination; (5) elicit a sense of moral obligation and personal responsibility.[2]

These five objectives fit nicely on the course syllabus, and help keep the student and professor focused throughout the semester. (Indeed, this author has listed these objectives on the syllabus, discussed them in the first week of classes, and then asked students on the final exam to assess the extent to which any or all of the objectives were achieved in their own cases, and, if not, why not. The essays are usually highly revealing.) We will consider each of the objectives in turn as they apply to the mass media ethics course, borrowing insights from the 1980 Hastings Center monograph and a separate study by Clifford Christians and Catherine Covert.[3]

The first three objectives are especially adaptable to mass media education, whereas the other two are difficult to achieve.

Recognizing Ethical Issues. This objective is entirely consistent with a preprofessional curriculum. Being able to define problematic areas, recognizing that although something may be legal that does not necessarily make it ethical, understanding the duties of communicators and the impact communicators have on society—all are worthy enterprises.

The Socratic method works particularly well here, if we can create a classroom environment in which we can provide each other with ethically acceptable reactions to mass media problems and sharpen one another's ability to discover the ethical dimensions of various practices and policies.[4] This is a skill we are describing, and, like most skills, it is built upon insight and knowledge. (When done well, in an open classroom, such discussions or dialogues have a natural tendency to move from "moralizing" toward "moral philosophy.")

Those with experience in mass media—summer internships, work on student publications or media, for instance—seem to have less difficulty recognizing ethical issues in mass media than do those whose exposure to media is only as consumers or as classroom students of media. While becoming aware of their own inherent insights into or ignorance of various topics, through the media ethics course students can become much more precise in their definitions of concepts and principles.

Developing Analytical Skills. This objective, which is high on most taxonomies of educational objectives, is also quite compatible with media education. The subject matter of ethics is often in dispute, and the dynamic tension arising from an open marketplace of philosophical positions becomes very stimulating. It is not easy for some students to connect issues raised in this course with such ethical theories as relativism, egoism, utilitarianism, and deontology (to be discussed later in this chapter). However, when the connections are made and the case studies can be analyzed in accordance with the new vocabularies that such ethical theories provide, a significant growth in the intellectual endeavor is likely to be shown. Likewise, intellectual and analytical skills come with learning and applying various decision-making models or justificatory processes (also to be discussed momentarily).

Students of mass media ethics have probably already learned practical skills such as newsgathering and reporting, developing public relations and advertising campaigns, photography, and the like. However, it may well be that such skills were learned more through instruction and rote than through individual exploration. It is surprising how often media ethics students will exclaim, "This is the first time I've ever been asked to really analyze why we do what we do." In developing analytical skills, students are encouraged to demonstrate intellectual coherence and consistency. As Christians and Covert have said,[5] the mass media profession demands powerful skills for interpreting very complex events. Therefore, analytical abilities should be sought to varying degrees in all media courses; the ethics course is a natural vehicle for honing these abilities.

It has been said elsewhere in this book, but let us repeat it here: The traditional lecture method and testing through regurgitation are surefire ways to guarantee that this course objective is never met. Analytical skills develop from engaging students in decision-making processes. They do not develop from random discussion in class, although bull sessions have their value in helping clarify some of the issues (objective #1, above). The decision-making process being described here may be tedious, but it is a highly effective way of understanding and resolving complex problems. Rigorous argumentation with attention to evidence, not rampant moralizing, is the key.

Students should be motivated to state why a particular problem has ethical dimensions, and to formulate a hypothesis. Possible solutions to the problem should be explored during a brainstorming session, but a halt to brainstorming should then be called and students asked to provide careful systematic attention to detail—to causes and consequences, to persons affected by ethical or nonethical decisions, to institutional norms and values. The solutions should then be tested against "the wisdom of the ages," that is, against traditional philosophic principles.

To make all of this happen takes careful monitoring and mentoring, not lecturing. To measure its effectiveness, instructors cannot rely upon multiple choice tests; they need to watch and listen with all their antennae, and to rely upon essay exams or case study analyses for other feedback. A class developing such analytical skills will probably be a lively, even at times a rowdy, class. It needs a combination coach and referee, not a traditional lecturer.

Tolerating—and Resisting—Disagreement and Ambiguity. The mass media ethics classroom has a natural proclivity toward open discourse. It is only normal for such discourse to entail a great deal of disagreement and ambiguity. Many of the questions appear at first to have no clear answers, and the articulation of opinions is likely to take up much class time. However, we must bear in mind that not all opinions have equal intellectual or ethical weight. To put the disagreements in their proper pedagogical perspective, the instructor must probe beneath the surface, asking the "why" about the "what." Students who rely upon convention and the "of course" syndrome, arguing that something "just is because it just is," should be asked to peel back other layers of that anti-intellectual moralistic onion.

Instructors conversant with epistemology—how we know what we think we know—might help students clarify the nature of their own and others' opinion and belief formations. At some point in the course, in discussions of moral development theory, instructors might help students recognize how natural it is for maturing individuals to move away from opinions and beliefs based on tenacity or authority, and into a position of tolerance for disagreement and ambiguity, followed, in some cases, by developing an individual commitment and sense of personal responsibility.

Many students become uncomfortable with the recognition that there may be no single "right" answers to many of the questions raised in class. Why, they ask, if philosophers have been working for two millennia on these issues, aren't there more absolutes? "Immature" students of moral philosophy, frustrated with the inherent disagreements among various schools of philosophic thought, tend to revert to relativism, arguing that if there are no clearly articulated, universally moral absolutes governing media ethics, then all opinions have equal value. This juncture (or, more likely, these many junctures) in the course provides marvelous "teachable moments." A skilled instructor capitalizes upon this frustration to widen the arena of investigation, to help students work through various moral points of view to discern for themselves a justifiable system of ethical decision making. If the class members are willing to grapple honestly with their areas of disagreement, they will be receptive to the analytical skills-building exercises and likely move toward having their individual and collective moral imaginations stimulated. Perhaps they will even take steps toward developing a sense of moral obligation and personal responsibility.

It would be nice to say that the call for tolerance of disagreement needs little further comment at this juncture. We are trying in our schools and colleges of journalism and mass communication to avoid mindlessly promoting ideological ethics and undisputed conventions, and assume that students will naturally appreciate the need for some discussion, disagreement, and tolerance. However, in this day and age of "politically correct speech," with institutional intolerance for extreme utterances, faculty and students may be unnecessarily restricted in exploring the natural boundaries of their ideologies and value-based words, ideas, and behaviors. An intellectually honest course in media ethics is a natural venue for such an exploration.

Stimulating the Moral Imagination. Unlike the first three objectives outlined above, this fourth goal of media ethics instruction is not fully compatible with typical mass communication practice and instruction. Stimulation of the moral imagination demands that the course-work involve more than practical skills or even abstract intellectual exercises. It also means that students' feelings and imagination must be stimulated.[6]

According to Christians and Covert, students' moral imagination will not be stimulated until live human beings and their welfare become central to the classroom enterprise.[7] And that is an extremely difficult task to achieve, given the "realities" of journalism, advertising, public relations, and broadcasting as they are taught and practiced today.

Mass communicators tend to lack one central characteristic shared by other professionals. Whereas other professionals have individual clients with articulated needs and expectations, mass communicators tend to deal with customers—undifferentiated members of the public. As a result mass communicators have a difficult time sensing empathy for individuals they report about, persuade, entertain, and report to—their sources and audiences. They may pay lip service to meeting the needs of "T. C. Pits" (The Celebrated Person in the Street), but in everyday practice mass communicators are more likely to operate in terms of appealing to a vast, anonymous, heterogeneous, and undifferentiated mass audience. In today's increasingly depersonalized mass media institutions, where neophyte practitioners sense their own role to be that of interchangeable cogs in the corporate machine, it is hard to be idealistic and empathic. To many students worried about finding a media job that pays a living wage, let alone one that offers occupational if not moral autonomy, the professional trait of "servant" or "steward" does not come naturally. Media ethics courses should reinforce the fact that the public has a right to the best information, entertainment, and persuasion the students will provide them, and that producing these "products" in accordance with moral principles often entails suffering or unhappiness on the part of "real" people.

By definition, serving the mass media audience means practitioners will have to help them make sense out of the myriad of conflicting messages that clutter the airwaves and print channels. Doing so means the communicator has to take a long, hard look at the world, to understand insofar as possible the forces that make it work, and to choose a position from which to communicate. Raising such questions in the media ethics class invariably means students begin questioning such standard operating principles as objectivity, or such bromides as "go with what you've got," "if the competition's going with it, so should we," or "if it's legal, it's ethical." Stimulating the moral imagination means asking why deadlines and technological or economic constraints seem to produce certain sets of behaviors that would be less tolerable if such pressures were absent or lessened. In the quiet after the deadline has been met, introspection and second guessing may give rise to questions of impact and empathy. If an ethics course meets its objective of stimulating the moral imagination, such questions will become internalized and media practitioners might consider their permutations before the next deadline. (A typical concern expressed by students in this class is that it's all well and good to sit around and discuss these issues at our leisure over the course of a semester, but that in "the real world" there is scarcely time to tend to the task at hand, let alone play abstract intellectual games. A logical response from the instructor is that if the process is undertaken in the classroom often and well enough, the synapses will be in place for much more rapid and sophisticated decision making under pressure, so that each new dilemma is not written upon a blank tablet.)

There's another problem with stimulating the moral imagination of mass media students and practitioners: We tend to be convinced that it is the public's responsibility, not the communicators', to impose meaning and deal with consequences of news, persuasion, and entertainment. Journalists, for instance, tend to think that their major responsibility is to meet the deadline, to be published; they think very little about the consequences of everything they write. They provide the "facts"; once they are published, it is assumed that an abundance of ideas competing in the marketplace will make all come out right— as suggested by such utilitarians and libertarians as John Stuart Mill, Thomas Jefferson, and John Milton. If individuals' rights are considered, they are often thought of in terms of *legal* rights (privacy, intrusion, libel, fair trial, etc.) instead of *moral* rights (dignity, well-being, peace of mind, etc.).[8] Likewise, advertisers and public relations folks are motivated by the sometimes contradictory goals of informing and persuading, and are quick to turn from one campaign to the next, without taking stock of the impact of the first. Often, persuaders claim it is not their responsibility to control the effects of their messages—they just throw them out for public consideration, hoping their messages will get through and bring about the desired results. Given this attitude, and the pressures of the moment, advertisers and public relations practitioners may be acting irresponsibly—and not even know it.

In the ethics course, the moral imagination can be stimulated by having students deal with real people who are consumers of the media or perhaps those who may have been "hurt" by the media. Community leaders or individuals with power who are experienced in dealing with the media offer quite a different perspective than do ordinary citizens who have found themselves somehow affected by media—by news stories or public relations or advertising campaigns or perhaps by fictional treatments that may have had dysfunctional effects. Bringing such individuals into the classroom, or sending media students out to speak with them, is useful pedagogy. If time and circumstances do not permit the exposure to media consumers, the same results can be obtained through various role-playing exercises, in which empathy is demanded as students work their way through realistic issues.

Another popular means of stimulating the moral imagination is to use various films, TV shows, or novels that have dealt with media issues. *Citizen Kane, The Front Page, The Man in the Gray Flannel Suit, Absence of Malice, Under Fire, All the President's Men, Broadcast News, The Mean Seasons,* and *Crazy People* are among nearly 2,000 films (some based on books) Hollywood has made about media people in the past three-quarters of a century. Television shows such as "Murphy Brown," "E. N. G.," "Lou Grant," and "L. A. Law," and any of the hundreds of novels that have used journalists and other media personnel as central characters, often stimulate the moral imagination. In using such media in the ethics class, however, care must be taken that the fun of viewing and discussing the fictional incidents does not overshadow the more important mission of clarifying the import of the messages.

Of course, students of mass communication can be provoked into considering their own effects on the public, and those who have not yet practiced journalism or public relations or advertising can benefit by being exposed to working practitioners whose work has impacted society. That is why in this course we frequently invite guest speakers from the professional world to speak with us. In one recent semester, this instructor had stimulating class visits from a former Latin American executive with Nestle's corporation, who discussed his firm's marketing of infant formula, and a black editor/publisher who shared his agony of dealing with a boycott against one of his major advertisers, an inner-city grocer who had been selling day-old bread as fresh. Such visits go a long way toward stimulating students' moral imaginations. (After the visitors have gone, students are eager to analyze the visitors' decision-making processes, attempting to discern which philosopher(s) seemed to share the offices with the visitors, and what stages of moral development seemed to be reflected in the visitors' decisions and actions.)

Eliciting a Sense of Moral Obligation and Personal Responsibility. This final objective, like the previous one discussed, is difficult for us to attain in this type of class, but it is one well worth attempting. At several points throughout the semester, students do well to face such questions as "Why should I be moral? What are my ethical duties and obligations as an individual, as a student, and as a professional mass communicator? Given my freedoms, what are my responsibilities?" The questions are obviously abstract, but they cut to the quick of the enterprise. They ask students to take ethics seriously and to recognize that there is more to ethics than recognizing ethical problems, having analytical abilities, staying open-minded, and being morally stimulated. At the same time, this fifth objective may be the most problematic, because it opens the Pandora's box in which reside all the concerns about education vis-à-vis indoctrination, learning-about-ethics vis-à-vis being-expected-to-be-ethical.

As Christians and Covert explained it, in order to elicit moral obligation, it is necessary that ethics instruction "appeal to the will, expect some sort of action, and engage volition. For all practical purposes, it is presupposed that individuals are free to make moral choices and be held responsible for them."[9] But this freedom to make moral choices may be somewhat limited in mass media because practitioners are operating within profit-centered institutions, they carry out their chores under conditions of controlled pandemonium, and they are somewhat removed from the people affected by their actions—factors which tend to isolate ethical decisions from other routine decisions. If, as more than one philosopher has said, the ultimate ethical decision may be whether to accept the universe or to protest against it, many mass media practitioners are not routinely in the position to make ultimate ethical decisions. (We have already dealt with some ramifications of these factors, in discussing ways to stimulate students' moral imaginations.)

Honing a sense of moral obligation and personal responsibility goes hand in hand with leading an examined life—surely a worthy goal for any university experience. Studies in moral psychology, particularly those by William Perry[10] and Lawrence Kohlberg,[11] tell us that acting out of a sense of commitment and principled behavior occurs only at a higher stage of moral development. This stage of development reflects the internalization and operationalization of moral principles, the refinement of conscience. When it occurs, it does so after individuals have progressed through stages of egoism, relativism, and culturally defined goals and rules. The process of internalization may appear on the surface to be somewhat irrational and may differ enormously from case to case, individual to individual. But it tends to occur as individuals move from an illusory kind of inner direction to a more rational and realistic one in which they achieve an examined life and a kind of autonomy, become moral agents on their own, and even reach a point at which they can criticize the rules and values of their society.[12]

Instructors who hope that in one semester their students will progress through these stages and emerge as "moral heroes" may be setting their sights unrealistically high. The overwhelming majority of us operate at conventional stages of morality, motivated largely by convention and temporal pressures. Professors themselves are not immune to such forces, so why should they expect to see miracles in their students?

Thoughtful mass media educators and mass media practitioners tend to share certain values, such as truth telling, minimizing harm, optimizing good, and acting out of principle. These values are not always well articulated. However, when scratched deeply enough, most folks in the mass media world will admit to believing in them, at least to a degree. If these are seen as universal moral principles that are expected of new employees, there is a tendency also to expect our students to arrive already holding them—or, at least, to hold to them by the end of the semester. And if our students do not arrive holding such values, we may have the tendency to "profess" the essential shared values, lest our students seek to enter the workforce without knowing the passwords. Because we believe so deeply in those few fundamental truths, we have difficulty fathoming anyone staking a claim in mass media without also sharing these values. Those who cross that line arouse the ire of observers such as Lou Hodges, director of Washington and Lee University's Center for the Study of Society and the Professions, who complain that such inculcation is moral imperialism of the worst sort.[13] We do well to note the observation of mathematics professor G. V. Ramanathan, who laments the blurring of the distinction between "education" and "teaching":

We do not look upon education as a means of elevating the child's soul, but as a list of skills to be mastered in order to test well and please us. . . . Education, in the true sense of leading the child, has given way to teaching, where the focus is on the instructor. You teach a dog to do tricks. You do not teach a human being; you must lead him or her through a process of discovery. To teach is to dehumanize.[14]

Even though Hodges and others conclude that values per se are caught, not taught, the mass media ethics instructor who has assumed the values of the profession faces a particularly difficult challenge if he or she is to remain true to the philosophic challenge of truth-seeking and genuine inquiry and to avoid dehumanizing his or her students. If one is to meet the challenge, one must encourage students to develop the capacity to recognize the difference between moralizing, bromides, war stories, and the "of course" syndrome (i.e., acting out of unquestioned adherence to institutional conventions) on the one hand and moral philosophy on the other. As Michael J. Collins argued in *Teaching Values and Ethics in College*:

We cannot teach people to be virtuous. We cannot eradicate evil and injustice with a liberal arts education. But when we develop in bright, talented young men and women the skills to succeed in the marketplace, we give them power, and we should, therefore, as Socrates recognized in *The Gorgias*, give some attention to how they will use it—help them, through our teaching, to become just, generous, and compassionate.[15]

Alternative Approaches to Values Instruction. One final note about the teaching of values. Regardless of the approaches we take to our courses or the way we format or package them, our objectives, or our individual and educational philosophy, we are constantly teaching values, even when we claim we are being objective or value-free.[16] Our approaches to the subject matter, to students, to one another—in short, our citizenship—inform our students as to our values. What we do probably speaks more loudly than what we say.

Consciously, on the surface, we may be employing any of a half dozen approaches to teaching values and ethics, while beneath the surface, perhaps even unbeknownst to ourselves, we are still expressing a value system, a set of beliefs about what ought to be.

Six traditional approaches to teaching values have been described by Albert Howard Carter III in a recent book on teaching values and ethics in college.[17] They are introduced as separate and distinct, but as can be inferred from the previous discussion of course objectives, there can be a great deal of overlap in the typical mass media ethics course. The approaches:

1. The Inculcative Approach. This approach assumes there to be a certain set of acceptable values which authorities are to instill in students. It is the "moral imperialism" rejected by Hodges and most other contemporary libertarian philosophers, but it has a long tradition, particularly within private or church-run colleges.

2. The Classical Approach. This approach draws from the wisdom of the ages, and is typical of courses taught in philosophy departments. A survey of Western thinkers from Plato to John Rawls is "objectively" presented, in an abstract manner, for students' information. Usually there is no conscious effort to force-feed correctness, and often the exams and papers lack application to contemporary issues.

3. The Experiential Approach. American pragmatists, inspired by Dewey and Plato, hold that educated individuals (philosopher-kings at many levels) can and should become moral leaders. Highly relevant experiences in philosophic arts and skills can develop moral character, according to this view. Case studies, hands-on experiences such as field trips and internships, teach-ins, conferences, workshops, and other experimental courses are typical of the experiential approach. While this approach offers a vivid, stimulating, and "relevant" study of values, care must be taken that the results are not a polarization of tenaciously held alternatives and a lack of philosophically sound insights.

4. The Growth-Oriented Approach. A focus on values clarification gained widespread popularity in the 1960s and 1970s, particularly among high school and college students. Based on works by Carl Jung and Carl Rogers, this approach stressed individualism and relevance, but as put into practice often lacked historical, social, or philosophical breadth. "Lifeboat ethics" and a fixation on individual decision making about sex and drug use were seen by traditional professors as being overly frivolous and trendy.

5. The Developmental Approach. Developmental psychology, as influenced by Jean Piaget, William Perry, Lawrence Kohlberg, Carol Gilligan, and others, offers another approach to understanding values. As suggested earlier, research indicates that individuals progress through a series of logical stages of moral and intellectual development. In the classroom this research can be presented either as theory or as an impetus for individual development. Several of us who have introduced moral development into the media ethics course have noticed the efforts made by students not only to understand the constructs, but to test themselves against what they see to be standards or challenges for growth. This is particularly evident when the class is exposed to real-world scenarios and is asked to analyze the moral development evidenced by guest speakers or characters in case studies. Obviously, care must be taken when dealing with feelings of guilt or inadequacy; it may be dysfunctional for an individual to discern that he or she is a moral troglodyte.

6. The Preprofessional Approach. "Ethics and . . . " courses are experiencing a growth spurt in the 1980s and 1990s—a boomlet of sorts. Biomedical ethics, business ethics, ethics and education, ethics and law, and ethics and journalism are typically offered as separate courses to advanced

undergraduates or graduate students majoring in a preprofessional field. They are transitional courses, connecting the academy to the real world. Obviously, the courses described throughout this chapter could fall under this category, given the "target audience" and general objectives.

A review of these half dozen approaches shows that each has its strengths and weaknesses, and suggests that the skilled pedagogue will draw from a combination of them in designing a successful ethics course. We will now consider some practical ways in which these objectives and approaches can be handled.

ORGANIZATION

Because the bulk of this chapter stresses flexibility in pedagogy, this is no time to propose *the* way to teach this course. There are many successful organizations to be followed. Each instructor will play to his or her own strengths. Those more conversant with political or economic or social or philosophic theory will undoubtedly put that particular spin on the syllabus. Of all the courses in the curriculum, however, this one may offer the most intellectual fun, because it places a premium on intellectual kleptomania.

A decade or so of teaching the course, coupled with participation in numerous workshops and research projects, has led this instructor to the following general course organization. This is not to impose a syllabus on others, but to indicate how the aforementioned objectives and approaches can be put into practice. As is frequently the case with other instructors, years of teaching this course have resulted in an individualized package of materials made available to students, supplementing the textbooks.[18] At present, the course averages fifty students per semester, too large to handle as a seminar, but not too large for plenty of student involvement. A review of major topics in the supplementary package can serve as a tour through the semester's work.

1. Introduction to the Study of Mass Media Ethics. Not unlike the first several pages of this chapter, the introduction outlines course objectives and indicates various ways in which they can be met. The first week is also a good time to show a video such as the ABC documentary "Lying, Cheating and Stealing in America" or a section of the PBS series "Ethics in America" to help sensitize students to the general issues and open channels of communication.

2. On Doing Ethics. Ethics and morality are defined. Questions are raised: Why be good? What are the forces for good? Differences between law and ethics are explored, as are concerns about codes, individual judgments, conscience, and ethics and relationships. Various approaches to ethics scholarship are outlined. Philosophical ethics are contrasted with other forms of ethics; moral philosophy and moralizing are explored. Justification models and other systematic methods of decision making are introduced, starting with Sissela Bok's test for veracity and the Potter Box, which explores the nature of values, principles, and loyalties.

3. On Freedom and Communication. Students work through some lessons in civics; a special case is made that freedoms to communicate are coupled with responsibilities. First Amendment mandates and privileges are put into libertarian perspectives (Milton, Mill, Locke, Hume, etc.), and problems with the open marketplace are investigated.

4. Advice from Philosophers. Moving more seriously into philosophic ethics, students are introduced to ideas of Aristotle, Mill, Kant, Rawls, Ross, and others, plus the Judeo-Christian perspective and, when possible, alternative non-Western traditions. This is not a full-blown discussion, but a brief introduction. Individual philosophers are given much more extensive coverage later in the course.

5. More Decision-Making Models. Epistemology is introduced. Authority, precedent, logic, emotion and other means of "fixing beliefs" are studied, and students are involved in rethinking some of the "truisms" they have learned about their professions.

6. Values and Priorities. The nature of values and value systems, as outlined by Milton Rokeach and others, is covered. Students take a personal values inventory, and later in the course take it again, to see what underlies their attitudes and behaviors and how, although there are some universal values, individuals prioritize those values differently depending on a variety of circumstances. Such values as individualism, altruism, idealism, and pragmatism, as discussed by Sanford Krolick, are identified.

7. The Moral Law. Just as there are universal values that shake out differently in different individuals, so are there some universal laws or principles, some hierarchies of virtues. Lawrence Kohlberg's list of virtues (life, liberties, truth, contract, law, character, authority, affiliation, property, and punishment) is introduced and put into mass media perspectives.

8. On Egoism and Relativism. We begin at this point to systematically cover various ethical principles. Students have probably already defended many media practices in terms of ethical egoism and relativism, so this is a good juncture to put these constructs in perspective. Strengths and weaknesses of each system are investigated; through case studies and writing in "ethics journals" (a sort of academic diary turned in to the

instructor every three weeks) students tend to recognize the problems with egoism and relativism as guiding principles.

9. On Utilitarianism. Students grapple with the media's profit orientation and concern with reaching audiences, and the problems that this utilitarian approach creates. Various theories of consequentialism or teleological thinking are covered, including act, general, and rule utilitarianism, so alternatives to relativism or situationalism are understood. Bentham, Mill, and others are applied to media scenarios.

10. On Deontology. A dramatic shift from consequences to duties occurs at this point. Students study W. D. Ross, Immanuel Kant, Bernard Gert, and others who ask and then answer: "What makes right acts right? What are our inherent duties? What does it mean to be a responsible and morally autonomous individual?" The rigors of Kant's categorical imperative and the logic of Ross's "prima facie duties" and "duties proper" are assessed and, insofar as possible, applied to mass media cases.

By this point we have reached the midterm. Much of the foundation has been laid, students have been provoked into examining their conventional wisdoms, and we are ready for much more application.

11. On Defining Truth. Because truth telling is a fundamental "given" in the communications world, cutting across journalism, public relations, advertising, and entertainment media, we devote special attention to it. Students are exposed to a "truth continuum" which goes from "capital-T Truth" down through blatant lies, with all sorts of subcategories in between. Veracity, truth telling, and various forms of deception are covered in this unit, including the nature and problems of propaganda. Case studies range from the use and misuse of quotes and sources (the Janet Malcolm case, coverage of the Persian Gulf War, etc.) to news stories and public relations releases, puffery and deceit in advertising, commercial product placement in movies, and the role of government agencies and individual media in regulating such problems. Semantics and other principles of communication are employed.

12. On Credibility. A discussion of truth telling leads to a discussion of credibility in communications. The traits of credibility, comparisons of different individuals' and media's credibility, are covered. Students are made aware of the significant difference between credibility (what people think of you) and ethics (your basic character/what you are), and consider the natural tugs between the two forces. It is appropriate here to study the place of media councils, ombudsmen, corrections systems, or other agencies to assure credibility and ethical behavior of media.

13. Intellectual and Ethical Development. Insights from Perry, Kohlberg, Gilligan, and others are given. Discussions cover stages and sequences of moral development, justice, gender, conformity, individualism, personhood, citizenship, commitment, stewardship, and moral autonomy. Natural topics to arise include the extent to which mass media businesses impede rather than enhance moral development, and contemporary concerns over value-based education vis-à-vis training.

14. Codes of Ethics. Now that we have covered ethical theory and moral development, the time is right for a serious discussion of the pros and cons of codes of ethics. By now students are aware that codes may not be the panacea others believe, and they are ready to investigate the media's claims for code-based morality. Minimalistic and "ideal standards" codes are assessed. A valuable exercise at this point is for students to design their own codes, to be applied to their chosen media fields, and then to critique one another's efforts.

15. On Professionalism. The final topic of the semester is that of professionalism: what does it mean, what are the criteria, what are the limitations—is professionalism a set of individualistic character traits, or can it be institutional—are the media "professions," can they be, should they be? The idea is that thoughtful students, upon completing a personal and institutional examination—an "ethics audit," if you will—are ready for a realistic assessment of their chosen careers.

TEXTS

The past decade has seen a virtual plethora of books and materials to help professors and students succeed in the teaching and learning of mass media ethics. The very fact that most textbook publishing houses either have published or are planning to publish materials for this course indicates that it has reached critical mass. No completely up-to-date figures are available on the numbers of courses and student enrollment, but it is safe to say that hundreds of universities and colleges are now offering this course, and thousands of students are exposed to this material annually.

Reviews of textbooks and relevant professional materials are found in the quarterly *Journal of Mass Media Ethics*, published by Lawrence Erlbaum Associates. The journal also offers case studies and commentaries, and both qualitative and quantitative studies by academics and media practitioners about the teaching and practice of media ethics.

Three 1991 textbooks seem to provide the best "complete package" for the media ethics course:

Clifford Christians, Kim B. Rotzoll, and Mark Fackler, *Media Ethics: Cases & Moral Reasoning* (New York: Longman, 1991). This publication is the best-selling textbook in the field. It provides an excellent albeit brief introduction to ethical theory, then eighty-six case studies from all areas of media.

Louis A. Day, *Ethics in Mass Communications: Cases and Controversies* (Belmont, CA: Wadsworth, 1991). The book offers an extensive "Foundations and Principles" section, covering such topics as ethics and moral development, ethics and society, and ethics and moral reasoning; the second and much larger part of the text deals with case studies.

Philip Patterson and Lee Wilkins, *Media Ethics: Issues and Cases* (Dubuque, IA: William C. Brown, 1991). Patterson and Wilkins have edited case studies submitted by thirty-seven different authors. The cases are tied together into a solid philosophical and pedagogical package, with a series of "discussion starters" following each case.

All three of these media ethics texts have valuable reference lists or bibliographies; the Patterson and Wilkins book even has short pieces on how to use Hollywood films or novels about media people to enhance the learning experience.

Faculty members who wish to introduce their students to classical ethical theory would do well to consider augmenting their textbook with any of several good small books. Among the strong contenders:

William Frankena, *Ethics* (Englewood Cliffs, NJ: Prentice-Hall, 1973).

Louis P. Pojman, *Ethics: Discovering Right and Wrong* (Belmont, CA: Wadsworth, 1990).

Richard C. Purtill, *Thinking About Ethics* (Englewood Cliffs, NJ: Prentice-Hall, 1976).

CONCLUSION

All of the forgoing might indicate that the task of teaching the mass media ethics course is daunting, that only a Renaissance philosopher with years of contemporary and interdisciplinary media work experience and teaching could handle the chore. Such is not necessarily the case. Where these courses have blossomed, they often have been taught by senior faculty members who are conversant with media issues, sensitive to student needs, and skilled at creating a classroom environment in which learning rather than teaching is at the forefront. Handling the course well, however, also demands an appreciation of philosophy. Although it would be nice, one need not have an advanced degree in the subject. It is probably enough to be a competent amateur philosopher.

In 1978 and again in 1985, Clifford Christians took stock of the nature and scope of mass media ethics courses, and most recently declared the existence of a true "boomlet" in the enterprise.[19] However, Christians expressed some concern that the enterprise may not be growing as rapidly in theoretical and philosophical sophistication as it is in enrollment. He noted a great increase in courses called "Journalism Ethics," along with a general tendency of administrators who had not added such courses to their catalogs to insist that all other courses in the curriculum introduce students to journalism ethics through "the pervasive" approach. But Christians was not convinced that ethics was actually learned in all those courses, particularly under the scattershot conditions of the pervasive courses.

Where, we might ask, are journalism and other mass media instructors to learn how to teach moral philosophy, to help students understand the virtues of applied normative ethics? Is it reasonable to expect a cadre of former news reporters and editors or public relations and advertising practitioners, or instructors whose graduate training consisted primarily of social science research and theory, to transmogrify into Kantian or Aristotelian scholars? Or is it enough for them to become "competent amateur philosophers"? Believing the latter to be a realistic goal, Edmund Lambeth and the staff of the Poynter Institute for Mass Media Studies have led the charge throughout much of the past decade.

Since 1984 Lambeth, first at the University of Kentucky and recently at the University of Missouri–Columbia, has held week-long workshops on the teaching of journalism ethics. Underwritten by the Gannett Foundation, Lambeth's philosophically based workshops have attracted between 90 and 100 applications each year for the 15 open slots. Meanwhile, the Poynter Institute staff has effectively covered similar territory with professors, college students, and media professionals. Lambeth and Poynter associates have noted a slow but marked trend, based on their participants' course syllabi and anecdotal evidence, away from the war stories and "of course" syndromes of yore and toward the creation of substantial case studies and applied moral philosophy for today's and tomorrow's complex mass media environment.

As Christians concluded in 1985, the teaching of journalism and mass communication ethics may always remain an ambiguous enterprise, living in some degree of tension on the fringes of mass media education.

Those involved in this area undoubtedly will continue to believe it is eminently worth doing, but there are not indications anywhere that the prestige, energy and resources will shift decisively to ethics. To date it has not attracted the considerable status of law or the money of research or the good minds of communication theory or even the fascination of the new technologies. And media ethics may never do so.[20]

There are slow but definite signs that the enterprise is being taken more seriously throughout the nation's journalism and mass communication schools and colleges. Whether it ever gains the academic respectability and resources of other enterprises remains to be seen, but the increased attention, enthusiasm, and scholarship in the field bode well for the future.

NOTES

1. William Frankena, *Ethics*, 2nd ed. (Englewood Cliffs, NJ: Prentice-Hall, 1973), 8.

2. Hastings Center Institute of Society, Ethics and The Life Sciences, *The Teaching of Ethics in Higher Education* (Hastings-on-Hudson, NY: Institute of Society, Ethics and The Life Sciences, 1980).

3. Clifford C. Christians and Catherine L. Covert, *Teaching Ethics in Journalism Education* (Hastings-on-Hudson, NY: Institute of Society, Ethics and The Life Sciences, 1980).

4. Ibid., 38.

5. Ibid., 39.

6. Hastings Center, 48

7. Christians and Covert, 40.

8. Ibid., 41–42.

9. Ibid., 43.

10. William Perry, *Intellectual and Moral Development in the College Years* (New York: Holt, Rinehart & Winston, 1970).

11. Lawrence Kohlberg, *Stages in Development of Moral Thought and Action* (New York: Holt, Rinehart & Winston, 1963); and "Stage and Sequence: The Cognitive-Development Approach to Socialization," in D. Goslin, ed., *Handbook of Socialization Theory and Research* (Chicago: Rand McNally College Publishing Co., 1963).

12. Jay Black and Ralph Barney, "The Case Against Mass Media Codes of Ethics," *Journal of Mass Media Ethics* 1 (Fall-Winter 1985–86): 32.

13. Lou Hodges, in panel discussion "Bridging Morality Gap: Doing Newsroom Ethics," Mass Media Ethics in the Information Age Conference, Tuscaloosa, AL (March 30, 1990).

14. G. V. Ramanathan, "Selling Our Kids to Business . . . and Insulting College Students," *Chicago Tribune* (July 5, 1990): 19.

15. Michael J. Collins, "Values and Teaching," in Michael J. Collins, ed., *Teaching Values and Ethics in College, New Directions for Teaching and Learning, No. 13* (San Francisco: Josey-Bass, 1983), 8.

16. Albert Howard Carter, III, "The Teaching of Values in Colleges and Universities," in Michael J. Collins, ed., *Teaching Values and Ethics*, 15.

17. Ibid., 11–15.

18. Jay Black and Frank Deaver, colleagues in the University of Alabama College of Communication, have written and edited a Kinko's text of some 200 pages that is available upon request.

19. Clifford G. Christians, "Variety of Approaches Used in Teaching Media Ethics," *Journalism Educator* (April 1978): 3–8; and "Media Ethics Courses Have Increased Since 1977," *Journalism Educator* (Summer 1985): 17–19, 51.

20. Christians, "Media Ethics Courses," 19.

SUGGESTED READINGS

BOOKS

Alder, Richard, and Douglas Cater, eds. *Television as a Cultural Force.* New York: Praeger, 1976.

Allen, Robert C., and Douglas Gomery. *Film History Theory and Practice.* New York: Alfred A. Knopf, 1985.

Blyskal, Jeff, and Marie Blyskal. *How the Public Relations Industry Writes the News.* New York, NY: William Morrow and Company, 1985.

Botan, Carl H., and Vincent Hazleton, Jr., eds. *Public Relations Theory.* Hillsdale, NJ: Lawrence Erlbaum Associates, 1989.

Broom, Glen M., and David M. Dozier. *Using Research in Public Relations: Applications to Program Management.* Englewood Cliffs, NJ: Prentice-Hall, 1990.

Brown, Les. *Television: The Business Behind the Box.* New York: Harcourt, Brace, Jovanovich, 1971.

Campbell, Douglas S.C. *The Supreme Court and the Mass Media: Selected Cases, Summaries and Analyses.* New York: Praeger, 1990.

Christians, Clifford G., Kim B. Rotzoll, and Mark Fackler. *Media Ethics: Cases and Moral Reasoning.* New York: Longman, 1991.

Deal, Terrence E., and Allen A. Kennedy. *Corporate Cultures: The Rites and Rituals of Corporate Life.* Reading, MA: Addison-Wesley, 1982.

DeFleur, Melvin L., and Everette E. Dennis. *The Media Society: Evidence About Mass Communication in America.* Dubuque, IA: William C. Brown, 1991.

Eastman, Susan, Sydney Head, and Lewis Klein. *Broadcast Programming,* 3rd ed. Belmont, CA: Wadsworth, 1989.

Ellmore, Garland C. *The Communication Discipline in Higher Education.* Indianapolis, IN: Association for Communication Administration, 1990.

Esslin, Martin. *The Age of Television.* San Francisco: W. H. Freeman, 1982.

Farrar, Ronald T. *Mass Communication.* Saint Paul, MN: West, 1988.

Fowler, Floyd J., Jr. *Survey Research Methods,* rev. ed. Newbury Park, CA: Sage, 1988.

Godfrey, Donald G. *A Directory of Broadcast Archives.* Washington, DC: Broadcast Education Association, 1983.

Head, Sydney, and Christopher Sterling. *Broadcasting in America.* Boston: Houghton Mifflin, 1990.

Heighton, Elizabeth J., and Don R. Cunningham. *Advertising in Broadcast and Cable Media,* 2nd ed. Belmont, CA: Wadsworth, 1984.

Kruckeberg, Dean, and Kenneth Starck. *Public Relations and Community: A Reconstructed Theory.* New York: Praeger, 1988.

Krueger, Richard A. *Focus Groups: A Practical Guide for Applied Research.* Newbury Park, CA: Sage, 1988.

Larson, Charles U. *Persuasion: Reception and Responsibility,* 5th ed. Belmont, CA: Wadsworth, 1989.

Mankiewicz, Frank, and Joel Swerdlow. *Remote Control: Television and Manipulation of American Life.* New York: Ballantine Books, 1978.

Newcomb, Horace, ed. *Television: The Critical View,* 3rd ed. New York: Oxford Press, 1982.

Newcomb, Horace, and Robert S. Alley. *The Producer's Medium: Conversations with Creators of American TV.* New York: Oxford University Press, 1983.

Patterson, Phillip, and Lee Wilkins. *Media Ethics: Issues and Cases.* Dubuque, IA: William C. Brown, 1991.

Pavlik, John V. *Public Relations: What Research Tells Us.* Newbury Park, CA: Sage, 1987.

Pojman, Louis P. *Ethics: Discovering Right and Wrong.* Belmont, CA: Wadsworth, 1990.

Purtill, Richard L. *Thinking About Ethics.* Englewood Cliffs, NJ: Prentice-Hall, 1976.

Quall, Ward L., and James A. Brown. *Broadcast Management.* New York: Hastings House, 1976.

Shanks, Bob. *The Cool Fire: How to Make It in Television.* New York: W. W. Norton, 1976.

Squire, Jason E., ed. *The Movie Business Book.* New York: Simon and Schuster, 1983.

Utz, Peter. *The Video Users Handbook: Completely Revised & Expanded,* 3rd ed. Englewood Cliffs, NJ: Prentice-Hall, 1987.

Williams, Frederick. *The New Communications.* Belmont, CA: Wadsworth, 1984.

Zettl, Herbert. *Television Production Handbook,* 4th ed. Belmont, CA: Wadsworth, 1984.

ARTICLES

Behnke, Ralph R., and Phyllis Miller. "Information in Syllabus May Build Class Interest." *Journalism Educator* 44 (Autumn 1989): 45–47.

Berg, David. "Graduate Education in Communication: A Department Chairman's View." *Association for Communication Administration Bulletin* 34 (October 1980): 23–25.

Blanchard, Robert O., and William G. Christ. "In Search of the Unit Core: Commonalities in Curricula." *Journalism Educator* 40 (Autumn 1985): 28–33.

Blanchard, Robert O., and William G. Christ. "The Third Revolution: Integration in Research, Curricula." *Feedback* 28 (Winter 1987): 7–10.

Bradley, Patricia. "Teacher vs. Textbook." *Clio Among the Media* 21 (January 1989): 4–5.

Carroll, Raymond L. "Context in the Study of Mass Communication." *Feedback* 27 (Winter 1985): 3–8.

Caudill, Edward, Paul Ashdown, and Susan Caudill. "Assessing Learning in the News, Public Relations Curricula." *Journalism Educator* 45 (Summer 1990): 13–19.

Crook, James A. "Taking a Closer Look at Teaching, Leadership and Curriculum Design." *Journalism Educator* 43 (Autumn 1988): 54–56.

Davis, Leslie K. "Mass Communication Education and the Practical Course." *Communication Education* 27 (January 1978): 18–24.

De Mott, John. "Journalism Courses are an Essential Part of Liberal Education." *Journalism Educator* 39 (Autumn 1984): 31–33.

Dennis, Everette E. "Journalism Education: Failing Grades for a Dream." *ASNE Bulletin* (October 1983): 27–28.

Dennis, Everette E. "Journalism Education: Storm Swirls on Campus, Changes Coming." *Presstime* (September 1983): 4–7.

Eastman, S., and B. Adams. "A Radio-TV Program Profile." *Feedback,* 27 (Summer 1986): 10–12.

Fedler, Fred, and Tim Counts. "National J-Faculty Survey Reveals Job Likes, Dislikes." *Journalism Educator* 37 (Autumn 1982): 3–6.

Gomery, Douglas. "Media Education Economics." *Feedback* 27 (Summer 1986): 3–6.

———. "Radio, Television and Film: The State of Study in the 1980's." *Feedback* 27 (Fall 1985): 12–16.

Hanson, Jarice. "Internships and the Individual: Suggestions for Implementing or Improving an Internship Program." *Communication Education* 33 (January 1984): 53–61.

Head, Sydney W. "The Telecommunications Curriculum: A Personal View." *Feedback* 27 (Winter 1985): 9–11.

Lev, Peter, and Barry Moore. "Introduction to Film—An Integrative Approach." *Journal of Film and Video* 38 (Spring 1986): 81–87.

Limberg, Val E. "Administrative Structures and Program Orientation in Broadcast Communications Curricula." *Feedback* 28 (Summer 1987): 22–28.

Meiss, Guy T. "Help Your Students Read Their Textbooks More Profitably." *Journalism Educator* 37 (Summer 1983): 3–10.

Mitchell, Catherine. "Greeley as Journalism Teacher." *Journalism Educator* 44 (Autumn 1989): 16–19.

Murphy, Sharon. "Challenges and Opportunities in Journalism and Mass Communication Education." *Journalism Educator* 44 (Spring 1989): A1–A24.

Murray, Michael D. "Internships: Rural, City Markets." *Feedback* 15 (August 1977): 25–26.

Newsom, Douglas Ann. "Journalism/Mass Comm as an Academic Discipline." *Journalism Educator* 40 (Autumn 1985): 23–24.

Picard, Robert G. "Students Must be Taught to Think About Journalism." *Journalism Educator* 39 (Winter 1985): 30–33.

Shaw, Donald Lewis, and Sylvia L. Zack. "Rethinking Journalism History: How Some Recent Studies Support One Approach." *Journalism History* 14 (Winter 1987): 111–17.

Sterling, Christopher H. "The Meaning is the Name." *Feedback* 27 (Winter 1985): 13–14.

Stone, Gerald. "Measurement of Excellence in Newspaper Writing Classes." *Journalism Educator* 44 (Winter 1990): 4–19.

Stovall, James Glen. "Reflections on the Difficult Task of Grading Writing Assignments." *Journalism Educator* 41 (Autumn 1986): 4–7.

Ward, Jean. "Journalism Skills Courses Require Different Approach." *Journalism Educator* 36 (July 1981): 55–59.

Weaver, David, and G. Cleveland Wilhoit. "A Profile of the JMC Educator." *Journalism Educator* 42 (Summer 1988): 30–33.

Whitlow, S. Scott. "Early Imitation Eases Anxiety in Creative Course." *Journalism Educator* 40 (Winter 1986): 24–26.

INDEX

EDITORS AND CONTRIBUTORS

EDITORS

MICHAEL D. MURRAY is director of the mass communication program at the University of Missouri–St. Louis. He worked briefly for CBS News before receiving his doctorate from the University of Missouri–Columbia. He was founder of the communication program at the University of Louisville and also taught at Virginia Tech, where he received a teaching excellence award. He recently received fellowships from the National Endowment for the Humanities, Poynter Institute, and C-SPAN, the cable network. His articles have appeared in *American Journalism, Communication Education, Journalism Educator, Journalism History, Communication Quarterly*, and *Journalism Quarterly*.

ANTHONY J. FERRI is the executive assistant to the director of the Greenspun School of Communication at the University of Nevada, Las Vegas. He received his Ph.D. from Wayne State University. He has taught public relations courses for about ten years and has extensive consulting experience in various industries including utility, financial, chemical, and automotive. He is immediate past vice president of the American Heart Association, Nevada affiliate, and is on its board currently, holding the position of secretary. He is the recipient of the 1990 Rita Deanin Abbey Teacher of the Year Award (UNLV) and was nominated for the 1989 Donald McGannon Communication Research Center's Communication Policy and Ethics Research Award (Fordham University). His research articles have appeared in *Journalism Quarterly* and *Mass Comm Review*.

CONTRIBUTORS

MAURINE H. BEASLEY is professor of journalism at the University of Maryland–College Park, where she teaches graduate and undergraduate courses in journalism history and reporting. She is past head of the History Division of the Association for Education in Journalism and Mass Communication and immediate past president of the American Journalism Historians Association. Her books include *The White House Press Conferences of Eleanor Roosevelt* (1983) and *Eleanor Roosevelt and the Media: A Public Quest for Self-Fulfillment* (1987). A former staff writer for the *Washington Post*, she holds a Ph.D. in American civilization from George Washington University.

DAVID BENNETT, who left the newsroom for the classroom in 1980, teaches journalism at Indiana State University. Bennett won a fellowship to newspaper management at the Poynter Institute in 1989, and a Gannett Foundation fellowship to study journalism education in 1984. In 1987 he developed specialized mass media coursework for students traveling to China and South Korea. Formerly a newspaper editor, he has also worked as a wire service reporter, government reporter, environmental writer, and military journalist.

JAY BLACK is professor and former chair of the department of journalism at the University of Alabama. He is coeditor of the scholarly journal *Mass Media Ethics*, coauthor with Jennings Bryant of *Introduction to Mass Communication* (William C. Brown, 1991), and former chair of the professional freedom and responsibility committee for the Association for Education in Journalism and Mass Communication.

GARY BURNS is associate professor of communication studies at Northern Illinois University and has taught at University of Missouri–St. Louis and Northwestern University. He has published in a number of journals including *Feedback* and has given scholarly presentations at conventions of Broadcast Education Association, University Film and Video Association, and Central States Speech Association.

ELLIE CHAPMAN is coordinator of the writing certificate program at the University of Missouri–St. Louis, where she has been a member of the faculty since 1971. She supervises writing interns and teaches courses in editing, and news and business writing. Her writing consultancies include major midwestern business, industrial, and social service organizations.

STEVE CRAIG received his Ph.D. from Florida State University and has taught audio, video, and film production courses at the college level for over fourteen years. Graduates from his classes now include television network and corporate personnel. He teaches at the University of Maine.

JOHN DE MOTT is professor of journalism at Memphis State University and a former editor for the *Kansas City Star and Times*. He has taught media management courses at Northwestern, Northern Illinois, and Temple universities. He has served on education committees of the American Society of Newspaper Editors and Associated Press Managing Editors.

DONALD G. GODFREY is an associate professor in the Walter Cronkite School of Journalism and Telecommunication at Arizona State University. He has taught the introductory broadcast course in settings as large as the University of Washington and as small as Southern Utah University. He has authored numerous scholarly articles appearing in the *Journal of Broadcasting, Journalism Quarterly, Journalism History*, and the *Canadian Journal of Communication*.

ROY L. MOORE is associate professor of journalism and director of graduate studies in the College of Communications at the University of Kentucky. He is a practicing attorney specializing in media law, copyright, and libel. His doctorate is from the University of Wisconsin and his J.D. is from Georgia State University. He is writing a text, *Mass Communication Law and Ethics*, for Lawrence Erlbaum Associates.

JON D. MORRIS teaches in the College of Journalism and Communications at the University of Florida, where he completed his doctorate. Prior to that he taught at the University of Louisville and as visiting professor at Syracuse University. Before joining academia, he worked as account executive and media planning supervisor for Doyle Dane Bernbach and Dancer Fitzgerald Sample. In 1973 he received the award for best television campaign from the American Federation of Television and Radio Artists. He is consultant to a number of organizations, and serves on the editorial advisory board of *Journalism Educator*.

ROBERT MUSBURGER is associate director of the School of Communication at the University of Houston. He has twenty years of experience in broadcasting and recently published *Electronic News*

Gathering: A Guide to ENG. He is chair of the courses and curriculum division of the Broadcast Education Association and is the secretary/treasurer of the Society of Motion Picture and Television Engineers (Houston).

DAN NIMMO is a political scientist and professor of communication at the University of Oklahoma. He teaches courses in mass, political, and international communication. His most recent books include *Mediated Political Realities*, 2nd edition, *Cordial Consensus: Orchestrating National Party Conventions in the Telepolitical Age*, *Politics in Familiar Contexts*, *The Orwellian Moment*, and *New Directions in Political Communication: A Resource Book*.

FRANK N. PIERCE is founding chairman of the University of Florida department of advertising and has been a member of that faculty for the past eighteen years. Prior to that he taught at The University of Texas at Austin and the University of Illinois, where he was a James Webb Young scholar while completing his doctorate. His professional experience includes fourteen years in sales promotion and advertising. In the past fifteen years he has taught more than 2,300 students in fifty-eight different classes. Nationally known firms have served as "clients" for his campaigns class, including DuPont, Frito-Lay, Radio City Music Hall, Rubbermaid, Sea World, and Harte-Hanks newspapers.

MICHAEL A. RUSSO is chair of the communications department at Saint Mary's College of California. He received his doctorate from New York University and has worked as both a producer and consultant for CBS News in New York. His research specialty is media history and criticism and he recently served as a fellow at Joan Shorenstein Barone Center on Press, Politics and Public Policy, the John F. Kennedy School of Government, Harvard University.

KIM A. SMITH holds a Ph.D. in mass communication from the University of Wisconsin–Madison. He is associate professor and coordinator of graduate studies in the department of journalism and mass communication at Iowa State University. His research on political communication, agenda setting, and perceptions of community media, among other topics, has appeared in *Journalism Quarterly*, *Communication Research*, *Journalism Monographs*, and the *Newspaper Research Journal*. He has taught undergraduate and graduate methodology courses for the past twelve years.

S. SCOTT WHITLOW, Ph.D. from Southern Illinois University, is associate professor in the School of Journalism at the University of Kentucky and is coordinator of the advertising program and director of the school's internship program. Her articles have appeared in *Journalism Educator, Mass Comm Review, Educational Communication and Technology, Journalism Quarterly*, and *Media Development*.